Brackish-Water Fishes

An Aquarist's Guide to Indentification, Care & Husbandry

A complete guide to the most common and easy-to-obtain species for home aquariums.

Neale Monks, Editor

Brackish-Water Fishes
An Aquarist's Gudie to Indentification, Care & Husbandry

Project Team
Editors: Ryan Greene and David Boruchowitz
Copy Editor: Ann Fusz
Design: Angela Stanford

T.F.H. Publications, Inc.
President/CEO: Glen S. Axelrod
Executive Vice President: Mark E. Johnson
Publisher: Christopher T. Reggio
Production Manager: Kathy Bontz

T.F.H. Publications, Inc.
One TFH Plaza
Third and Union Avenues
Neptune City, NJ 07753

06 07 08 09 10 1 3 5 7 9 8 6 4 2
Printed and bound in China
Library of Congress Cataloging-in-Publication Data

Monks, Neale.
Brackish-Water Fishes : An Aquarist's Guide to Identification, Care & Husbandry / Neale Monks.
    p. cm.
 Includes bibliographical references.
  ISBN-13: 978-0-7938-0564-8 (alk. paper)
 1. Aquarium fishes. I. Title.
SF457.M66 2006
639.34--dc22
2006027185

This book has been published with the intent to provide accurate and authoritative information in
regard to the subject matter within. While every precaution has been taken in preparation of this
book, the author and publisher expressly disclaim responsibility for any errors, omissions, or adverse
effects arising from the use or application of the information contained herein. The techniques
and suggestions are used at the reader's discretion and are not to be considered a substitute for
veterinary care. If you suspect a medical problem consult your veterinarian.

The Leader In Responsible Animal Care For Over 50 Years.™
www.tfh.com

Brackish-Water Fishes

An Aquarist's Guide to Indentification, Care & Husbandry

TABLE OF CONTENTS

Preface
By Neale Monks

Brackish-water habitats are less well known to most aquarists compared to, say, coral reefs or the Rift Valley lakes of East Africa, but they are significant nevertheless. Indeed, marine biologists often refer to brackish-water habitats, especially estuaries and mangrove swamps, as the "nurseries of the sea" because so many marine fishes use them as spawning grounds or as feeding grounds when immature.

For the aquarist, the attraction of brackish-water fishes is that on the whole, they are hardy and active, and are often interesting and colorful as well. Among the roster of frequently imported brackish-water fishes are sailfin mollies, puffers, gobies, orange chromides, and killifish. But even more compelling for the advanced aquarist are less frequently seen—but still very desirable—oddballs like the "freshwater" flounders, morays, and lionfish, archerfish, garpikes, sleeper gobies, and tigerfish. Rounding out the collection are those species that straddle the boundary between freshwater and marine habitats, such as monos, scats, and shark catfish, which can be easily combined with marine fishes as well as more traditional brackish-water ones.

Rare is the aquarist who has not come across one or more of these fascinating fishes and fancied creating an aquarium just for them, but any aquarist interested in these unusual fishes will be dismayed to find that very few of the standard aquarium books offer much insight into their care and husbandry. It isn't that these fish aren't well known. Indeed, many are hobby staples, and even the most basic aquarium manuals will mention that mollies and gobies need a little salt in their water to do well. What's missing from the hobby is a comprehensive guide to brackish-water fishes, one that shows off their tremendous diversity while pinning down their exact requirements and tolerances in terms of water chemistry and salinity, companionability with other fishes, and so on. This is where *Brackish-Water Fishes* comes in.

To no small degree, this book is the offspring of the Brackish Water Aquarium mailing list started in the mid-1990s by Jim Horton, at that time at the University of Missouri School of Law, and currently managed by P. Douglas McKinney. In 1997, I decided to put together a section for the mailing list answering frequently asked questions, pulling together my own experiences with those of other members of the list. This FAQ was widely circulated on the Internet, and still exists in various forms, but there are limitations to what is possible with text-based articles on the web. Missouri School of Law, and currently managed by P. Douglas McKinney. In 1997 I decided to put together a section for the mailing list answering frequently asked questions, pulling together my own experiences with those of other members of the list. This FAQ was widely circulated on the Internet, and still exists in various forms, but there are limitations to what is possible with text-based articles on the web. What the fishkeeping hobby needed was a thorough, easy-to-read book dedicated to brackish-water species, something the aquarist could take along to the local fish store to help identify and describe the best way to keep brackish-water species.

To this end, I've brought together aquarists who have developed expertise in one or more areas of brackish-water fishkeeping. *Brackish-Water Fishes* covers both general topics and numerous specific groups of fish, and in every case the authors have worked hard to keep the content accessible as well as authoritative. We hope you find this book useful.

We would like to thank all the people who have helped us along the way, in particular Doug McKinney for maintaining the Brackish Water Aquarium mailing list.

Neale Monks, Ph.D.
University of Nebraska—Lincoln, Lincoln, USA
& Natural History Museum, London, England

An Introduction to Brackish-Water Aquariums

By Michele Kraft

Brackish-water enthusiasts tend to be mavericks. We love the different. We don't depend entirely on what we're told at the fish store, preferring to look, muse, and research things ourselves. Gleaning information from books and the Internet, we compile our data and sometimes, if we're lucky enough to find like minds, conspire and co-educate. Recently, more usable information has become is available for fishkeepers in general, thanks in large part to the wonder of the Internet, and it seems the brackish movement is gaining in popularity. In most cases, the fish stores I visit now even have at least one aquarium devoted to brackish water.

I blame the pufferfish for this rise in popularity. It was this cutie—er, rather, this interesting carnivore—that turned me to the brackish side. She made me do it!

She was cute—undeniably cute, in fact. Hovering like a rotund hummingbird, she had inquisitive, independently operating, iridescent blue eyes and the whisper of a smile surrounding nubby little teeth. I had to have her. But she was a brackish-water fish; she was from the wrong side of the aquarium tracks. She was no good for me. And, I thought, there

Introduction

The cute and personable pufferfish may be fueling the rising popularity of brackish-water fish.

just isn't enough variety in the brackish aquarium category to keep my interest up. Wrong. I went home that day and started poking around the Internet, only to find that some of the fish I'm most fond of—and already owned—just happen to be brackish-water inhabitants. After I found a home for my immense apple snail, the remaining inhabitants in my 20-gallon (70-liter) aquarium were, in fact, brackish fishes. I bought my first bag of marine salt and have not looked back since.

Like me, aquarists who have discovered the secret joys of brackish aquaria on their own have had a difficult time getting reliable information on the topic due to the short supply of reference materials and knowledgeable brackish enthusiasts at the local fish store. In this book, we hope to dispel the mystery surrounding this specialized but fun and interesting area of the aquarium hobby.

WHAT IS BRACKISH WATER, AND WHY WOULD I WANT AN AQUARIUM FULL OF IT?

For some folks, the word "brackish" brings images of sodden swamps, greasy black water, and the pungent smell of rotting vegetation. Those people often ask if fish can even live in brackish water, believing "brackish" means polluted or stagnant. Brackish water is simply fresh water and seawater mixed together. Every place in the world where a river meets the sea is a brackish environment. Brackish water teems with life—it is home to many independently developed evolutionary niches, all filled with interesting species—and these fishes are collected from tropical and subtropical zones around the world.

Unfortunately, you will not find representatives from every brackish water body in the world at your local fish store, but quite a diverse selection is available. In fact, many species commonly kept as freshwater fishes are actually native to a brackish environment. If only people knew! Some brackish species, such as mollies, have developed a reputation for being susceptible to ich. Commonly kept in freshwater community tanks, it is not surprising that they are prone to illness; while fresh water alone probably won't kill mollies, it is not the best environment for them. Mollies need a bit of the sea—a brackish fish in a freshwater aquarium is not having its needs met, leaving it susceptible to disease.

WHERE BRACKISH WATER OCCURS

From the Arctic to the Antarctic, there exist countless coastal habitats where fresh water meets ocean water. Just as important to humans as they are to aquatic species, brackish water bodies are home to some of the most important cities in the world; in the United States alone these include New York City, San Francisco, and Washington, D.C.

Brackish water occurs wherever saltwater and freshwater bodies meet—like in New York Bay.

11

Introduction

Growing up in Maryland, on the eastern seaboard of the United States, I was fortunate to have experienced the diversity of life found in the Chesapeake Bay. The Chesapeake is the largest body of brackish water in the United States and, like all estuaries, supports a wide variety of unique species, as well as serving as a nursery for many marine fishes.

Unfortunately, we come into contact with nontropical brackish species more often as food than as pets. These cold-water species are as interesting as their warm-water cousins, and share many adaptations with them. Among these traits is the ability to tolerate frequent but gradual changes in salinity, since the very nature of their habitat causes slight changes in salinity hour by hour. The sea pushes into the mouths of rivers and, over time, erosion creates large, shallow bodies of water where the two forces of fresh and marine water join. As the tide goes in and out, the salinity rises and falls. The outgoing tide relieves the pressure against the fresh water entering the bay, so more fresh water fills the basin. High tide pushes against the freshwater flow and forces salt water inland.

Additionally, large amounts of rainfall, and the resulting high water in rivers and streams draining into the estuary, cause salinity to drop throughout the system. Conversely, drought conditions cause the salinity to rise, because there is not as much fresh water available to push against the seawater.

Species often move to an area with the salinity they prefer, especially when breeding. I saw this myself during occasional hot, dry summers on the Chesapeake, when it would seem the bay emptied of fish entirely. Now I know they were all still there—they had just gone further upriver or deeper into the channels until normal conditions returned.

SO WHAT ARE THESE CRAZY BRACKISH-WATER FISHES ANYWAY?

As we'll explain throughout this book, brackish-water fishes are members of many families. The catfish, cichlid, eel, goby, livebearer, mudskipper, and rainbowfish families all have brackish species. For those of you living near a sea coast, the list includes all the fishes native to your estuary, since estuaries are actually brackish-water environments. (Be sure to check local and state rules and regulations before collecting native species; you might be surprised to find it's illegal to collect or keep some indigenous fishes as pets.) Importantly, not all members of these families are from brackish environments—for example, not all cichlids are brackish-water fishes, but some cichlids are naturally found in brackish habitats.

Determining which species you can keep and which ones you can't is one of the most difficult aspects of keeping a brackish-water aquarium. Even most experienced saltwater experts, respected among aquarists as having a great depth of skill and expertise, commonly know little about maintaining brackish-water species. Many reference books don't mention brackish species at all—and if they do, it's only a note about the usual archers, puffers, and scats.

We fishkeepers often have to take responsibility for educating ourselves. In the brackish-fish hobby, the appeal is in looking beyond the common species and discovering the many enjoyable creatures that thrive in brackish water. Of course, the species commonly available will be covered herein, and we'll describe where they are from and what is required to keep them. With the exception of salinity, everything involved in maintaining a brackish aquarium, including pH and temperature requirements, is just like keeping a freshwater aquarium. If you've mastered that, a brackish-water tank is a piece of cake.

SALT REGULATION AND FLUCTUATION

Natural fluctuations in salinity are important in understanding the basics of your brackish-water aquarium. The first question asked by freshwater fishkeepers usually regards the regulation of salt. Most people assume that, as with marine aquariums, salinity will be under very rigid control. Although it is true that changes in your aquarium should always be gradual, it is actually beneficial to vary the salinity. The fishes you keep will have specific needs that must be taken into account; for example, some species enjoy only mildly brackish water, while others can accept anything from mild to full marine conditions. Generally, there is room for flexibility here, as long as the optimum conditions for your species are the norm. As an added bonus, salinity changes help extinguish parasites, since they are commonly adapted to either fresh or marine conditions; a shift too far either way will kill them off.

The Expert Says...

Brackish water is seawater mixed with fresh water. It is imperative that you use packaged marine-aquarium salts in your brackish aquarium. Any other kind of salt does not have the complex variety of compounds found in the natural brackish-water environment. You will not be making a brackish aquarium if you do not use marine salt—you will be creating brine. This is fine if you are planning to cook your fish, but not so good for a life-sustaining habitat.

PLANNING AND IMPLEMENTATION

Planning the brackish-water aquarium is one of the most difficult tests of the aquarium hobby. As all aquarists know, you can't simply buy pretty fishes and expect everything to go swimmingly. The first thing you'll have to do is determine what kind of brackish-water fishes you want to keep. The habits of the fishes you focus on will determine the filtration, lighting, and substrate requirements for your tank.

Selecting a filtration system is especially critical. Although guppies will do well in a formerly freshwater tank with added sea salt, many popular brackish fishes are sloppy carnivores and thus require much better filtration than a typical community-tank setup. Research the fishes you plan to keep, know their eating habits, and plan your filtration accordingly, just as you would for a freshwater aquarium. It is best to plan for the worst and provide more-than-adequate filtration.

HOW MUCH SALT? WHAT IS SPECIFIC GRAVITY?

The most common bad advice about the making of brackish water is to add a number of tablespoons of salt per gallon of fresh water. While these formulas sound appealing because they are easy, they are not to be trusted. Salt does not always measure accurately by the spoonful. For example, if you measured a pail full of limestone sand and a pail full of limestone rock, the pail of sand would weigh more than the pail of rock because there is more limestone in the pail of sand. If the sand is damp, it will be even heavier. The same is true for salt; the grains can be many different sizes, and humidity affects their size and weight. The only way to know how much salt to use is to check the density of the water after you add the salt. It is a bit more challenging, but not that difficult.

Introduction

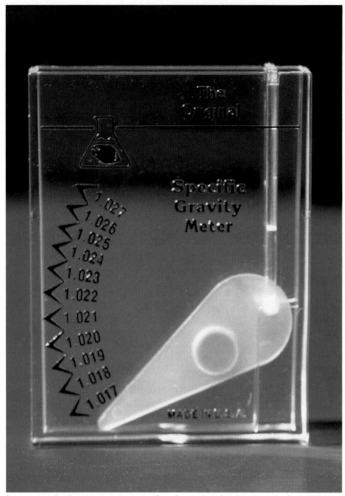

Swing-arm hydrometers are a popular choice for checking water density.

To check water density, you need a *hydrometer.* Two kinds of hydrometers are on the market today: floating and swing arm.

FLOATING HYDROMETERS

Most floating hydrometers are inexpensive, and some even have a built-in thermometer, making them especially tempting purchases. On the downside, the cheaper floating hydrometers are not especially accurate, and even the best ones can be difficult to read. Because they must float in the tank, any turbulence (from the filter or an air pump for example) will bob the hydrometer up and down, making it difficult to get an exact reading. After struggling with one of these units for many years, I eventually bought a swing-arm hydrometer. It was a revelation to find out just how much easier it was to use.

SWING-ARM HYDROMETERS

Being made of plastic, swing-arm hydrometers are much more durable than floating hydrometers (which invariably are made of glass), so you won't accidentally break one while you're doing a water change. With age and use, the swing arm may deteriorate, so handle your hydrometer carefully.

When purchasing your swing-arm hydrometer, make certain the calibrated readings include levels of at least 1.000 to 1.025. Now let's examine what these numbers mean.

RAISING, LOWERING, AND MAINTAINING SPECIFIC GRAVITY

For a successful brackish aquarium, you must maintain the specific gravity within the best range for the species you're keeping.

The specific-gravity number essentially describes the weight of the water. A liter of fresh water with no salt in it weighs 1 kilogram and has a density of 1.000, and a liter of seawater weighs 1.025 kilograms has a density of 1.025. The gravity of brackish water can be anywhere in between.

Test the specific gravity of the water in your tank and of any water you are adding during a water change. Before measuring specific gravity, always fully dissolve the salts before adding them to the water. (Also make sure that salt is fully dissolved before adding it to any aquarium with life in it.) Remember, always make changes in specific gravity very gradually.

Dissolving Salt

If you don't already have a bucket dedicated to aquarium use, you need to acquire at least one in which to dissolve the salt before adding it to your tank. This is called *premixing,* and it is an important step in successful brackish-aquarium care—it will come in handy time and time again. Dissolving salts before you begin a water change can take some time, so try to get it going the night before a water change. The easiest way to accomplish this is to just let the water and salt sit in the bucket. Put an air stone in the bucket to provide circulation, which will help dissolve the salt.

One method is to use two large buckets, one holding highly salted water and one holding fresh water. To achieve the proper specific gravity, add a little of the salt water to the freshwater bucket, and then add that to the tank. In time, you'll be able to judge about how much you'll need for a typical water change. To replace water lost by normal evaporation, use fresh water to *maintain the specific gravity.* Salt will not evaporate with the water, so the specific gravity rises slightly over time because less water is in your aquarium to mix with the salt already present.

To *raise the specific gravity*, top off your tank with brackish water as evaporation makes room for it.

To *lower the specific gravity*, siphon off small amounts of brackish aquarium water and replace it with fresh water.

Salinity, like many water parameters, is invisible.

Introduction

INTRODUCING NEW FISHES

When bringing new fishes into your aquarium, slowly introduce them to the brackish water—particularly if they were kept in straight fresh water. Place the fishes and the water in which they arrived into a glass or plastic container large enough to be less than half full. Add a small amount of water from your aquarium to the container. Repeat every 15 to 20 minutes until the amount of water added is more than the amount of water originally from the bag. Net the fishes out and release them into the tank. Observe them to be sure no violent reactions occur. Feeding the fishes already in the tank and turning off the lights prior to beginning the acclimation process is usually a good idea, too, since it calms the current tank inhabitants.

It is my hope that enthusiasm for brackish-water fishes will spread as more information on the topic becomes available. I look forward to the day when I walk into my local fish store and see mollies on display in a brackish setup, or perhaps a nice mudskipper soiree, or even just some guppies in a brackish tank.

Because it can tolerate some salt, the ever-popular guppy can be kept in brackish-water tanks.

The Biology of Brackish-Water Fishes and Plants

By Neale Monks

Above all else, the environments in which brackish fish live are characterized by change, which means that, unlike the fishes of the Red Sea, Lake Tanganyika, or the Rio Negro, brackish fish cannot rely on constant water conditions. This sets them apart from the majority of commonly kept aquarium fishes, which are adapted to very specific water conditions and will not do well if conditions deviate very far from them. Instead, brackish-water fishes are able to handle dramatic changes in pH, hardness, temperature, and salinity that would kill other fish very quickly. This adaptability makes them very hardy and has endeared them to generations of hobbyists.

BRACKISH WATER

Fresh water is easy enough to understand, and so is normal marine water, but what do we mean by "strongly brackish" or "weakly brackish" water? These vague terms reflect the fact that brackish waters constitute a continuum running from fresh water containing essentially no salt to seawater with a salinity of 35. When we talk about a fish enjoying weakly brackish

Brackish-Water Fishes and Plants

The Expert Says...
While it might taste a bit odd, you actually could drink slightly brackish water without ill effect.

conditions, what we really mean is that it will do well in a range of salinities close to that of fresh water. Conversely, a fish that needs strongly brackish water requires salinities approaching normal marine.

In fact, aquarists hardly ever measure salinity directly, instead using a much more handy proxy, specific gravity. Specific gravity (or density) is the weight of a given volume of water. The more salt that water contains, the denser it becomes. Pure water weighs 1,000 grams per liter, and 1 liter of water occupies exactly 1,000 cm^3. Since 1,000 divided by 1,000 is 1, the specific gravity of pure water is 1.000. For all practical purposes, fresh water contains too few minerals to raise its density above that of pure water, and so the specific gravity of fresh water is also 1.000. Seawater, on the other hand, is slightly heavier per liter than pure water because it contains more dissolved minerals. It weighs in at around 1,023 to 1,025 grams per liter, resulting in a specific gravity of 1.023 to 1.025.

There are countless brackish habitats throughout the world.

We don't normally use the term "brackish" for waters in the entire range between 1.000 and 1.025, however. Salinities below about 10 percent of normal marine conditions (a specific gravity of 1.002 or less) are considered to be an extension of the freshwater habitat. Generally speaking, freshwater-only fish, invertebrates, and plants will tolerate salinities as low as these.

At the other end of the scale, marine fish generally do well in water with salinities as low as 80 percent of normal marine (a specific gravity of 1.018). Indeed, it used to be rather common for aquarists to keep the salinity of fish-only tanks significantly lower than those containing fish and invertebrates. While marine invertebrates are stressed by less-than-fully-marine conditions, many marine fish seem to do quite well, the assumption being that a lower salinity places less of a demand on their osmoregulatory system. (While the wisdom of this practice has lost credibility, temporarily lowering salinity is still popular as a way to combat marine parasites, which cannot tolerate the reduced salinity.) Even in the wild, many marine fish, from herrings to great white sharks, routinely enter the estuaries of rivers and other areas of strongly brackish waters. So while technically brackish, salinities between 80 and 100 percent of normal marine (a specific gravity range of 1.018 to 1.023) can be thought of as essentially marine.

With the bottom end and the top end of the salinity range removed, this leaves salinities between 10 and 80 percent of normal marine conditions to be considered brackish. In other words, a brackish-water aquarium is one with a specific gravity between 1.002 and 1.018.

BRACKISH ENVIRONMENTS

Brackish water is found primarily where freshwater bodies meet the sea. While brackish-water habitats are very varied, they all share some common characteristics. Most are highly productive habitats with plenty of plant and animal life. Rivers in particular are often loaded with mineral nutrients, such as nitrate and phosphate, which have been washed off the surrounding land by rainfall. (This is in stark contrast to seawater, which usually lacks nutrients.) As soon as the nutrients reach the estuary, they feed a bloom of algae and plants, which in turn supports a rich diversity of animal life. The river also brings silt that is deposited as thick mud wherever the flow of water slows down, such as between the stems of plants. As the mud collects, it helps support yet more plant life, including salt marshes and seagrass meadows in the temperate zones and mangroves in the tropics.

Buried inside the mud are vast numbers of worms, crustaceans, and mollusks. These in turn become food for a huge variety of predators, of which wading birds like plovers are among the most obvious. In tidal brackish habitats, like most estuaries, animal life operates in two distinct phases: those that hunt underwater when the tide is in, and those that walk on the mud once the tide is out. Flatfish, such as flounders and soles, are examples of hunters that fall into the first category, following the tide up the estuary to hunt for worms and clams. Mudskippers, on the other hand, are largely dormant when the tide is in, and only feed on the exposed mudflats once the tide has receded.

Almost without exception, brackish-water habitats have ecological value far greater than their size would suggest. Many migratory birds use estuaries as resting places—plenty of food is available, the close proximity of the sea moderates extremes of heat and cold, and open expanses of sticky mud make it difficult for terrestrial

Brackish-Water Fishes and Plants

Tidal estuaries are the most common type of brackish habitat.

predators to get too close to them. Large numbers of marine species of fishes use estuaries as nursery grounds, either spawning there (as with herrings and flatfish) or migrating there when young to take advantage of the abundant food and relative security away from open-water predators (as with many snappers, tarpon, tuna, and other game fish). Still other fishes use estuaries as stopovers between their feeding and spawning grounds. In some cases, as with salmon, they pass through the estuary relatively quickly; other fish, like sea trout, eels, and sturgeons, can spend months or even years in an estuary. All this makes brackish-water habitats rank among the most important environments in terms of their influence beyond their immediate extent, putting them in the same category as rainforests and coral reefs.

Classifying brackish habitats is quite a complicated exercise, but aquarists need only know the basic types. Each provides inspiration for themed aquaria, in particular for selecting the types of fish that can be used and what plants and other materials should be used for decoration.

TIDAL ESTUARIES

Tidal estuaries are the most common brackish habitats and occur wherever rivers flow into the sea. We often consider estuaries to be divided into upper and lower regions. The upper estuary is dominated by the freshwater component of the system and has a low salinity; as a result, most of the fishes seen are freshwater and brackish-water species. Often, the low-lying nature of the land causes the river to spread out laterally far more than it does upstream, producing a delta consisting of a maze of streams and channels. As the river spreads out, it slows down, depositing sediment and producing a very rich soil known as alluvium. Plant growth is vigorous, and these habitats are highly productive, with lots of snails, insects, and crustaceans for the fish to feed on. The Nile Delta is the most well-known example of this type of estuary, but another delta, that of the River Niger, is home to two popular aquarium fish, the kribensis, *Pelvicachromis pulcher,* and the ropefish, *Erpetoichthys calabaricus.*

The lower estuary is much more marine in nature, with the higher salinity excluding many types of fish and plants. Instead, it typically features marine fish swimming into the estuary to feed on worms, clams, and other burrowing animals that inhabit the deep, silty sediment.

REED AND SALT MARSHES

Reed marshes and salt marshes are brackish meadows most characteristic of temperate zones. While they can be part of a tidal estuary, they don't have to be, and many fringe the sea directly. Rain water, ground water, and small streams feed fresh water into them on an irregular basis, while seawater flushes in with each tide.

Marshes are home to many fish, wading birds, and insects.

Brackish-Water Fishes and Plants

Together these influences create a brackish habitat of varying salinity. As a rule, reeds prefer a lower average salinity than do salt marshes, and so the communities of fish and invertebrates that are found in each will be rather different. With few exceptions, the fishes found in either tend to be small— for example, gobies, sticklebacks, and killifish. This is important, because most of the time the only water of use to fishes is found in freshwater streams and small pools. The only time a marsh is completely underwater is during periods of flooding or tidal inundation.

Besides small fish, marshes are home to vast numbers of insects, particularly mosquitoes, and snails. These in turn support large populations of wading birds and other predators.

SEAGRASS MEADOWS

In contrast to marshes, seagrass meadows often are permanently submerged or only exposed during low tides. Salinity is normally at least half that of normal seawater, and usually much higher. So whereas the fishes in marsh habitats include many that are also found in fresh water, the fauna in seagrass meadows is dominated by marine families. Gobies, flatfish, seahorses, and pipefish are among the most typical seagrass species.

MANGROVE FORESTS

Finally, mangrove forests (or mangals) constitute a very distinctive brackish habitat, one that is very interesting to aquarists. Mangroves occur throughout the tropics, from Florida to Australia, but the exact species that make up the mangrove forest vary from place to place. Some species can tolerate saltier water than others. They form a complex habitat both above and below the water line, supporting a huge variety of fish and other animals. Many of the most popular brackish-water fishes in the hobby, like monos, scats, and archers, are predominantly fishes of the mangrove.

OSMOREGULATION

Generally speaking, brackish fishes encounter changes in water conditions either because of the regular cycles of the tides or by actively swimming through regions where different water bodies are mixing (such as estuaries). Less mobile fishes, like gobies and cichlids, tend to hold territories; as the tide goes in and out, the salinity of the water around them can change. As a result, these fishes must deal with changes in water conditions that are rapid and regular—in the case of tides, taking place four times a day.

Mangroves are perhaps the most unique and, for many, the most exotic of brackish environments.

Brackish-Water Fishes and Plants

Some brackish species, like true eels, are migratory but may be kept in brackish aquaria.

More-active fishes are not tied to a single spot in a river or lagoon, and swim freely from high- to low-salinity areas for a variety of reasons. Archerfish, for example, hunt for insects in mangrove swamps, and will swim through waters of widely varying salinity without any particular preferences.

Other fishes only enter brackish water for a particular stage of their life cycle and are rarely found there at other times. Such fish include salmon, which migrate through estuaries to their spawning grounds, and others like the tarpon, which inhabit brackish-water nurseries as juveniles but move off into the sea as they get older.

In this book, we are mostly concerned with those fishes that spend their entire lives in brackish water, as these are the types best suited to life in a brackish-water aquarium. Of course, some migratory species can be kept in aquaria, such as the true eels, *Anguilla* spp., as well as a few marine fishes that, at least as juveniles, do well in brackish aquaria. But on the other hand, the vast majority of marine fishes, not to mention virtually all the freshwater species, cannot be kept in brackish-water aquaria.

Why is this? What makes brackish fishes so adaptable?

Although the variations in water temperature, pH, and hardness are significant, salinity is the crucial factor that keeps marine and freshwater fish out of habitats like estuaries and mangrove swamps. Salinity is simply the amount of salt dissolved in the water. Sea salt is primarily sodium chloride, but it also includes a large number of other mineral salts including calcium carbonate, a powerful buffering agent that keeps the pH and hardness of seawater high. Normal seawater contains about 35 grams of salt per liter of water (this is commonly referred to as normal marine salinity). This may alternately be described as 35 parts of salt per thousand parts of water, or 35‰ (35 per mil). Because the measurement is a proportion, it is reported technically without units—a salinity of 35.

Animals also contain salt and water—in the cytoplasm inside their cells and in the blood and other fluids moving around their bodies. The vast majority of marine invertebrates, such as corals, shrimps, and starfish, maintain body tissues with a salinity identical to that of normal seawater. As a result, no overall movement of salt or water occurs between their bodies and the seawater around them. Fish, on the other hand, do not have the same concentration of salt and water inside them as the sea around them, and so there is a tendency for them to gain salt and lose water. This is because of a process called *diffusion*, whereby chemicals move from places of high concentration to places of low concentration. A classic example of diffusion is what happens when a drop of ink is placed into a glass of water. Even without stirring, the ink will gradually spread out, coloring all the water.

Diffusion is a slow but inexorable process. If marine fish didn't reverse its effects somehow, they would effectively dehydrate. Their cells would lose water to the sea, and they would take in much more salt than they need. To prevent this from happening, marine fishes *osmoregulate*. Essentially what they do is drink seawater but remove the salt from it, thereby gaining the water they need to make up the losses from diffusion. The excess sea salt is excreted in two ways: the smaller ions, like sodium, by special cells in the gills, and the larger ions, like carbonate, in the urine.

Freshwater fishes face the opposite problem: They live in an environment generally lacking in salts of any kind, and the salinity of the cells and tissues inside their bodies is distinctly higher than that of the water around them. As a result, they tend to gain water as it diffuses into their bodies and lose salts as they diffuse out. Consequently, freshwater fish need systems that do the opposite of those of the marine fish—namely collect and conserve salts while removing the excess water. In contrast to marine fish, which produce only a little, highly concentrated urine, freshwater fish produce large amounts of diluted urine containing hardly any salt at all.

It is obvious that what works in fresh water would be fatal in the sea, and vice versa. More than anything else, it is this fundamental difference between their osmoregulatory systems that keeps freshwater fishes in ponds, lakes, and rivers, and marine fishes in the sea. Ichthyologists commonly refer to these fishes as *stenohaline*, meaning they are adapted to a narrow range of salinities (practically 0 for freshwater fish and 35 for marine fish).

But brackish fishes are different. They are *euryhaline*, tolerant of a broader range of salinities than stenohaline species, and so able to live where the salinity varies, such as in estuaries, mangrove swamps, coastal streams, and other places where fresh and salt water mix.

The Expert Says...

Different bodies of salt water vary in salinity based on numerous factors. The Red Sea, for example, has a slightly higher concentration of salt because of high levels of evaporation, whereas the Baltic Sea has significantly less salt, being essentially brackish in nature for much of its extent.

Brackish-Water Fishes and Plants

Some fish that are considered brackish, like the popular kribensis, really are freshwater fish that can tolerate a little salt.

VARIATION AMONG BRACKISH-WATER FISHES

Not all brackish fishes tolerate the same range of salinities, and understanding this is very important when it comes to selecting fish for the brackish-water aquarium. To begin with, some of the species often described as brackish-water fishes really aren't. It is perhaps more accurate to say they are freshwater fishes that tolerate a little salt. Among these are the ever-popular kribensis and various species of spiny eel (Table 2.1).

Table 2.1: Salt-tolerant freshwater fish

These are freshwater fishes that have some salt tolerance and so can be kept in slightly brackish water indefinitely, and so could be combined with brackish-water fishes that are tolerant of low salinities, such as archerfish, gobies, and flatfish. Generally speaking, the salinity should be kept below 10 percent that of normal seawater (a specific gravity of less than 1.002). Note that while these fishes have similar water requirements, they may not be compatible for other reasons, such as predatory behavior and aggression.

Eel-like fishes

Erpetoichthys calabaricus	Ropefish
Macrognathus aculeatus	Peacock spiny eel
Mastacembelus armatus	Tire-track spiny eel
Mastacembelus erythrotaenia	Fire spiny eel

Tetras

Pristella maxillaris	Pristella tetra

Carps

Carassius auratus	Goldfish (fancy varieties often more delicate)
Cyprinus carpio	Carp (including koi)

Catfish

Glyptoperichthys gibbiceps	Leopard sailfin suckermouth catfish
Hemibagrus nemurus	Asian red-tailed catfish
Hypostomus punctatus	Common spotted suckermouth catfish
Ictalurus punctatus	Channel catfish
Liposarcus pardalis	Giant sucker-mouth catfish
Mystus armatus	Kerala mystus
Mystus vittatus	Striped dwarf catfish

Livebearers

Poecilia reticulata	Guppy
Xiphophorus hellerii	Swordtail
Xiphophorus maculatus	Common platy (including fancy platies)
Xiphophorus variatus	Variatus platy

Killifish

Aplocheilus spp.	South Asian killifish or "panchax" rainbowfish
Melanotaenia spp.	Australian rainbowfish

Labyrinth fish

Anabas spp.	Asian climbing perch
Channa orientalis	Asian snakehead
Osphronemus goramy	Giant gourami

Nandidae

Nandus nandus	Asian leaffish

Cichlids

Aequidens pulcher	Blue acara
Archocentrus nigrofasciatus	Convict cichlid
Thorichthys meeki	Firemouth cichlid

Pufferfish

Colomesus asellus	South American pufferfish
Tetraodon lineatus	Fahaka puffer

Atherines

Bedotia geayi	Madagascar rainbowfish
Telmatherina ladigesi	Celebes rainbowfish

Miscellaneous species

Acipenser ruthenus	Sterlet
Esox lucius	Northern pike
Onchorhynchus mykiss	Rainbow trout

Brackish-Water Fishes and Plants

Table 2.2: Brackish-tolerant marine fish

Several marine fishes will tolerate salinities below normal marine conditions indefinitely, and can make good companions for brackish-water species. When sold, these fishes are normally adapted to marine conditions, and care should be taken while adapting them to a lower salinity. Depending on the species, a salinity between 50 and 75 percent that of normal marine conditions will be adequate (a specific gravity between 1.012 and 1.017). Note that while these fishes have similar water requirements, they may not be compatible for other reasons, such as predatory behavior and aggression.

Catfish
Plotosus lineatus	Striped marine catfish

Damselfish
Neopomacentrus taeniurus	Freshwater demoiselle
Pomacentrus taeniometopon	Freshwater damselfish
Stegastes otophorus	Freshwater gregory

Pufferfish
Arothron hispidus	Dog-faced puffer
Chelonodon patoca	Milk-spotted puffer

Miscellaneous species
Lutjanus argentimaculatus	Mangrove snapper
Lutjanus sebae	Emperor snapper
Micrognathus strigtus	Stripey
Platax orbicularis	Round batfish
Platax teira	Long-finned batfish

Xenentodon cancila is a recognizable euryhaline fish.

Then there are species that are usually traded as marine fish, such as some of the batfish and the dog-faced puffer, which will do well in a high-salinity brackish-water aquarium (Table 2.2). Finally, there are those species that tolerate fresh water, salt water, and anything in between, like scats and monos, and these are typically sold as true brackish-water fish (Table 2.3).

Inevitably, some fish blur the boundaries between these groups. Sailfin mollies, for example, although usually sold as freshwater fish and perfectly healthy in hard, basic, fresh water, do well in both brackish and marine aquaria. In fact, they are widely used during the maturation process of new marine aquaria, since they are more tolerant of nitrite and ammonia than most other species of ornamental marine fish.

Table 2.3: Adaptable euryhaline fish

These species are tolerant of wide salinity ranges, in some cases being able to adapt to fresh, brackish, and fully marine conditions. Typically, keeping the salinity between one-quarter and one-half the strength of seawater (a specific gravity between 1.006 and 1.012) will suit them fine. Note that while these fishes have similar water requirements, they may not be compatible for other reasons, such as predatory behavior and aggression.

Eels
Anguilla spp.	True eels
Echidna rhodochilus	Freshwater moray eel
Gymnothorax spp.	Brackish-water moray eels

Killifish
Cyprinodon and *Fundulus* spp.	North American killifish
Jordanella floridae	Florida flag killifish
Jordanella pulchra	Yucatan pupfish

Catfish
Aspredo aspredo	Estuarine, or eel-tailed, banjo catfish
Hexanematichthys seemani	Arius, or Colombian shark catfish
Mystus gulio	Estuarine mystus

Livebearers
Anableps anableps	Four-eyed fish
Belonesox belizanus	Pike livebearer
Gambusia spp.	Mosquitofish
Poecilia hybrid	Black molly
Poecilia latipinna	Common sailfin molly
Poecilia mexicana	Mexican shortfin molly
Poecilia sphenops	Shortfin molly
Poecilia velifera	Giant sailfin molly

Gobies and sleepers
Boleophthalmus spp.	Mudskippers
Brachygobius spp.	Bumblebee gobies
Butis butis	Crazyfish
Dormitator maculatus	Common sleeper
Gobioides broussonnetii	Violet goby
Periophthalmus spp.	Common mudskippers
Pomatoschistus spp.	European gobies
Stigmatogobius sadanundio	Knight goby
Salaria pavo	Peacock blenny

Cichlids
Cichlasoma urophthalmus	Mayan cichlid
Etroplus maculatus	Orange chromide
Etroplus suratensis	Green chromide
Hemichromis bimaculatus	Jewel cichlid
Herichthys carpintis	Texas cichlid
Oreochromis spp.	Tilapia
Nandopsis spp.	Cuban and Haitian cichlids
Sarotherodon spp.	Tilapia
Tilapia spp.	Tilapia
Vieja maculicauda	Black belt cichlid

Pufferfish
Tetraodon fluviatilis	Common spotted puffer

Flatfish
Achirus lineatus	Freshwater sole
Cynoglossus bilineatus	Brackish-water tongue sole
Trinectes fasciatus	Hogchoker sole

Miscellaneous species
Atractosteus tristoechus	Alligator gar
Datnioides spp.	Siamese tigerfish
Cynoglossus microlepis	Freshwater tongue sole
Dermogenys pusilla	Wrestling halfbeak
Gasterosteus aculeatus	Stickleback (brackish-water variety)
Lepisosteus oculatus	Short-nosed gar
Lepisosteus osseus	Long-nosed gar
Microphis brachyurus	African freshwater pipefish
Monodactylus spp.	Malayan angels, or monos
Notesthes robusta	Australian freshwater bullrout
Parambassis ranga	Common glassfish
Parambassis wolffi	Giant or Wolff's glassfish
Rhinomugil corsula	False four-eyed fish
Scatophagus spp.	Common scats
Selenotoca spp.	Silver scats
Toxotes spp.	Archerfish (some species strictly freshwater)
Terapon jarbua	Targetfish
Xenentodon cancila	Needle-nose halfbeak

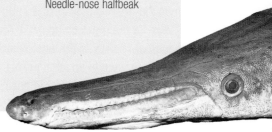

Brackish-Water Fishes and Plants

PRIMARY, SECONDARY, AND PERIPHERAL FRESHWATER FISHES

Ichthyologists categorize the different families of freshwater fish into those that are primary freshwater fish, secondary freshwater fish, and peripheral freshwater fish (Table 2.4).

PRIMARY

Primary freshwater fish are those families that have been in fresh water for most of their evolutionary history and have little or no tolerance for salt water. Unsurprisingly, many of the more primitive freshwater fish belong to this group, including the Lepidosirenidae (lungfishes), Osteoglossidae (arowanas), and Mormyridae (mormyrids). Also included among the primary freshwater fish are the Characidae (characins), Cyprinidae (carps), Cobitidae (loaches), Loricariidae (suckermouth catfishes), and Osphronemidae (gouramis). Although one or two exceptions exist, including certain Mastacembelidae (spiny eels) and Esocidae (pikes), generally speaking, primary freshwater fish are best excluded from brackish-water aquaria.

The Expert Says...

Note that while as families these primary and secondary groups might be salt tolerant, it can be a whole different story at the species level. It would be a bad idea to keep soft-water cichlids like discus, *Symphysodon* spp., or angels, *Pterophyllum* spp., in brackish water, for example. On the other hand, you will find that many familiar freshwater fishes discussed later in this book can be adapted easily to brackish water.

SECONDARY

In contrast to the primary freshwater fish families, many species among the secondary freshwater fish are distinctly salt tolerant. Although normally inhabiting fresh water, these fish can generally tolerate brackish or marine conditions for short periods. Some can actually adapt to marine conditions permanently, even being able to reproduce in salt water. The Cichlidae (cichlids), Cyprinodontidae (killifish), and Poeciliidae (livebearers) are the most important secondary freshwater fish as far as aquarists are concerned, though several others exist as well. Their tolerance for salt has been exploited for many years by fishkeepers—as with the therapeutic use of salt dips, the theory being that the salty water will kill external parasites and fungi long before it will do any harm to the fish. Many aquarists routinely add salt to killifish and livebearer aquaria even if they don't naturally come from brackish waters. Again, the idea is that it won't do any harm, and it may do some good in suppressing parasites and moderating the effects of nitrite and ammonium in the aquarium.

PERIPHERAL

The peripheral freshwater fish families are closely related to marine groups, but have become more or less entirely adapted to life in fresh water. In some cases they are normally only found in fresh water, as with the Potamotrygonidae (freshwater stingrays), but most peripheral freshwater families include species that can be found in fresh, brackish, and marine environments. Consequently, these include many of the most adaptable fishes for the brackish aquarist. Among the peripheral freshwater fish families, several are important to aquarists—such as the Gasterosteidae (sticklebacks), Toxotidae (archers), and Scatophagidae (scats). Although not widely kept in aquaria, the Salmonidae (salmons and trouts) and Galaxiidae (galaxiids) are peripheral freshwater fish of interest to advanced aquarists.

Avoid keeping soft-water cichlids like discus in brackish tanks.

Table 2.4: Primary, Secondary, and Peripheral Freshwater Fish Families

The following is a list of primary, secondary, and peripheral freshwater fish families important to aquarists. As a very general rule, primary freshwater fish are intolerant of brackish water, while secondary and peripheral freshwater fish are tolerant of it. There are plenty of exceptions, however, so this is only a very rough guide. Note also that while this list contains only those families of prime importance to aquarists, there are numerous freshwater fish families not included here.

Primary Families

Protopteridae	African lungfish
Lepiodsirenidae	South American lungfish
Polypteridae	Bichirs
Amiidae	Bowfin
Osteoglossidae	Arowanas
Mormyridae	Elephant noses
Characidae	Characins
Gasteropelecidae	Freshwater hatchetfish
Anostomidae	Headstanders and pencilfish
Citharinidae	African characins
Cyprinidae	Carps and minnows
Cobitidae	Loaches
Ictaluridae	Channel catfish
Bagridae	Asian catfish
Siluridae	Eurasian catfish
Clariidae	African walking catfish
Mochokidae	Upside-down catfish
Doradidae	Talking catfish
Aspredinidae	Banjo catfish
Pimelodontidae	South American catfish
Callichthyidae	*Corydoras* catfish and relatives
Loricariidae	Plecos and other suckermouth catfish
Channidae	Snakeheads
Centrarchidae	North American sunfish
Percidae	Perches
Nandidae	Leaffish
Anabantidae	Climbing perches
Belontiidae	Bettas and gouramis
Helostomatidae	Kissing gourami
Mastacembelidae	Spiny eels

Secondary Families

Lepisosteidae	Garpikes
Cyprinodontidae	Killifish and egg-laying toothcarps
Anablepidae	Four-eyed fish
Poecilidae	Livebearers
Melanotaeniidae	Australian rainbowfish
Cichlidae	Cichlids

Peripheral Families

Potamotrygonidae	Freshwater stingrays
Acipenseridae	Sturgeons
Gasterosteidae	Sticklebacks
Synbranchidae	Swamp eels
Cottidae	Bullheads
Toxotidae	Archerfish
Scatophagidae	Scats

Also, numerous marine families include species that inhabit fresh waters (Table 2.5). Of prime interest to the aquarist are the Gobiidae (gobies) and Tetraodontidae (pufferfish), but several others of lesser but still significant importance are available.

CATADROMY, ANADROMY, AND BRACKISH-WATER NURSERY GROUNDS

Classifications of primary, secondary, and peripheral freshwater fish families apply to those fish that are resident in fresh water on a more or less permanent basis. If these species ever do make excursions into the marine realm, they are restricted to coastal habitats such as mangroves and reefs. But numerous other fishes migrate freely between the open sea and fresh waters, and some of these fishes can have their place in the brackish-water aquarium. The true eels, Anguillidae, are among the most well known of these. They have what is referred to as a catadromous life history—although the adults spawn in the depths of the ocean, after hatching, the young fish migrate into rivers and eventually into the streams, swamps, and lakes where they spend most of their lives. They only return to the ocean after several years have passed, and once they have spawned, they die. (The life cycle of the eel is a fascinating subject and is discussed in more depth in Chapter 11.) In addition to the eels, many of the flounders (Pleuronectidae), basses (Moronidae), and mullets (Mugilidae) found in fresh water are catadromous as well, although they spawn in shallower water than do the eels, and they reproduce several times over their lives rather than just once.

The reverse of catadromy is anadromy, in which the adult fish spawns in fresh water but the young go to the sea to grow. The Salmonidae are the most well-known examples of these fishes, but also listed among the anadromous fishes are the sturgeons (Acipenseridae), sea catfish (Ariidae), and Cottidae (sculpins).

While these fishes pass through brackish waters, yet other fishes use brackish waters as spawning grounds or as a place for their juveniles to feed and grow. Many herrings, snappers, groupers, and jacks spawn or grow up in brackish water, and since these are commercially important fishes, the health of estuaries and mangroves can influence the quality of fisheries hundreds of miles away. Unlike catadromous and anadromous fish, these species will not tolerate freshwater conditions. As a result, few have become popular among

Scats like *Scatophagus argus* are popular peripheral freshwater fish.

Many of the flounders, bass, and mullets found in fresh water are catadromous.

aquarists. One notable exception is the batfish, *Platax* sp., which is a common inhabitant of mangroves as a juvenile, but a primarily marine fish as an adult.

MARINE FISH IN BRACKISH-WATER HABITATS

In addition to the batfish, a few other marine fishes make excursions into brackish waters from time to time. These can be viable, permanent residents of a brackish-water aquarium (Table 2.5). Among these, the most durable are the "freshwater" damsels, *Neopomacentrus taeniurus*, *Pomacentrus taeniometopon*, and *Stegastes otophorus*. All three will survive in unsalted water for a while, and this is often how they are kept in aquarium stores. But they are truly brackish-water and marine fish, and although none is as brightly colored as the typical coral-reef damsels, they are just as active and easy to keep, and are well worth looking out for. The striped catfish, *Plotosus lineatus*, is another marine fish that can be acclimated to a brackish-water aquarium. The youngsters are quite commonly seen for sale in marine-aquarium stores. Also widely traded is the dog-faced puffer, *Arothron hispidus*, a large but relatively peaceful puffer that will do well in either brackish or marine conditions.

The key to adapting any of these fish to a brackish-water system is to acclimate them gradually, preferably over several days, so they can get used to the lower salinity. This won't be an issue if fish are being offered for sale from fresh or brackish water. If not, then adapting them too quickly to brackish water can stress or even kill them. The first thing to do is ask the aquarium store at what specific gravity they keep their tanks. Then get your aquarium within one or two points of it. For example, if the dealer has his tanks at a specific gravity of 1.018, then taking your brackish-water tank to a gravity of 1.016 to 1.017 will be adequate.

While "freshwater" damsels can survive in fresh water for some time, they truly are brackish or marine fish.

Any fish already in your aquarium that are suitable for keeping with these marine species will do fine at this elevated salinity. (Do not, however, buy these marine fish with a view to combining them with low-salinity brackish-water species like kribensis or spiny eels.) Introduce the marine fish by placing the bag it comes in on the surface of the aquarium and making small slits in the bag. This will allow aquarium water to seep slowly into the bag, gently changing the salinity and giving the fish plenty of time to become accustomed to it. After 20 to 30 minutes, open the bag and gently lower the opening into the water so the fish can swim into its new home.

Over the next weeks, with each water change, lower the salinity a point or two. Keep an eye on the new fish to see that it is happy and feeding. As a general rule, these marine fish are a bit more demanding than the average brackish fish in that the aquarist must keep a closer eye on things like oxygenation levels, pH, and hardness. Aside from the lower salinity, treat an aquarium containing these brackish-marine fishes as you would a marine aquarium, provide the best filtration you can, and carry out regular water changes. But keep in mind that while these fishes have much to recommend them, they are species for the advanced aquarist rather than the beginner.

Table 2.5 Notable marine families with significant numbers of freshwater or brackish species

This list contains several marine families that include numerous freshwater and brackish species, which can make viable residents of a brackish aquarium.

Muraenidae	Morays	Eleotridae	Sleepers
Ariidae	Sea catfish	Monodactylidae	Monos
Plotosidae	Reef catfish	Pomacentridae	Damselfish
Mugilidae	Mullets	Tetraodontidae	Pufferfish
Syngnathidae	Pipefish	Cynoglossidae	Hogchoker and other
Scorpaenidae	Scorpionfish		tonguefish
Ambassidae	Glassfish	Pleuronectidae	Flounders
Blennidae	Blennies	Soleidae	Soles
Gobiidae	Gobies		

Brackish-Water Fishes and Plants

Anubias, a favorite choice for cichlid tanks, also can be used in low-salinity brackish tanks.

BRACKISH-WATER PLANTS

Many people believe that brackish-water aquaria cannot be planted, and that you are stuck with using plastic plants. While it is true that none of the commonly traded freshwater plants is able to tolerate strongly brackish or marine conditions, many species will adapt well to lower-salinity systems. Such plants can be kept in aquaria with a specific gravity of up to 1.005, making them suitable for combining with cichlids, livebearers,

gobies, killifish, halfbeaks, spiny eels—indeed, all the smaller fish species that you would probably want to keep in a planted tank. Many of these fish actually do better in planted aquaria, being more likely to swim outside their caves or burrows and, in the case of livebearers and killifish especially, more likely to breed successfully.

Several problems face freshwater plants in brackish water, but one of the most serious is that hard, alkaline water does not contain much free carbon dioxide, which the plants need for photosynthesis. Pumping CO_2 into the aquarium isn't a worthwhile option, because all that does is reduce the hardness and pH, making the fish uncomfortable. The only freshwater plants that do well in brackish-water systems are those that are tolerant of hard, alkaline water, because they are able to use the carbonate compounds in the water for photosynthesis as an alternative to CO_2. Typically, these species tolerate brackish water up to a specific gravity of 1.003. A handful of other species that naturally come from slightly brackish waters can be used in aquaria with a specific gravity up to 1.005.

BRACKISH-TOLERANT FRESHWATER PLANTS (SPECIFIC GRAVITY UP TO 1.003)

Anubias barteri

The African epiphyte *Anubias barteri* var. *nana* is one of the most popular members of this genus among aquarists, and can do very well in low-salinity brackish aquaria. It is indifferent to substrate type or whether an undergravel filter is used because it grows attached to rocks or bogwood, rather than in the soil. Though small and slow growing, it is attractive, with sturdy, dark green leaves. Also, it will put up with lower levels of ambient light than will most other aquarium plants. In many ways, it is very similar to the ever-popular Java fern and can be cared for in the same way. Like Java ferns, it is sometimes sold as a potted plant. Although these might do well, the main stem of the plant often rots when buried in substrate. Instead, remove potted *Anubias* and attach them to small pieces of bogwood with black cotton thread, taking care not to tighten the thread too much. After a few months, the *Anubias* will have attached firmly to the wood with their roots, and the thread can be cut or left to rot away.

Ceratophyllum demersum is a good choice for use in some brackish aquaria.

Ceratophyllum demersum

In aquaria with small fish, particularly livebearers, killifish, and gobies, the hornwort *Ceratophyllum demersum* can be an excellent choice for providing floating cover. While brittle and apparently delicious to large, vegetarian fish such as cichlids and scats, small fish will not affect the normally rapid growth of this species. It requires a great deal of light and regular feeding using an iron-rich plant food to do well. Sometimes sold in pots, it does not do well buried in the sediment; however, large plants will throw down long, white roots from the green stems, and these roots will anchor the plant to the substrate. Because this species absorbs nutrients directly from the water, it is not bothered by the type of substrate used. It also will do well in aquaria using undergravel filters.

Ceratopteris cornuta

Like *Ceratophyllum demersum*, *Ceratopteris cornuta* is a fast-growing, floating plant that is easy to care for. Because it is a floater, it doesn't care about the substrate used or whether an undergravel filter is employed, but it does require fairly strong lighting. This is a popular species for use with livebearers, giving the baby fish plenty of places to hide from potential predators.

Vallisneria are among the most useful freshwater plants for brackish aquarists.

Brackish-Water Fishes and Plants

Echinodorus tenellus is a good choice for use in some brackish aquaria.

Crinum thaianum

Crinum thaianum is widely known as the onion plant, because of the bulb from which the long, strap-like leaves grow. It is fairly hardy, and can be used as an alternative to the larger species of *Vallisneria*. This plant needs a deep, laterite-enriched sediment and strong lighting. Although it grows slowly, it benefits from regular feeding with an iron-rich plant food. It will not do well in plain, washed gravel or in aquaria with undergravel filters.

Cryptocoryne wendtii

This is one of the few *Cryptocorynes* that will do well in brackish-water aquaria. It is a somber, slow-growing plant, but is hardy and reliable in slightly brackish water. Being relatively small, this isn't a plant to use in aquaria with big fish like cichlids or the larger spiny eels that engage in massive earth-moving operations, but it can be an excellent specimen with small gobies and dwarf cichlids. It prefers a laterite-rich soil and will not do well if planted directly into the plain gravel used as part of an undergravel filter.

Hygrophila spp.

Common hygrophila, *Hygrophila polysperma*, and the giant hygrophila, *Hygrophila corymbosa*, can both adapt successfully to slightly brackish water. Like giant vals, they need strong lighting and regular feeding, but they also need a laterite-rich substrate and will not do well in plain gravel. If kept improperly, these plants become etiolated and the few small leaves turn pale green. Such plants are fragile and snap apart easily—and when that happens, they don't look attractive. On the other hand, if kept well, these plants are vigorous, hardy, and grow very quickly. They tend to grow upward rather than outward, so regular pruning is important if you want to create a bushier-looking plant. Propagation occurs through cuttings, which should take root when placed in the sediment.

Vallisneria spp.

Among the most useful freshwater plants available to the brackish aquarist are the giant val species, most commonly either *Vallisneria gigantea* or *Vallisneria asiatica*. These big plants work very well with large fish that like thickets to hide in and appreciate some cover at the top of the aquarium. Such species include gars, pike livebearers, Siamese tigerfish, archerfish, and spiny eels. These are big plants, with leaves that grow to over 3 feet (1 meter) in length. As such, they are best used in comparably large aquaria. Both these *Vallisneria* species are hardy, fast growing, and undemanding. They will do well even in plain gravel (although a mixture of laterite, sand, and gravel works better), provided that it is at least 3 inches (8 cm) deep and not part of an undergravel filter. About the only demands they place on the aquarist is for strong lighting and regular feeding with a quality plant food.

Like most other plants, they can take a few weeks to settle in, but once adjusted to your aquarium, vals usually grow vigorously, producing numerous daughter plants that can be cut off from the runner once they have developed a good root system and planted elsewhere. Some pruning is essential, but simply trimming the leaves back halfway often causes the plant to die back. Instead, cut overly long leaves back as close to the base as you can without damaging other leaves. Use a razor blade or sharp knife to make sure the cut is clean, and take care not to allow sand or gravel to enter the crown of the plant (the point just above the roots, where the leaves sprout). All *Vallisneria* do better when the crown is well above the gravel or sand, so allow about half an inch (1 cm or so) of the roots to remain *above* the level of substrate. (Incidentally, the

Brackish-Water Fishes and Plants

Jave ferns are possibly the best all-around choice for a planted brackish aquarium.

smaller species of *Vallisneria*, such as *Vallisneria spiralis*, do not adapt quite as well to brackish water and tend to be rather delicate.)

NATURALLY OCCURRING BRACKISH-WATER PLANTS (SPECIFIC GRAVITY UP TO 1.005)

Bacopa monnieri

This popular plant is usually kept in freshwater aquaria, but in the wild is most commonly found in slightly brackish waters.

Crinum calamistratum and *Crinum pedunculatum*

These two onion-plant species are kept in the same way as *Crinum thaianum*, but because they naturally occur in slightly brackish waters, they can be expected to tolerate a little more salt in the aquarium.

Echinodorus tenellus

Like *Cryptocoryne wendtii*, this is a good choice for an aquarium with small fish. It requires a rich substrate (a mix of fine gravel and laterite is ideal) and plenty of light. Some care must be taken to prevent other, faster-growing species from overshadowing this species, but otherwise it is not particularly demanding. Runners will spread out from the mother plant across the bottom of the tank.

Lilaeopsis brasiliensis

A rather demanding plant that needs a laterite-rich substrate and very strong light to do well, it is a more compact, bushier alternative to *Echinodorus tenellus* for creating low-lying vegetation across large areas of the substrate. Although not fast growing, the resulting lawn-like effect is exceptionally attractive when paired with smaller, bottom-dwelling fish such as gobies and dwarf cichlids.

Microsorium pteropus (Java fern)

Considered by many brackish aquarists as the best all around, this plant has many attributes in its favor. First, it naturally occurs in brackish water and so adapts readily to such conditions in aquaria. It is also tolerant of hard, alkaline water, and will put up with low light levels and undergravel filters. It is an epiphyte (like *Anubias* spp.) and should not be planted in the substrate; instead, allow it to grow over stones or rocks. It is possible to buy large specimens already growing on small pieces of bogwood; although expensive, they represent excellent value for the money because they are hardy and reliable.

Many varieties of Java fern are available, but all seem equally robust. Because these plants are poisonous, they should not be kept with fishes that will eat them (such as scats). Otherwise, their foul taste is enough to put off casual plant nibblers, such as cichlids, without causing harm.

Mangroves and Seagrasses

Mangroves and seagrasses are among the relatively few flowering plants that normally inhabit strongly brackish waters. While seagrasses do not adapt well to aquaria, mangroves do, provided that some care is taken to allow for their very special needs.

Brackish for Beginners

By Rory McDaniel

Experienced aquarists will probably find much of what is covered in this chapter familiar, but it is well worth saying that maintaining a brackish-water tank isn't beyond the ability of even an ambitious newcomer to the fishkeeping hobby, provided that he adheres to a few basic rules. While some people are surprised to discover that brackish-water aquaria exist alongside freshwater and marine ones, they very quickly learn that a brackish aquarium is the best way to keep a variety of truly fascinating species, from mudskippers and four-eyed fish to archers and puffers.

SETTING UP THE BRACKISH-WATER AQUARIUM

THE TANK

While some brackish fish can be kept in small aquaria, it is broadly the case that, compared with most freshwater community fishes, brackish-water

Brackish for Beginners

Though many are tolerant of salt, some cichlids that have adapted to very specific water conditions, like the *Xenotilapia flavipinnins* of Lake Tanganyika, are not.

species tend to be large and very active, often needing relatively large aquaria. For smaller aquaria—around the 10- to 20-gallon (30- to 70-liter) mark—gobies, glassfish, halfbeaks, and killifish are the best options. Pipefish, soles, and flatfish are somewhat bigger than these species, but being relatively inactive, they can also work well in small tanks. However, for the classic brackish species, such as monos, scats, archers, and pufferfish, the bigger the tank you set up, the better. A 50-gallon (200-liter) aquarium is probably the minimum aquarium for many of these species.

A perennial question is whether freshwater species can be kept in the brackish-water aquarium. Generally, the answer is no. With few exceptions, catfish, tetras, loaches, gouramis, and barbs all have a very low salt tolerance. They will not do well in even slightly brackish water. Cichlids, killifish, halfbeaks, and livebearers, on the other hand, are often quite tolerant of salt. Of course, those species that have adapted to very specific water conditions, such as Amazonian and Lake Tanganyika cichlids, do not do well in brackish water, but generalists, such as blue acara and guppies, are often far more adaptable. Later chapters of this book, particularly those on cichlids, catfish, and livebearers, identify some of the versatile species suitable for inclusion in low-salinity brackish-water aquaria.

Filtration

Brackish-water fish vary from species largely indifferent to water quality, such as mudskippers, to others that are very sensitive to low oxygen and high nitrate levels, like pufferfish. While there is no one-size-fits-all approach to filtering the brackish-water aquarium, the best approach usually is to overfilter the aquarium to take into account the fact that brackish-water fish are often large, greedy, and rather messy feeders.

A good rule of thumb is to choose a filter device that provides 50 to 100 percent more filtration than your aquarium needs. It is usual for electric internal or external filters to be rated in terms of *turnover*, in either gallons or liters per hour. In a standard freshwater aquarium, it is usually recommended that a filter be used that will turn the water over (that is, pass the entire volume of water through

Even with the help of an aerator, mid- to high-salinity brackish tanks should not be densely stocked.

the filter media) at least four times per hour or more. For a 20-gallon (70-liter) tank, a filter rated at 80 gallons (280 liters) per hour would therefore be the acceptable minimum. Increasing this for a brackish-water system means the aquarist should choose a filter rated at least at 120 to 160 gallons (420 to 560 liters) per hour.

Air-powered undergravel filters can be used in brackish-water aquaria very effectively, but they have their shortcomings. Solid waste, for example, accumulates on the surface of the substrate and must be siphoned away, usually at least once a week. Undergravel filters also interfere with plant growth, so it is best to use undergravel filters only in tanks without plants or with species that absorb minerals directly from the water (like Java fern, *Anubias*, and hornwort).

A few other factors must be considered when choosing a filter. First, zeolite (ammonia remover) will not work in brackish water. Salty water absorbs ammonia from the zeolite, making it useless in this type of aquarium. The second issue to consider is the lower oxygen concentration in brackish water compared with fresh water: the higher the salinity, the lower the oxygen concentration. Therefore, in mid- to high-salinity systems, you must use a stocking density closer to that of a marine aquarium than of a freshwater aquarium. This can be mitigated somewhat by using additional aeration methods, but even so, compared with a freshwater community tank, a brackish-water aquarium must not be densely stocked.

Obvious exceptions to the rule of overfiltering are small, slow-moving species, such as gobies and pipefish, which tend to do best in tanks with a relatively modest water current, if only because they depend on supplies of live foods such as *Artemia* that would be quickly sucked up by power filters. For these types of fish, basic air-powered sponge filters are often the best choice.

Substrate

When it comes to choosing a substrate, the deciding factor will be the fishes you intend to keep. Species requiring a high pH and hardness, such as monos, scats, and green spotted pufferfish, invariably do best in tanks where a calcareous substrate such as coral sand or crushed coral is used. Calcareous substrates buffer the water, neutralizing the tendency of most aquaria to acidify over time.

For fishes that like neutral to slightly alkaline water conditions with only a little salt added, as is the case with spiny eels, bumblebee gobies, glassfish, halfbeaks, and orange chromides, different substrate types should be used. Silica sand is one option that is particularly favored by many aquarists because it is chemically inert and so has no effect on water chemistry. River sand, which is usually a mix of silica and calcareous sands, also works well, but it will slightly raise the pH and hardness levels, although not to the same degree as coral sand. Plain gravel is another good option. Like silica sand, it is chemically inert, and because it's inexpensive and easy to clean, it is an ideal choice for use in large tanks and with messy fishes.

Water chemistry aside, the other key factor will be the behavior of the fishes you intend to keep. Burrowing species, such as spiny eels and flatfish, must be kept in tanks with a soft substrate. Silica sand, river sand, or coral sand should be used, depending on the particular

> ### The Expert Says...
> Bottom-dwellers that don't burrow tend to prefer dark-colored substrates. In tanks with a bright substrate, these fish become nervous, and their colors are often relatively muted compared with specimens kept under the correct conditions.

Silica sand and plain gravel are both good substrates for use in brackish aquaria.

water-chemistry requirements of the species involved. If forced to dig into a hard, gravelly substrate, these fish quickly scratch their delicate skins and become vulnerable to bacterial and fungal infections. Bottom-dwelling fish that don't burrow but do like to stay close to the substrate, as is the case with many cichlids and catfish, can be kept in tanks with either sand or gravel.

Midwater fish like monos, and fishes that stay close to the surface, such as halfbeaks, are usually indifferent to the substrate type. In these cases, water-chemistry constraints alone will be the deciding factor.

MAKING BRACKISH WATER

Several methods for making brackish water have been described over the years, but the only reliable technique is to use proper marine-aquarium salt. These marine mixes provide both the salinity and the buffering capacity that brackish aquarium water needs. As mentioned earlier, brackish-water fishes usually must be maintained in water with a high pH and hardness. Marine salt mixes usually ensure that this is the case without needing to add extra hardening agents, such as coral sand or crushed coral, to the filter.

Preparing brackish water using marine salt mix isn't difficult (the exact process is described in Chapters 1 and 2). Simply follow the instructions in this book or on the box, using a

The Expert Says...

Using table salt in the brackish aquarium is not recommended, although as a stopgap measure it can be better than nothing. Likewise, the aquarium tonic salt sold in many tropical fish stores isn't really suitable for long-term use with brackish-water fishes.

Brackish for Beginners

Hardy fish like black mollies are very effective in maturing aquaria.

hydrometer to measure the specific gravity of the water as you go along. Typically, low-salinity fishes, such as bumblebee gobies, need a specific gravity of around 1.005, or about one-fifth the amount of salt per gallon (or liter) of water necessary for marine fishes. Higher-salinity fishes, such as monos and green spotted puffers, require more salt. A specific gravity of 1.012 is about right: This corresponds to a concentration of salt about one-half that used in a marine aquarium.

CYCLING THE BRACKISH-WATER AQUARIUM

A key stage in setting up any aquarium is maturing it—specifically, building up the populations of bacteria in the filtration system. These bacteria eventually convert the ammonium and other wastes produced by the fishes into the comparatively nontoxic nitrates that can be removed with each water change. Cycling aquaria can be done in two ways: with or without live fishes.

Hardy fishes, such as black mollies, can be used very effectively to mature aquaria. A starter culture of bacteria also should be added to the aquarium to speed things up: You can either use gravel or filter medium from another aquarium, or buy bottles containing the bacteria from your retailer. For a low-salinity aquarium (specific gravity 1.005 or less), freshwater bacteria will do fine. Otherwise, use bacteria adapted to marine-aquarium conditions. The mollies provide a source of ammonium for the bacteria to feed on, and this gives the boost the bacterial populations need to grow rapidly. Because mollies can thrive at any salinity from freshwater to marine

Feeding brackish-water fish generally is easier than feeding freshwater fish—scats, for example, are shameless gluttons.

Brackish for Beginners

Beware overfeeding. It's not good for the fish or the aquarium.

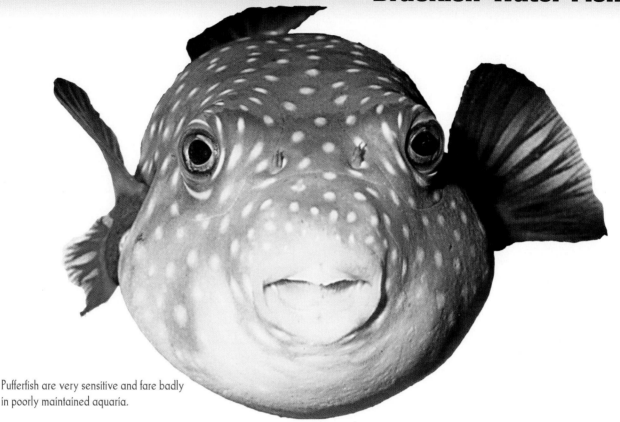

Pufferfish are very sensitive and fare badly in poorly maintained aquaria.

conditions, they are a particularly versatile choice. While the aquarium is still immature, the mollies should be fed only sparingly, and any uneaten food must be removed at once. Don't worry about starving them: Fishes need far less food to survive than most aquarists believe!

A nitrite test kit is especially useful during the maturation phase of an aquarium's life. Nitrite levels typically rise rapidly during the first few weeks. After about six to eight weeks, however, the nitrite level should have dropped to zero. Only after this point is reached is it safe to start adding a few more fish. (And even then, it is still important not to overfeed the fishes.) The downside to this approach is that these fish are effectively living in toxic conditions; at the very least, they may be more prone to diseases.

Cycling without fish present is an alternative approach that doesn't put fish at any risk. Again, a bacteria starter culture is needed to get things going, but instead of using fishes, chemicals are added to the tank to provide the bacteria with ammonium. Pharmaceutical-grade ammonium hydroxide is the preferred ammonium source for many hobbyists, and can be obtained inexpensively from drugstores and hardware stores. It is critical to make sure the ammonium hydroxide solution is pure, though, because any additional chemicals in the solution may be toxic to the fishes or even the bacteria. Exactly how much ammonium hydroxide you should add is a bit of a dark art, but a good rule of thumb is to use approximately 2 drops per 10 gallons (30 liters) per day. Measure the nitrite level each day so you can observe when the nitrites reach their peak and then drop to zero. Once you're at zero, the tank is ready for its first, preferably hardy, residents.

Brackish for Beginners

Avoid painted glassfish—those striking colors are inhumanely injected into their bodies via syringe.

MAINTAINING THE BRACKISH AQUARIUM

Once the aquarium is running properly, maintaining the tank is straightforward. The basic rules are the same as those for the freshwater aquarium. Regular water changes of at least 10 to 20 percent of the water in the aquarium are important, and should be carried out at least twice a month–preferably more often. Pufferfish in particular are sensitive to old water with a high concentration of nitrates, and these fishes respond well to weekly water changes of 50 percent. Likewise, big, messy species, such as scats and Colombian shark catfish, also require substantial water changes if they are to be kept healthy over the long term.

Generally, brackish-water fishes are tolerant of salinity changes, so keeping a constant specific-gravity level is irrelevant. A few exceptions exist, however. Fish tolerant of only very low salinities, such as spiny eels, should not be exposed to high salinities, while halfbeaks and needlefish are notoriously sensitive to sudden changes in salinity, pH, or hardness, to the point where stressed fish can die within hours. However, the vast majority of brackish species not only tolerate changes in salinity with each water change, but positively thrive in them, as they are adapted to environments where salinity changes all the time. Monos, scats, mudskippers, archerfish, orange and green chromides, green spotted pufferfish, and freshwater soles and flatfish are all examples of species that adapt to changes in salinity very easily, provided they are not too great.

In general, going up or down two points on the specific-gravity scale (for example, from 1.010 to 1.012) does these fish no harm at all.

Feeding brackish fishes often prevents even fewer problems than feeding freshwater fishes does. By their very nature, most of these species are opportunists, taking whatever they can find. Scats in particular are legendary gluttons and eat anything from floating pellets to aquarium plants—even hair algae. Most brackish-water fish can be maintained on a mixed diet of flake, pellet, and frozen foods.

CHOOSING YOUR FIRST BRACKISH-WATER FISHES

Newcomers to the brackish side of the fishkeeping hobby are often drawn to species such as puffers and mudskippers, true characters that make very worthwhile and engaging pets. However, these are not necessarily easy fish to maintain. (Although as later chapters in this book will make clear, with the right care they can do well in home aquaria.)

Pufferfish in particular have very strong personalities, and many aquarists consider them by far the most intelligent of all the fishes, cichlids notwithstanding. Individual pufferfish certainly can have very distinct personalities, and within a group of one species, some will be more outgoing while others remain shy. Many people give them names and treat them as they would a cat or dog. All pufferfish seem to learn to recognize their owner, and most adopt obvious begging behaviors whenever they suspect a meal might be forthcoming. In this regard, pufferfish often manage to train their owners remarkably well! However, pufferfish are aggressive toward other fishes, both of their own species and of others, and some specimens become persistent fin nippers, taking chunks out of the fins of other fish. For this reason, they rarely work well in community tank settings.

Mudskippers are another of the brackish-water fishes that earn star billing in many aquaria—but again, these are tricky fishes to keep in community tanks. They need an extensive area of dry land, for one thing, and are often rather territorial, so they need plenty of space.

On the other hand, many of the smaller gobies make excellent fish for the beginner with a relatively small aquarium. Knight gobies and bumblebee gobies don't swim around much and hold very small territories, and so are particularly accommodating. Candy-stripe gobies, *Awaous strigatus,* are another good choice, as they are lively and very entertaining to watch. Another peaceable fish is the violet goby, quite commonly seen in fish stores, perhaps because of its rather fearsome appearance. Looks aside, it is singularly inoffensive, and nippy fishes like puffers and dwarf cichlids can easily worry it to death.

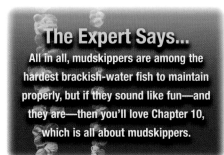

The Expert Says...

All in all, mudskippers are among the hardest brackish-water fish to maintain properly, but if they sound like fun—and they are—then you'll love Chapter 10, which is all about mudskippers.

Colombian shark catfish are perhaps the most well known and most popular of the brackish-water predators. They are, however, very large—quickly reaching lengths of over 8 inches (20 cm) in captivity. They also must be kept in groups, and are very sensitive to poor water quality. While an outstanding subject for the ambitious aquarist, this species is perhaps not the best choice for the absolute beginner.

Spiny eels, by contrast, are predatory fish that do make good fish for beginners. They are relatively hardy, and do well in low-salinity aquaria alongside gobies and livebearers of similar size. The big species easily exceed 24 inches (60 cm) in length and will polish off fishes even as large as platies, but the smaller species much prefer earthworms, river shrimps, and other small invertebrates.

Finally, avoid painted glassfish. These fish have bright green, pink, and other fluorescent colors in their transparent bodies. The color is injected into the fish's bodys using a syringe, a process that is unquestionably stressful to the fish. Although this artificial color eventually fades, the fish are permanently weakened by the process. Do not reward those who do this by buying such fish.

CHOOSING HEALTHY FISH

Many brackish fishes are difficult to breed in captivity and therefore must be caught from the wild. This process leaves fish susceptible to contracting disease or being harassed by other fish when they arrive at shops. Their condition is further worsened because many fish shops keep brackish-water species in freshwater tanks, something that invariably weakens the fish, making them more prone to illness and less likely to feed properly.

You can tell a healthy fish from a sick or weak fish in two ways. First, look at how a fish swims and holds its fins. If the fins are fully extended and the fish is active and alert, it is usually in good condition. While the shyer species tend to hide, outgoing species like cichlids and scats often swim to the surface when someone approaches the aquarium, because the fish anticipate being fed. Fish that feed readily and have full stomachs are generally a safe purchase. When buying expensive or delicate fish, it is invariably a good idea to ask the sales clerk to feed the fish so you can gauge the animal's appetite.

The second clue to the health of a fish is its colors. Many species of fish can change colors—if they have gone through stressful conditions in the last day or two, their colors are often muted and their patterns have less contrast. Monos, for example, turn dark gray when stressed. In contrast, fish that are brightly colored, particularly if they are sporting their breeding colors or are displaying to one another, are likely to be in good shape.

Aquarists often believe that pufferfish are delicate and prone to mysterious deaths, but in fact, healthy specimens are relatively easy to spot. Checking their caudal fin is a quick and easy test: If it stays spread out the majority of the time, then it is probably a good specimen. Due to the aggressive nature of many pufferfish species, when they are crowded together in a store aquarium, weaker individuals often have had chunks of their fins bitten off by the more dominant specimens. These harassed fish have a greatly decreased survival rate; "rescuing" them can be a rather expensive act of kindness. On the other hand, the color of pufferfish is sometimes deceptive because when some of the species sleep, their colors fade to dark gray. (The two most common puffers, *Tetraodon biocellatus* and *T. fluviatilis*, both exhibit this trait).

As for mudskippers, you must watch them for a while to tell which ones are healthy and which ones are dominant. To see which ones are harassed, simply look for those that are too scared to get out of the water.

Avoid buying unhealthy fish. If usually lively fish are acting sluggish, or colorful fish, like monos, have dull colorations, chances are they're sick.

The Southeast Asian Staples

By Neale Monks

For many people, **Monodactylus argenteus** (the mono), *Scatophagus argus* (the scat), and *Toxotes jaculatrix* (the common archerfish) are the quintessential brackish-water fishes. These three species are abundant throughout southeastern Asia and so have been continually collected and shipped by the major exporters in Indonesia, Singapore, and Thailand. They can be found wherever brackish-water fish are sold. Indeed, few brackish-water aquaria don't include one of these species. In many ways, these species exemplify the best in brackish-water fishes: They are big, active, attractively patterned, and—above all—tough as nails.

The monos and scats in particular have a well-earned reputation for being among the best fishes with which to cycle a marine aquarium. Their extraordinary boldness and willingness to eat pretty much anything makes them ideal dither fish to help more nervous marine fish settle in and get used to life in captivity. Monos and scats mix well with each other too, and many people keep mixed schools of the two species with great success.

But monos, scats, and archers aren't the only southeast Asian brackish fish to turn up in pet stores. *Terapon jarbua* (targetfish) and *Datnioides* species (Siamese tigerfish) are highly

predatory fish that are seen at larger retailers from time to time. While the targetfish has never really caught on as an aquarium fish, advanced aquarists looking for something a bit special might appreciate the peaceful demeanor and rakish good looks of the tigerfish.

All these fishes are large by aquarium-fish standards, reaching at least 6 inches (15 cm) long—and often much longer—when mature. Consequently, they demand a large aquarium with plenty of swimming room. Because most will eat anything they can fit into their mouths, they shouldn't be trusted with small fish. Otherwise, they can be mixed well with one another or with any similarly sized brackish-water fish. Even though they are hardy, they shouldn't be abused—they all benefit from good filtration and well-oxygenated water.

MONOS—*MONODACTYLUS ARGENTEUS* AND *M. SEBAE*

Monos are bright, active fishes that are especially cute when small but grow into fairly large animals (around 6 inches, or 15 cm, is not uncommon) that must be kept in a large, strongly brackish or marine aquarium. Shaped rather like an angelfish, *Monodactylus argenteus* in particular has sometimes been called the Malayan angel after one of the places it can be found. But unlike the freshwater angelfish *Pterophyllum scalare*, these fishes are frenetically active schooling fish that must be kept in groups if they are to do well. Complicating this slightly is the fact that although they cannot be kept on their own—solitary specimens are at best very nervous and commonly die prematurely—aggression within a group is not uncommon. The smallest specimens may be chased and picked on, to the point where they cannot feed or rest and eventually die from either starvation or stress.

Mono

Name	*Monodactylus* spp.
Other names	Mono, Malayan angel, fingerfish, moony, silver mono, common mono, West African mono
Origin	Indo-West Pacific (*M. argenteus*); West Africa (*M. sebae*)
Size	Can reach at least 10 inches (25 cm) in length; dwelling notably deeper than most fishes, they need a spacious and deep aquarium
Water conditions	Fresh or slightly brackish (specific gravity <1.005) when small; adults need half- to full-strength seawater
Diet	Invertebrates; small fish; prepared fish foods; some vegetable matter such as algae, boiled peas, or blanched lettuce
Temperament	Peaceful schooling fish
Availability	Commonly traded, although may be seasonal; moderately priced
Ease of maintenance	Fairly easy
Specific problems	Must be kept in groups of six or more; will eat very small fish; sensitive to pollution and low oxygen levels; adults sensitive to shock

Monodactylus sebae

Southeast Asian Staples

Monodactylus argenteus lacks the rudimentary pelvic fins of *M. sebae*.

The solution to this is to keep a sufficiently large group of them in a tank with plenty of space: Pairs and triplets rarely work out well, but by keeping six or more, any aggression is diffused enough among all the fishes for each individual to do well. It is also important to make sure all the specimens are of roughly equal size and are introduced into the aquarium simultaneously. This of course is the same basic strategy familiar to fishkeepers who are used to aggressive cichlids such as mbuna, except for the fact that monos don't hold territories. A pecking order tends to emerge, however, and one or two fish will grow fastest and be the most forward at feeding time.

Having said all this, it would be wrong to give the idea that monos are aggressive fishes—they are not. They mix extremely well with fishes too large to be considered food, and constitute the heart of many community aquaria. They can frequently be seen in large public aquaria swimming alongside sharks and groupers, and home aquarists can rely on them to work well with shark catfish, gars, and other showpiece fishes.

Monos also mix very well with scats. In fact, many aquarists keep them together as mixed schools. In the wild they commonly inhabit the same places, so this is mimicking their natural behavior to a degree.

Two species of mono are seen in the hobby. The more common of the two species, the common or silver mono, *Monodactylus argenteus,* is a silvery fish with a rounded diamond shape, a yellowy tail, and a few short black stripes running across the head and flanks. It can be found in coastal waters right across southeastern Asia to Australia, where it is sometimes called the "moony." A second species, *M. sebae*, is from West Africa, so strictly speaking it falls outside the scope of this chapter. However, it is so similar to *M. argenteus* that it warrants a place here. The West African mono looks very much like the common mono, except that it is much taller than it is long, and so is often called the fingerfish. At first glance, it is very similar in appearance to the freshwater angelfish, even down to its basic coloration of dark grays and silver. It lacks the yellow tail of the common mono, but the dark vertical stripes are much more strongly developed and run across the head and body from the tip of the dorsal fin down to the very end of the anal fin. Another difference between the two monos is the presence of rudimentary pelvic fins in *M. sebae*, which are absent on *M. argenteus*.

One feature common to both species—and very rarely seen in any other fish—is the scales covering the anal and dorsal fins, giving them a rather fleshy appearance.

Because both species are relatively tall fish, a deep aquarium is useful; an ideal aquarium for six individuals is 48 inches (160 cm) long and 24 inches (60 cm) deep. This leaves a bit of room for some other comparably sized community fish, such as a big sleeper goby or a couple of scats or shark catfish.

Monos are open-water fish and aren't particularly fussy about having plants in their aquarium, though a bit of cover will be welcomed. Because these are fishes of mangrove and estuarine habitats, artificial roots are ideal, but large shells or water-worn stones can be used just as effectively.

Keeping monos should present no particular problems to the experienced aquarist. In addition to the space required to keep a good-size school, the only other demand they place on the hobbyist is a need for clean, well-filtered water. In common with the other fishes in this chapter, consistently hard, alkaline water is essential. Juveniles less than 2 inches (5 cm) long will do fine in fresh water, but salt is required as they mature. Brackish water that has a specific gravity of around 1.010 is ideal for long-term health, and monos can also be adapted to normal marine conditions. In high-salinity aquariums, a protein skimmer can be used to contribute to proper water management, but in any case a powerful filter is essential. These fish are greedy and fast growing, and produce a lot of waste, which puts a heavy burden on the filter. Monos also appreciate strong water currents, something air-powered filters tend not to be able to supply. Instead, use electric powerheads on an undergravel filter, or else opt for an external canister filter.

Monos are remarkably hardy. Although they occasionally come down with whitespot or get a bit of fungus on their fins, these diseases are easily treated by increasing the salinity of the aquarium. Freshwater parasites

The Expert Says...
Although it has happened from time to time, monos have rarely been spawned in captivity.

and fungi lack the adaptability of monos, and seawater quickly kills them off, leaving the monos in perfect health. Alternatively, use commercially produced remedies if the other fishes in the aquarium cannot be acclimated to full-strength seawater. Monos are a bit sensitive to stress, especially when mature, turning from their normal bright silver to dark gray or black when unhappy. Although they soon recover in the right conditions, stressed monos very occasionally die for no apparent reason. Consequently, it is essential to avoid stressful situations, such as netting the fish or transporting it from one aquarium to another. The aquarist should be aware, though, that monos may turn dark at night; this is perfectly normal and nothing to worry about.

Southeast Asian Staples

SCATS—*SCATOPHAGUS* AND *SELENOTOCA* SPP.

Scats, sometimes called argusfishes in older aquarium books, are some of the most adaptable and likeable fishes in the hobby. They generally mix well with all fishes, although they don't do well with aggressive fish like large cichlids, and while they will eat very small fishes, they are rather inept predators and are easily satisfied with commercially prepared foods. Indeed, scats have rightly earned a reputation for greedily eating pretty much anything, including aquarium plants, pellets, and insects shot down by any archerfishes housed in the tank with them. Unlike many other aquarium fish, scats are distinctly herbivorous, and plant matter of one sort or another should make up a significant part of their diet. Blanched lettuce leaves, thin slices of cucumber or zucchini, frozen peas, and algae flakes are all used with success. Because they eat aquarium plants, scats obviously cannot be kept in planted aquaria.

For the most part, these fish can be kept in exactly the same way as the monos described in the previous section. Many aquarists mix

Scatophagus tetracanthus

Scat

Name	*Scatophagus* and *Selenotoca* spp.
Other names	Scat, argusfish
Origin	Coastal waters and reefs of the Indo-West Pacific
Size	In captivity, typically 6 to 8 inches (15 to 20 cm); potentially as long as 1 foot (30 cm)
Water conditions	Fresh or slightly brackish (specific gravity <1.005) when small; adults need one-quarter to full-strength seawater
Diet	Omnivores—they do best with a varied diet including vegetarian flakes, cichlid pellets, fresh or frozen invertebrates, algae, cooked vegetables
Temperament	Peaceful schooling fish
Availability	Commonly traded, although may be seasonal; moderately priced
Ease of maintenance	Easy
Specific problems	Large size and greedy habits can put a strain on filters; will damage any live plants in the aquarium

monos and scats with great success. Scats are even larger than monos, however, and both types of fish appreciate a large aquarium with well-filtered water and plenty of swimming room. While certainly schooling animals, scats are significantly more curious and independent-minded than monos, and individuals can become quite tame. This makes them much better pets than monos, although monos probably have the edge as far as activity and prettiness go. Together, they make a winning combination.

Four species of scat are commonly imported. *Scatophagus argus* is probably the most commonly seen. The juveniles are rounded and either brown or green with a leopard-like pattern of spots, usually with a couple of stripes on the head. As the fish mature, these stripes disappear—the fish become much more bronze or silvery in color, and take on a more rectangular shape (very similar to their close relatives, the marine butterfly fishes). A popular variety of this species is the ruby scat, *Scatophagus argus atromaculatus,* sometimes called *S. rubifrons.* This fish is identical to the regular common scat when mature, but the juveniles enjoy a more brilliant coloration, with bright red or orange flashes on the dorsal fin.

The African scat, *S. tetracanthus,* is more rarely seen. It has a distinctive juvenile coloration, with vertical stripes instead of spots. As an adult, the African scat is identical to the adults of other species, all of which can grow up to 1 foot (30 cm) long.

Even less frequently seen are *Selenotoca multifasciata* and *Selenotoca papuensis.* Aquarists will be hard pressed to tell these fish apart from each other, but they are easily separated from species of *Scatophagus.* They are much more silvery, the basic color being a brilliant white-silver, against which their black stripes and

Selenotoca multifasciata is among the very rare brackish scats.

spots stand out dramatically. Juveniles and adults are rather similar, as the dorsal fins of all ages sport striking red or golden flecks.

All in all, they are beautiful fish, and the news just gets better: They are just as easy to keep as the common scats, but don't grow nearly so large. *Selenotoca multifasciata* typically reaches lengths of only 6 to 8 inches (15 to 20 cm) in captivity, and *S. papuensis* is even smaller, growing to no more than 4 inches (10 cm) in length.

None of the scats presents any particular problems as far as health care goes. Like all big fish, they are prone to physical damage if startled, often scratching their skin or eyes on rough objects in the aquarium. While damage to the fins heals quickly, the eyes are more sensitive, and pop-eye can be a problem. This isn't fatal and it doesn't appear to upset the fish much, but it is unsightly and takes a long time to heal. The best solution is prevention—make sure nothing in the aquarium could cause this type of damage (such as bleached coral). Poor water quality can lead to problems like hole-in-the-head disease and lymphocystis. Otherwise, regular water changes and variations in salinity from time to time help keep these fish healthy with minimal need for medications.

As with the monos, these fish rarely, if ever, spawn in captivity.

ARCHERFISH—*TOXOTES*

Although not as showy as the monos or as friendly as the scats, the archerfishes bow to neither when it comes to interesting behavior and adaptability. Archerfish get their name from their amazing ability to shoot

Toxotes jaculatrix

Half the fun of owning archerfish is watching them shoot down insects perched above the water line for dinner.

down insects and spiders from overhanging branches. Fully grown specimens can spit water up to 5 feet (150 cm) with remarkable accuracy. Fish biologists have found that they can even compensate for the refraction of light as it passes through the water. (From a fish's perspective, the fly or spider it is looking at through the water isn't where it seems to be. This is the same phenomenon that makes a spoon placed in a glass of water appear to be bent.) Even more amazingly, archers can predict where their prey will fall once hit, and set off toward that spot immediately after opening fire. This trick is undoubtedly useful because it saves time. If the archer waited to see where its prey fell, it would leave time for other fish in the school to snap up the prize before the shooter had a chance to get there.

Archerfish also jump for their food, like trout and salmon, and they choose whether to jump or spit depending on how far the food is above the surface of the water. If their prey is a body length or so above the water, they tend to jump, but if it is farther than that, they spit. They also eat anything they can catch in the midwater level too, including small fish. They do not *need* live foods though—archers readily adapt to frozen bloodworms, small pieces of shrimp and squid, cichlid pellets, and good-quality flake food. Vegetable matter of some sort, such as an algae-based flake food of the type frequently given to livebearers and cichlids, is important.

Easy as it is to keep archerfish well fed on traditional fish foods, the fun for most aquarists is in seeing them spit. For this to happen, they must be a bit hungry, so if you want them to work for their dinner, don't feed them breakfast. They also need to be at least 3 inches (8 cm) or so long; specimens smaller than that don't seem to spit at all.

The best arrangement is to keep archers in an aquarium that is only partially filled with water. For this to work, given the size of these relatively deep-bodied fish, a deep aquarium is necessary. A tank 18 inches (45 cm) deep but only two-thirds filled with water is probably the minimum for adults. This allows several inches of empty space above the water level for you to place morsels of food that the archers can spit down. Small pieces of prawn moistened with aquarium water will stick to the glass and make ideal targets. Some fish will spit at them without further prompting, but if they don't, a good trick is to begin by placing the prawns right at the water line so the fish can see and smell them. Each time they take the food, place the next bit of prawn a little higher up. At first, the archers will jump, but eventually they will begin spitting. Watching one take aim and then race over to its meal before another fish can steal it from them is terrific fun, and one of the most fascinating behaviors available for the home aquarist to watch. Take care not to overfeed them, though, tempting as it is.

Archerfish generally adapt well to any aquarium, but because most species reach 6 to 12 inches (15 to 30 cm) in length, they need plenty of space. They normally inhabit waters with overhanging branches and other

Archerfish

Name	*Toxotes* spp.
Other names	Archerfish, archers
Origin	Coastal waters of the Indo-West Pacific
Size	Generally around 6 inches (15 cm) in captivity, but can reach twice that size in the wild
Water conditions	*Toxotes jaculatrix* and *T. chatareus* require specific gravity around 1.010; *T. microlepis* requires fresh water or a specfic gravity around 1.005. All other species need fresh water.
Diet	Predatory, prefers live invertebrates and small fish; will take good-quality flakes and pellets, augmented with pieces of squid, frozen bloodworms, and other meaty foods
Temperament	Generally a quiet schooling fish; completely ignores other fishes too big to eat
Availability	Seasonal; only *T. jaculatrix* and *T. chatareus* are regularly seen; moderately priced
Ease of maintenance	Easy
Specific problems	Highly predatory; will jump out of uncovered aquaria; some specimens can become bullies toward conspecifics

sorts of vegetation, so the best way to help an archer settle into a new aquarium is to include plenty of real or artificial wood and plants, depending on the tank's salinity. (As noted, these fish jump well, and a secure aquarium lid is absolutely essential.)

Archers will not uproot or otherwise damage salt-tolerant plants like Java ferns, and provided that a reasonable amount of sea salt is in the water, the acidification effects of small amounts of bogwood will not be significant. Archerfish do not burrow into sand or move stones, although some may use their water jet to spray sand around when searching for food.

They are notably tolerant of other fish, provided that the other fish are not unduly aggressive and stay out of the upper levels of the tank, which the archers prefer. They can be kept well with predatory catfish and the more docile, bottom-dwelling cichlids. Even midwater swimmers, like scats and monos, are generally ignored.

Behavior toward conspecifics—fish of the same species—can be more unpredictable. In general, these are considered schooling fish, and that is certainly how they behave in the wild. However, in small aquaria, larger archerfish sometimes pick on smaller ones, and even under the best circumstances, a definite pecking order appears within the school. The best thing to do is ensure that they are not crowded and that all specimens are of similar size. In a very small aquarium, say 36 inches (90 cm) or less in length, it is wisest to keep just one. Having said this, they are certainly much less shy and much more active if kept in schools, and the serious aquarist will want to keep at least three specimens.

Keeping archers in good health presents no major problems. Like the scats and monos, these are intrinsically hardy fish. They rarely come down with external parasites like whitespot, and when they do, they respond well to commercial treatments or to a temporary elevation of the salinity to marine levels. Poor water conditions can lead to problems like fin rot, of course, but otherwise there is very little for the aquarist to worry about, assuming the fish are in good health when purchased. Archers have a reputation for being delicate when first imported. It is very wise to make sure any new fishes at the retailer are settled in and feeding well. Starved archers have a distinctive narrowing of the region just above the anal fin, and fish in this condition should be avoided. Good stock will be lively, alert, and have a pleasingly stocky appearance. One misleading indicator though is the position of the pelvic and dorsal fins. In many fish, when these are folded up close to the body, it is a sign of stress and bad health. In archers, however, it is relatively common and doesn't in itself mean anything is wrong.

Only two species of archerfish are commercially traded. Difficult to tell apart, the two species also are similar in temperament and water requirements. The most regularly seen species is probably the common archer, *Toxotes jaculatrix*, a bright, silvery fish with five to seven dark, triangular bands running halfway down its flanks. At least one of these bands usually passes over the eye, and another is located on the caudal

Archerfish are generally tolerant of other fishes and can be kept with predatory catfish like *Ictalurus punctatus*.

peduncle. There are no markings on the flanks below the level of the eye and pectoral fins, and the anal fin, if it bears any coloration at all, is a vague, silvery gray. The second species is *T. chatareus*, known variously as the spotted or seven-banded archerfish. It is basically similar in color to the common archer, but in addition to the dark bands, spots or blotches are present between the bands, and more markings are often seen on the lower half of the flanks. The anal fin is often a darker gray than that of the common archerfish. Both species occasionally have yellow or golden patches on the flanks, particularly when young.

A third species, *T. microlepis*, is sold increasingly often. It inhabits fresh and slightly brackish water, and only grows to about 5 inches (12.5 cm) long. It resembles *T. jaculatrix* in coloration, except for smalll black spots on the edge of the dorsal fin.

Although *T. jaculatrix* naturally swims freely among fresh, brackish, and marine habitats, it is very much a fish of estuaries and mangroves. Hard, alkaline water with a specific gravity between 1.005 and 1.010 is ideal for long-term health. The southeast Asian populations of *T. chatareus* that yield commercially traded specimens enjoy the same sorts of conditions, but some freshwater populations exist in Australia.

Very rarely, other species of *Toxotes* turn up. One of these is known as the primitive archerfish, *T. lorentzi*, and although similar to the other archers in its need for space and food preferences, it is a strictly freshwater species. It is brown, not silver-black like the other species in the genus, and so is easy to identify. *Toxotes oligolepis* is another freshwater-only species that is seen occasionally. It resembles *T. chatareus*, except that the black bands pass all the way down the flanks and the anal fin is solidly black in color. A third, as yet undescribed species from the Fitzroy River in Australia known as the Western archerfish is frequently confused

While *Toxotes jaculatrix* and *T. chatareus* are fairly common, finding other archer species can be very difficult.

with *T. oligolepis*, but can be distinguished by its flank scales, which are outlined in black.

TARGETFISH—*TERAPON JARBUA*

The targetfish is not a commonly traded fish, and while it's seen from time to time on dealers' lists, it doesn't really have a huge amount to recommend it as an aquarium fish. Part of the problem is that this is a big, very active predator. On the whole, these fishes don't fit in well with the placid pace of life in a home aquarium. They are also rather aggressive, and since they like to school, a mob of these fishes can easily terrorize any less aggressive animals in the tank with them (such as archers). A group of targetfish could be kept with other robust, fast-moving fish, like scats and monos, but this requires a large tank, something on the order of 180 gallons (700 liters). All this sounds rather negative, but this is a good-looking fish with a nice pattern of stripes along its body (which from above resembles the pattern on an archery target, hence the name). It is also very hardy and adaptable, and will eat practically any prepared or meaty foods.

While small juveniles do appear in fresh water, this fish is really a coastal marine animal, similar to the sea basses, *Morone* spp., which are familiar to fishkeepers who live in temperate zones. Targetfishes can be found in very shallow water, including the surf zone on sandy beaches, as well as in estuaries and mangroves. The ideal aquarium for these fish should reflect this by providing plenty of swimming room. They are not particularly bothered about plants or rocks, although a pile of large stones at one end of the aquarium would give less active fishes somewhere to go when they want to be away from the targetfish. Clean, washed sand is the substrate closest to that of their natural habitat, built into sand banks and illuminated with spotlights rather than fluorescent lights to create a speckled pattern of light and dark. Scatter a few large seashells or artificial

Targetfish

Name	*Terapon jarbua*
Other names	Targetfish, *Therapon jarbua*
Origin	Coastal waters of the Indo-West Pacific
Size	At least 6 inches (15 cm) in captivity; over 14 inches (36 cm) in the wild
Water conditions	Fresh or slightly brackish (specific gravity <1.005) when small; adults do best in half- to full-strength seawater
Diet	Primarily cichlid pellets and similar prepared foods, augmented with fresh foods such as earthworms and pieces of squid
Temperament	Active schooling fish; can be aggressive
Availability	Rare, but can usually be ordered
Ease of maintenance	Easy
Specific problems	Must be kept in groups of at least three; highly predatory

Terapon jarbua

corals on the sand for variety; this will very nicely mimic the shallow marine habitats these fish frequent.

SIAMESE TIGERFISH—*DATNIOIDES*

Siamese tigerfish are large carnivores that naturally inhabit fresh and brackish waters. They do not occur in seawater, and will not do well in strongly brackish water either. Although tigerfish can be adapted to a freshwater aquarium, their long-term health is best served by adding at least some salt to the water. Brackish water with a specific gravity of 1.003 to 1.005 is ideal. Not requiring much salt means the tigerfish aquarium can be planted with hardy plant species. In fact, tigerfish really like to hide among dense thickets of *Vallisneria* or *Sagittaria*. Like their namesakes, their stripes help them disappear in thick vegetation, where they can lurk and wait for their prey. If growing live plants isn't your strong point, use plastic plants, bamboo canes, artificial wood, bogwood, or pieces of slate to build shadowy tangles and crevices that the fish can hide in.

Although bright illumination of the aquarium is fine if plenty of plants are present, avoid it in a more sparsely decorated aquarium. Only when they feel secure in their new home will tigerfish venture into the front of the aquarium where you can admire them. These fish can jump well, so the aquarium must be securely covered. Otherwise, they do not cause any disruption, and will not dig, uproot plants, or move stones.

Physically, tigerfish resemble snappers—rather stocky with large mouths. Like snappers, they are voracious

Siamese tigerfish

Name	*Datnioides* spp.
Other names	Siamese tigerfish, *Coius* spp.
Origin	Coastal rivers and swamps of southeastern Asia
Size	Potentially 18 inches (45 cm), but in captivity generally much smaller—around 9 to 12 inches (20 to 30 cm); notably slow growing
Water conditions	Fresh or slightly brackish (specific gravity <1.005) depending on the species; *D. quadriasciatus, D. microlepis,* and *D.campbelli* will do well in a specific-gravity range of 1.005 to 1.010
Diet	Distinctly predatory; prefers live river shrimps, earthworms, and small fishes; can usually be weaned onto fresh meaty foods such as frozen prawns, whitebait, and mussels
Temperament	Peaceful; do well with other fish of similar size, including their own kind
Availability	Pretty rarely seen, but usually can be ordered
Ease of maintenance	Fairly easy
Specific problems	Very predatory; may be difficult getting the fish used to dead

Datnioides quadrifasciatus

Datnioides campbelli is particularly aggressive toward other tigerfish, no how matter how big the aquarium.

Southeast Asian Staples

predators and will eat surprisingly large prey. As such, it is best to keep them with fish of comparable size, such as archers, green chromides, or the bigger sleeper gobies; such fishes will be completely ignored and the tigerfish will make good community-tank residents. They also will do fine with monos and scats, but those species need higher salinities when mature than tigerfish, so they don't make ideal long-term companions.

Generally, adult tigerfish are territorial and somewhat aggressive toward one another, but provided that each fish has enough swimming space and a cave or thicket to call home, more than one specimen can be kept in one big aquarium. If the aquarium is too small, however, the largest specimens will pick on the others. As with African cichlids, either keep one or keep a decent-size school—not two or three—to diffuse some of this aggression. The level of aggression actually varies between species. *Datnioides campbelli* has a particular reputation for being aggressive toward its own and other species of tigerfish, regardless of the size of the aquarium, although it is peaceful toward other, similarly sized fishes, such as cichlids or catfish.

Although tigerfish do have a preference for live fish, it is not a good idea to use feeder goldfish and other live fish to support predatory species like these in captivity—the risk of introducing parasites and other infections is just too high. If your tigerfish refuses to take frozen foods, large live invertebrates such as river shrimps, *Gammarus*, earthworms, and insect larvae make an excellent alternative to live fish.

Two species are commonly traded: the fine-scale or Indonesian tigerfish, *Datnioides microlepis*, and the four-barred tigerfish, *D. quadrifasciatus*, which is occasionally called the American tigerfish (quite paradoxically, since it comes from southeastern Asia, not the Americas). Both species require a large aquarium with well-filtered water, preferably planted with large, robust species. These are big fish, reaching lengths of up to 18 inches (45 cm) and 1 foot (30 cm) respectively. In their natural habitats, both are considered good food fish.

These two types of tigerfish are among the most handsome fishes in the brackish aquarium hobby, particularly when young, with dark vertical stripes set off against a silvery or bronze-colored body. These stripes give them their common name. *Datnioides microlepis* has a more mottled appearance—the bands are broken up into patches and spots, particularly away from the head—whereas the stripes on *D. quadrifasciatus* are completely solid.

Very occasionally, other species, such as the New Guinea tigerfish, *D. campbelli*, turn up in aquarium stores, and all tigerfish can be kept in the same way.

BUILDING A SOUTHEAST ASIAN ESTUARY BIOTOPE TANK

A southeast Asian estuary is in some ways one of the easiest brackish-water aquaria to put together because so many of the species that work well in it are commonly traded, relatively inexpensive, and remarkably hardy. These species are adaptable, but a middling salinity with a specific gravity between 1.010

Putting together an aquarium based on an Asian estuary can be a fun but huge undertaking.

The hardy and popular marine macroalgae *Caulerpa* will be readily eaten by many fish.

and 1.015 is ideal. The only real problem is their need for space: A 55-gallon (210-liter) aquarium should be considered the minimum if you want to keep a small school of scats or monos. If you want a group of both, plus some oddballs as well (like a moray eel, puffer, or sleeper goby), then a 180-gallon (680-liter) tank is going to be much closer to the mark. Combine the requirement for space with the need for a powerful filter that will turn over the water quickly enough to keep pace with these active, messy fishes, and you have quite a project on your hands. Offsetting this is the fact that these are all very nice fishes, combining bright colors, personality, and a certain *joie de vivre* that few other aquarium fishes can match.

The basic requirement is for a big tank with a large filter. Canister filters provide the best value and effectiveness when it comes to keeping big fishes, and they are almost definitely the way to go here. Undergravel filters are a viable option as well, with two caveats. First, air pumps simply don't produce the strong water currents scats and monos like, so powerheads must be used instead. These cost about the same as a high-capacity air pump but produce a much more vigorous water flow, and many also include some sort of venturi device for adding turbulence by sucking air into the outgoing water flow. The second thing to remember about undergravel filters is that they are not terribly good at dealing with the solid wastes and leftover food that large fish tend to produce. If you use an undergravel filter, you will probably need to siphon off the muck from the sand at the bottom of the tank at least once a week if you want to keep it looking clean and white.

Because our aquarium is based on a wide, sandy estuary where the environment is more coastal marine than freshwater, we will use sand instead of gravel to give the tank a much more "seashore" feel. Coral sand is ideal because it not only has the right look, but also helps keep the pH and hardness levels high. If you are using an undergravel filter, coral sand has the additional advantage of being highly porous, making it an excellent medium for biological filtration. In aquaria without an undergravel filter, you only need a shallow bed of sand: 1 to 1.5 inches (2 to 3 cm) is fine. A few well-chosen shells help reinforce the image of a tidal estuary by breaking up the monotony of the clean, white sand. In the wild, seashells often get piled up into little drifts by the current, so rather than just scattering them around, arrange the shells in small heaps.

Planting such an aquarium is problematic, because none of the commonly available freshwater species will adapt to a high-salinity system such as this one. The marine algae of the genus *Caulerpa* sometimes survive in brackish water with a specific gravity of 1.015 or more, and they are inexpensive enough to make it worth

Asian Estuary Tank

Theme	Southeast Asian tidal estuary
Specific gravity	1.010 to 1.015
pH and hardness	Hard, alkaline conditions
Lighting	Not important
Filtration	External canister filter
Substrate	Coral sand
Planting	Primarily artificial plants, if any
Possible fish	Monos, scats, archers, brackish-water puffers, sleeper gobies, moray eels, flounders, freshwater damselfish

Southeast Asian Staples

Make sure you don't clutter the tank too much, as your fish will want plenty of open space.

trying, but scats will eat *Caulerpa* as eagerly as any other plant or alga.

Plastic plants are a better proposition, particularly those that look like brown seaweeds, which would be entirely appropriate for the habitat you are trying to recreate. Bamboo stems can be used to create thickets along the back, but because they float, they must be attached to something heavy. The easiest way to do this is to use aquarium sealant (silicone) and stick them to small pieces of slate, then bury the slate under the sand. This keeps the bamboo in place very effectively.

Artificial wood and other ornaments can be used to add a focal point to the aquarium. One of the nicest tricks is to place an airstone inside an ornament and use it to add some movement to the aquarium. Various manufacturers produce artificial urns and amphorae, and these are especially good in this regard. A wooden airstone is the nicest if you have a powerful air pump because of the fine mist it creates. Placing one of these inside the urn creates a brilliant, rising column of bubbles that isn't just aesthetically pleasing but also helps

aerate the water.

Don't clutter up the sea bed too much, though; what you want is plenty of open space for the fish to enjoy. Also, with the right lighting the sand itself adds to the drama. Instead of using full-length fluorescent lights, choose a few bright spotlights instead. They don't need to be the high-output ones used by aquarists raising plants; ordinary household halogen bulbs will do fine. Place the lights 24 inches (60 cm) or so above the surface of the water, and make sure you use a glass cover over the aquarium to prevent the bulbs from getting splashed. (Obviously, you don't want to use an aquarium hood.) When small, bright lights are used instead of full-length ones, the whole atmosphere of the aquarium changes. Instead of illuminating the tank uniformly, the light only strikes the water in a few places and looks much more broken up. The sand becomes dappled, constantly changing as the surface of the water moves, looking exactly like the real sea floor. The effect is truly magical: As the bright, silvery fishes swim in and out of the streams of light, they shimmer beautifully.

Livebearers
By Catherine Burnett

While it is true that many fish—from sharks to seahorses—give birth to live young, aquarists often use the term "livebearers" to refer to the family Poeciliidae, which includes such well-known aquarium fish as guppies, platies, swordtails, and mollies. These are among the most adaptable fishes available to the aquarist. They are generally peaceful and hardy, and many do well in brackish-water aquaria. They have also been bred into a variety of colorful strains. Less commonly seen members of the group include the mosquitofish and the pike livebearer, both of which can be kept in aquaria but need special care, the mosquitofish because it is aggressive, and the pike livebearer because it grows quite large and is highly predatory.

The Poeciliidae as a group tend to have long yet stocky bodies, with rounded rather than forked caudal fins. Even the wild varieties tend toward being brightly colored, with males usually bearing some sort of pattern on their tails, which they use to attract the attention of females. The females are usually much larger and not as colorful, although both sexes are active and lively and bring plenty of activity to the aquarium. Livebearers also tend to have upward-pointing mouths, which they use in the wild to feed on insect larvae, such as

Livebearers

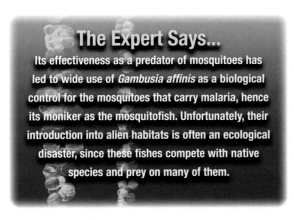
mosquito larvae and bloodworms (chironomids).

Although livebearers lack adipose fins or barbels, they do have one very special feature that is obvious to the aquarist—the gonopodium. Found on males, the gonopodium is a highly modified anal fin that can rotate a full 360 degrees and is used to place sperm inside the females. The fertilized eggs develop inside the mother for a month or so, and fry are born as small but fully formed versions of their parents—and their prodigious appetites help them grow very quickly.

Unlike most other aquarium fish, the young of livebearers settle into aquarium life easily, eating algae and finely divided fish flake, as well as commercially prepared livebearer fry food. Even so, some species of livebearers think nothing of eating their own young, so serious breeders tend to set up breeding tanks in which the female and male can be left together to mate; the male is removed once his job is done, and the female is taken out after she has released the fry. Some species, like mollies, are singularly indifferent toward their fry and will rarely if ever eat them, but none extends the sort of brood care toward its young that cichlids do.

Two other families of livebearing fish are of interest to the aquarist, the Anablepidae and the Hemiramphidae. The Anablepidae includes the four-eyed fish, *Anableps anableps*, a bizarre fish from the estuaries of South America well known for its specialized eyes, which allow it to see above and below the water line at the same time. The Hemiramphidae are a mostly marine family of fish that includes a large number of species known as halfbeaks and gars (unrelated to the gars of North America). A few halfbeaks, in particular the wrestling halfbeak, *Dermogenys pusilla,* occur in brackish and fresh water and have attained a modest degree of popularity. Both four-eyed fish and halfbeaks are discussed elsewhere in this book, but this

A close-up of a male livebearer's gonopodium, showing the minute details.

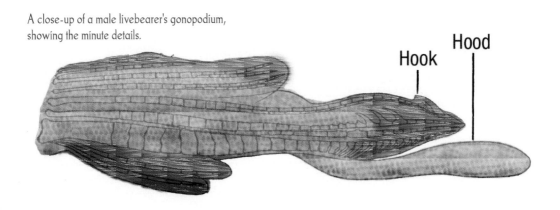

Hood

Hook

The Expert Says...

Besides insect larvae, all livebearers eat algae to some extent. The mollies especially need a good supply of vegetarian flake or some other plant matter to do well. Also, most species happily peck away at any algae in the aquarium, making them useful algae cleaners, if not quite in the same league as the more well-known suckermouth cats and flying foxes.

chapter focuses on the more common livebearers of the family Poeciliidae that are both widely available and tolerant of brackish water.

GUPPIES—*POECILIA RETICULATA*

Guppies are typically available as fancy varieties or, less expensively, as feeder stock intended as live food for predatory fish. While they may look different, both are kept in the same way and have the same tolerance for brackish water. And although guppies are most commonly traded as freshwater fish, they adapt to well brackish water. Indeed, if your local water is soft and acidic, then adding a little salt is probably essential.

Because they are small fish, guppies are best suited to aquaria containing similarly sized fishes, or species that are strict herbivores, such as mollies. Larger fish, like monos and archerfish, will simply view guppies as food. They are very inoffensive animals and make good companions for quiet fish like pipefish and gobies (although both of these will readily eat baby guppies given the chance). Guppies will occasionally nip at soft-leafed plants, but unlike mollies or scats, they are too small to do any damage and so make a good choice for inclusion in a planted aquarium. They also perform a modest amount of algae removal.

Poecilia reticulata

Livebearers

Guppies also can be adapted to full-strength seawater (a specific gravity of 1.023), but always acclimate them to the new salinity gradually. One interesting thing about keeping them in brackish or marine conditions is that they often tend to grow longer fins and develop brighter colors in the higher salinity. They will even breed in salt water, although other reef fish usually devour any baby guppies they find. Damselfish in particular are very good at ferreting out small fish from between rocks and inside caves, and they will also nip at the longer fins of the adult guppies.

Fancy guppies are bred to have colorful bodies and tails.

Although the feeder-grade guppies probably resemble the wild guppies more closely than anything else, fancy guppies hold the greatest attraction for many people. Fancy guppies have been bred with large tailfins in practically every color of the rainbow and with body types such as "tuxedo" (black body from the middle of the back) and "cobra" (snakeskin-like markings on the fish's entire body).

In contrast, male feeder guppies typically have colorful but random "war paint" markings on their tails. Although their tails are not as large or colorful as those of the fancy guppies, they can have extensions to the caudal fin and so sometimes resemble swordtails, *Xiphophorus hellerii*. These extensions, known as swords, sometimes occur at the top of the fin, other times at the bottom, and sometimes at both the top and bottom of the fin. Occasionally, a male might have the sword in the middle of the caudal fin instead.

This wonderful variety among guppies has allowed aquarists to breed many splendid varieties. A project for the dedicated aquarist is to find an interesting variation and create a strain of guppy with that feature that breeds true.

Guppies

Name	*Poecilia reticulata*
Other names	Guppy, millions fish
Origin	South America
Size	Females up to 2 inches (5 cm), males smaller
Water conditions	Fresh or slightly brackish (specific gravity <1.005); can be adapted to higher salinities with care
Diet	Flake, frozen bloodworms, live foods such as daphnia and brine shrimp, algae
Temperament	Peaceful
Availability	Commonly traded and inexpensive
Ease of maintenance	Easy
Specific problems	May be eaten by large fish; some fish are tempted to peck at the trailing fins of the males

MOLLIES—*POECILIA* SPP.

Mollies are very adaptable fishes, and although some are rather large, they are neither demanding nor predatory, and so make very good community fish. As a rule, they do well in anything from hard, alkaline fresh water to full-strength seawater. Inexpensive and fairly hardy, they are commonly used to cycle new marine tanks. The smaller species do fine in small aquaria, but the larger ones need their space; male sailfin mollies especially are noted for not growing their magnificent dorsal fins if housed in cramped conditions. All mollies are distinctly vegetarian, and their diet should be rich in plant material of some kind. Blanched lettuce, cucumber, and small pieces of spinach are readily taken, and it is always wise to leave some algae in the aquarium for them to graze on. Vegetarian flake is commercially available for mollies and other herbivorous fishes, and makes an excellent staple. Mollies also take meaty foods, including insect larvae like bloodworms, but generally they are not predatory and ignore even newborn livebearer fry.

Four species are of interest to aquarists, although few are ever seen as wild-caught stock, and hybrids between the species are common. Two of them are known as shortfin mollies and the other two as sailfin mollies. The shortfins, *Poecilia sphenops* and *P. mexicana*, are inhabitants of coastal streams and like well-filtered water with a reasonably strong current. They are the smaller of the molly species, with females typically growing to around 3 inches (7.5 cm) and males quite a bit less. They are known as shortfins because the males have normal-size dorsal fins not very different from those of the females, although they do use their dorsal fins when displaying to females or rival males. Male sailfins, in contrast, have much larger dorsal fins than do the females—when raised, the fin can appear almost as large as the fish itself!

Poecilia latipinna is the most commonly seen sailfin and has been bred into many different color versions. It is substantially larger than either of the shortfin mollies, with females reaching as much as 4 inches (10 cm) in length, though the males are smaller. Finally, females of the giant sailfin molly, *P. velifera*, can reach a whopping 6 inches (15 cm) in length, making them among the biggest of the livebearers. Adults of these species are very impressive, but sadly they are not often traded, and good-quality stock is hard to find.

Guppies will eat any standard aquarium fare.

Livebearers

Females of the giant sailfin molly, Poecilia velifera, *can reach a whopping 6 inches long.*

Both sailfin mollies prefer coastal and brackish environments to freshwater ones, and they are very commonly found in seawater, even significant distances off shore, where they feed on plankton. In my experience, sailfin mollies are slightly more likely to be jumpers than shortfins, but whatever species you have, a tight-fitting hood to stop these fish from throwing themselves out of your aquarium is a very good idea.

Most of the mollies commonly seen in the hobby are artificial varieties, often hybrids of two or more species. These hybrids fall into three basic types: regular short-finned mollies (they look a lot like scaled-up guppies); large sailfin mollies (distinguished by the dramatic sail-like fin of the males); and the bizarre balloon mollies that have been bred into a globose distortion of their original form. Each occurs in a wide variety of colors, including velvety black, chocolate, orange, and silver. Other forms feature mixtures of colors, such as those speckled in black and white, or those with orange bodies and black fins. The wild-type form can also be found from time to time; it is significantly drabber than these artificial forms, being basically silvery green.

Mollies

Name	*Poecilia latipinna, P. mexicana, P. sphenops, P. velifera*
Other names	Molly, shortfin molly, sailfin molly, plus numerous artificial strains such as the black molly
Origin	Southern United States, Central America, northern South America, many islands in the Gulf of Mexico
Size	Depending on the species, females up to 6 inches (15 cm), males usually smaller
Water conditions	Slightly brackish to marine conditions (specific gravity 1.005 to 1.023); will not do well in soft, acidic fresh water, or in water with high levels of dissolved wastes
Diet	Vegetarian flake and algae essential; also frozen bloodworms and live foods such as daphnia and brine shrimp
Temperament	Peaceful schooling fish
Availability	Commonly traded and inexpensive
Ease of maintenance	Easy in appropriate water conditions
Specific problems	Particularly sensitive to poor water conditions

Variations in fin shape also occur. A common short-finned variety is the lyretail molly, sometimes claimed to be a hybrid of shortfin and sailfin mollies: P. *sphenops* x *P. velifera*. It is a little bigger than the average shortfin molly, reaching around 3 inches (7.5 cm) in length. Balloon-belly mollies are regular mollies selectively bred in captivity to produce a deformed, rounded body shape. This body shape has been claimed by some to slightly reduce swimming ability, the ability to compete for food, and possibly life expectancy, but otherwise doesn't make them any more difficult to keep than regular mollies. They tend to reach a length of about 2 inches (5 cm).

Mollies are hardy fish, having no particular inherent health problems the aquarist need worry about. To a greater degree than with guppies, brackish conditions are very useful with mollies because they help prevent fungus. Kept in pure fresh water, mollies often develop fungus on their fins, as well as another complaint known as shimmying, in which the molly lurks in a corner, looking sad and wobbling instead of swimming.

Mollies are easy to breed and will do so in fresh, brackish, or marine water. About the only thing to remember is that pregnant mollies respond very badly to being netted (or being scooped into a breeding trap for that matter) and are liable to miscarry when stressed. The fry are larger than those of most livebearer young and are generally ignored by their mother, particularly if she is well fed. They grow rapidly, but as noted earlier, males only fully develop their sailfins if given plenty of swimming space.

SWORDTAILS—*XIPHOPHORUS HELLERII*

Swordtails are active, colorful fish that look good in any community tank, and they are big enough to do well with other medium-size fish that are not confirmed piscivores. So while they shouldn't be kept with tigerfish or archers, they will do fine with orange chromides, medium-size gobies and sleepers, and the smaller spiny eels. They prefer less salt than guppies and mollies, and so are not quite so useful as

Swordtails

Name	*Xiphophorus hellerii*
Other names	Swordtail
Origin	Central America
Size	Up to 6 inches (16 cm); males smaller, but with a sword-like extension on their tails
Water conditions	Fresh or slightly brackish (specific gravity <1.005)
Diet	Flake; frozen bloodworms; live foods such as daphnia and brine shrimp; algae
Temperament	A good community fish, though males can be quarrelsome
Availability	Commonly traded and inexpensive
Ease of maintenance	Easy
Specific problems	None

Xiphophorus hellerii, a domesticated lyretail strain.

brackish-water fish, but they do have their place in low-salinity systems. Male swordtails can be aggressive toward one another (and closely related species), but on the whole this species is peaceful.

Swordtails and platies are quite similar. Both belong to the same genus, and if kept together, they will hybridize. But important differences can be seen, espesially the sword at the bottom of the male swordtail's tail. Swordtails are also somewhat longer than platies and more likely to be jumpers. In addition, female swordtails will sometimes change to male, although only young swordtails genetically destined to be males will develop full-length swords.

The wild-type swordtail is basically green with a colored stripe running from about midway along the flank to the end of the sword (in the males at least—it is fainter in the females and absent from the tail). But as with most of the livebearers, many colorful artificial varieties are available to choose from. The orange or gold morph is very popular—both males and females are a bright shade of yellowy orange, and the male has a dark red sword as well. Another popular variety is the pineapple swordtail, a red to orange fish with the same sort of stripe and sword as the wild-type swordtail. The orange wagtail is similar to the orange swordtail but has black fins. Black swordtails, calico swordtails, and even albino swordtails also are available. Both platies and swordtails have been bred in highfin varieties, as well.

The male wild-type swordtail is basically green with a colored stripe running along the flank to the end of the sword.

Livebearers

Xiphophorus maculatus

Most platies are *Xiphophorus maculatus* or a hybrid of that and *X. variatus*, and are slightly shorter and rounder than swordtails. They come in a wider range of colors as well, including orange and blue, speckled and solid. A wagtail variety is also available. Many have sort of moon-shaped markings at the base of their tails, leading to their older name of "moon." Platies and swordtails are capable of interbreeding and will generally do so without hesitation if mixed in a tank.

As with swordtails, these fish do not normally inhabit brackish waters, and while they will tolerate low salinity, mollies or guppies should be used instead in aquaria with a specific gravity over 1.005.

Platy

Name	*Xiphophorus maculatus* and *X. variatus*
Other names	Platy, moon, variatus
Origin	Central America
Size	Up to 2.75 inches (7 cm)
Water conditions	Fresh or slightly brackish (specific gravity <1.005)
Diet	Flake; frozen bloodworms; live foods such as daphnia and brine shrimp; algae
Temperament	Peaceful
Availability	Commonly traded and inexpensive
Ease of maintenance	Easy
Specific problems	None

ENDLER'S LIVEBEARER—*POECILIA WINGEI*

Endler's livebearer

Although recently described as a new species, some believe the Endler's livebearer is a species in the making and not quite differentiated from the guppy. The female is virtually identical to the female feeder guppy, while the male essentially is a more colorful version of the male feeder guppy, although usually with a particular pattern that includes a dark, diagonal, mid-body stripe. In any case, they seem to tolerate salt water as well as any guppy, and those produced by crossbreeding with fancy guppies seem to grow longer, more brightly colored fins when kept in saltier water, just as ordinary guppies do. However, breeders do not advise crossbreeding Endler's livebearers with guppies, as they hope to keep the two strains pure.

Endlers

Name	*Poecilia wingei.*
Other names	*Poecilia* sp. "Endler," Endler's livebearer, endlers
Origin	South America
Size	Females up to 1.5 inches (3 cm), males smaller
Water conditions	Fresh or slightly brackish (specific gravity <1.005); can be adapted to higher salinities with care
Diet	Flake; frozen bloodworms; live foods such as daphnia and brine shrimp; algae
Temperament	Peaceful
Availability	Commonly traded and inexpensive
Ease of maintenance	Easy
Specific problems	May be eaten by large fish

Livebearers

PIKE LIVEBEARER—*BELONESOX BELIZANUS*

Compared to the other Poeciliidae, the pike livebearer is a fish apart—it is large, and big females often attack and eat the smaller males when they are kept together. Pike livebearers are so piscivorous that they rarely eat anything other than small live fish such as guppies. Unsurprisingly, very few aquarists ever bother with these fish, but for the dedicated brackish-water aquarist, these fish do have some attraction. They are undeniably handsome, being rather like miniature pike in shape and behavior, and when kept with fish of the same size or larger, they are completely peaceful. Pike livebearers only attack fish they can swallow whole, so they can be kept with large cichlids and catfish.

Because these fish rarely eat anything other than live foods (insect larvae and livebearer fry when young, and small fish as adults), they are not good for beginners and those without access to a continual supply of live food. As with any other piscivorous fish, offering feeder guppies and goldfish is the easiest way to feed them, but the potential for introducing parasites and diseases is an inherent risk in using these low-quality fishes as a staple diet. Feeder guppies and goldfish are invariably kept in crowded tanks and looked after less carefully than other ornamental fish, which makes it easy for pathogens to spread from fish to fish, contaminating every fish in the tank.

A better proposition is to maintain your own population of livebearers, such as guppies or mosquitofish, with which you can regularly feed your pike livebearers. This way you can keep a close eye on the quality of the fish you are feeding to the pike livebearers and make sure they are healthy and clear of parasites. However, because an adult pike livebearer eats about one small goldfish or half a dozen adult guppies a day, you will need a lot of food, and this makes them expensive pets. Unlike many other predatory fish, such as gars, these fish do not eat a big meal and then fast for a week; instead they need a regular supply of prey each and every day.

Pike livebearer

Name	*Belonesox belizanus*
Other names	Pike livebearer, pike topminnow
Origin	Central America
Size	Females up to 8 inches (20 cm), males about one-third smaller
Water conditions	Slightly brackish (specific gravity of 1.005), but can be adapted to higher salinities
Diet	Predominantly live foods—most easily fed small livebearers and other fish; may take to other live prey such as river shrimp
Temperament	Peaceful but highly predatory fish
Availability	Rare
Ease of maintenance	Difficult
Specific problems	Requires live foods; often cannibalistic

Belonesox belizanus

Livebearers

Most pike livebearers will starve rather than eat anything other than live feeder fish.

Some pike livebearers will adapt to nonliving foods. This is especially true if they have been raised in captivity their entire lives and fed bloodworms, brine shrimp, and other meaty invertebrate foods. If you can locate fish such as these, then they make an excellent subject for the advanced aquarist looking for a challenge.

Even with wild-caught fish, or captive-bred specimens that prefer live fish, it is certainly worth trying to get them to eat other foods, if only to be prepared for an emergency—if you or your pet store runs out of feeder fish, at least you'll have some alternatives to feed your pike livebearers until the stock can be replenished. Large river shrimp (often sold in bait shops) are well worth trying, as are some of the larger aquatic insects, such as backswimmers and waterboatmen (for example, *Notonecta* and *Corixa* spp.). With some coaxing, the larvae of terrestrial insects such as mealworms, *Tenebrio molitor*, also can be used by dangling the prey on pieces of thread or by holding them with tweezers. But do not bank on training your pike livebearer to accept these alternative foods: Most specimens will simply refuse to eat, or wil not eat enough and gradually starve to death.

As with many other predatory fishes, pike livebearers do not like being in open water and require plenty of cover if they are to feel secure. Brackish-water-tolerant floating plants like hornwort, *Ceratophyllum demersum*, are ideal, while the long, strap-leafed *Vallisneria* and *Sagittaria* make good alternatives, offering plenty of shade across the top of the tank. Without adequate cover, these fish become nervous and pretty frequently throw themselves at the glass when startled (for example, when lights are turned on). This accounts for the frequency of broken and damaged jaws seen on these fish in many retailers.

Note that although these fish like shade, they generally inhabit only the top level of the aquarium, so plants that are bushy at the base, such as Java fern, are less useful for providing cover than those that grow upward and spread out at the surface of the tank. Also, pike livebearers are jumpers, so in addition to providing the fish

Pike livebearers are the Central American equivalent of the Asian freshwater gars: stealthy ambush predators.

with plants to hide under, a tight-fitting aquarium hood is essential.

Pike livebearers are without question difficult fish. For the average aquarist who cannot (or does not want to) supply the live foods necessary to keep them alive, they do not make good pets.

CARING FOR LIVEBEARERS IN A BRACKISH-WATER ENVIRONMENT

Most livebearers—other than mollies—are quite tolerant of suboptimal water conditions. As long as the fish do not look visibly distressed or diseased, they are doing well. Even so, while most livebearers are remarkably tolerant of short-term lapses in the management of the nitrogen cycle, this doesn't mean they actually *like* being in water with high concentrations of ammonium and nitrite. When building a community of these fish, you should certainly add them slowly so the bacteria colonies in the filter can grow to accommodate them without causing an ammonia spike. Compared to messier fish, such as puffers and scats, livebearers are not gross feeders and do not require heavy filtration. For the most part, air-powered undergravel filters or box filters are perfectly suitable.

The salinity of the tank depends on the species of fish being kept. Salt water should preferably be made using a good-quality marine salt mix that provides the necessary trace minerals and buffering capacity that table or aquarium salt does not. While many aquarium books quote the required salinities for livebearers in terms of teaspoons of salt per gallon or liter, the most reliable way to keep a consistent salinity level with each water change is to measure the specific gravity of the water. Because livebearers are commonly kept at the lower end of specific-gravity range, you must have a hydrometer that measures specific gravity all the way down to 1.000. The floating-arm type is particularly easy to use, but be careful not to get one that only covers the upper part of the specific-gravity range.

One final thing to remember when making brackish water is to allow the salt to fully dissolve by mixing it well in water and then leaving it to sit for at least an hour or two before adding the newly made-up brackish water to the tank.

Reverse-osmosis water, which many saltwater aquarists use, is not particularly necessary in a brackish tank, which does not require the precise water chemistry of a reef tank. Salt creep is inevitable in any brackish tank, so make sure any metal parts in the light hood, if you have one, are shielded from splashes to prevent corrosion. Do not place the tank directly onto any stand or surface that could be damaged by contact with salt water. When cleaning the outside glass, do not use commercial cleaners, because these are toxic to fish; simply ensure that you clean the salt residue off and dry the outside very well.

> **The Expert Says...**
>
> Medications containing copper should never be used in a tank in which you might ever want to house saltwater invertebrates. The copper can be absorbed into the silicone seals, only to later leach back out and poison the invertebrates.

HEALTH

On the whole, livebearers are hardy animals, but because they are bred in large numbers and often kept in densely packed conditions at the wholesaler and retailer levels, it is not uncommon for specimens to arrive in

Livebearers are hardy and relatively clean feeders, so they don't need heavy filtration.

Livebearers

your aquarium with some sort of parasite or infection. Fortunately, their innate hardiness allows them to respond well to treatment—being able to use salt water on brackish fish for therapeutic purposes certainly helps. Freshwater whitespot, or ich, will not live in salt water, and saltwater whitespot will not live in fresh water. So if brackish-water fishes become infected with one of these parasites, it is simple enough to deal with. For ich, raise the salinity from freshwater levels to a specific gravity of 1.010 or more; if the problem is the marine parasite, lower the salinity down to near fresh water (a specific gravity of 1.005 will do the trick). Fungus normally only affects fish kept in fresh water (although some rare marine forms exist)—in particular, it might plague mollies kept in soft, acidic water. As with freshwater whitespot, increasing the salinity of the aquarium cures external fungal infections quickly. Even species that cannot tolerant high salinities, such as platies, will tolerate brief (30- to 60-second) immersions in full-strength seawater just fine. These saltwater dips, if carried out once or twice a day, are a tried and trusted solution.

Mouth fungus isn't really a fungus but a bacterial infection, and won't be cured by changing salinity. Commercial treatments are available for this and most other miscellaneous fish diseases, but be sure to get products that are safe in both fresh and salt water. When it comes to buying and using medications, treat brackish-water aquaria as you would saltwater ones. It also is a good idea to always contact your veterinarian for advice before administering any type of medication.

Water Testing

As with medications, when buying water-testing kits take care to not buy those that only work in fresh water. Freshwater test kits can give inaccurate readings, or even no reading at all. A bit of guesswork might be

necessary to determine the readings when separate color scales are provided for salt and fresh water, but these scales will give you a better idea of parameters than not testing at all. A high-range pH (that is, alkaline water conditions) kit usually is required to accurately test a brackish-water tank. Regular water changes using water made with a marine salt mix to the correct specific gravity usually ensures that the pH remains in a tolerable range, especially given the wide range in which these fish can survive—generally anything above 7.2 is fine.

Newborn mollies are large enough to be able to swim strongly, and their parents are pretty likely not to eat them.

Livebearers

BREEDING

Most livebearers usually take care of breeding themselves, but if your fish do not seem to be reproducing, first check to make sure you have adequate hiding places—preferably plants like Java moss or artificial spawning grass—for the fry, so they don't get eaten. (If you never see any fry, it's entirely possibly that your fish have bred but other fish in the tank, including their parents, have eaten the fry.) Another good tip is to make sure you have a ratio of at least two females per male. Males tend to try to mate with females whether or not they are pregnant, and if too few females are available, the males can easily stress them and cause miscarriages.

Also make sure the water parameters, especially the water temperature, are right, because most livebearers tend to breed more readily when it's a little warmer than normal—a range of 74° to 82°F (26° to 28°C) is about right.

Breeding traps are not recommended because they tend to stress the female excessively. Mollies in particular are a bit big for the average breeding trap; if they feel confined, they sometimes miscarry. It is far safer to mate the fishes in a small nursery tank, then remove the male and let the female spend the next few weeks on her own in the tank. Because these fish are relatively clean animals, a simple, air-powered box filter is perfectly adequate for filtration. There is no need to use gravel, which might harbor decaying organic matter and pathogenic bacteria.

The sturdier species of *Hypostomus* and *Ancistrus* will do well at a specific gravity around 1.002.

Sailfin mollies will thrive in brackish water with salinity all the way up to full marine.

On the other hand, floating plants and some sort of cave, like a flower pot, will give the female a sense of security, as well as some cover for the fry once they are born. With the fry swimming around happily, the female can be moved back to the community tank.

Guppies tend to eat their young more than other livebearers do, and they also tend to produce fewer fry at a time. In contrast, mollies are the least likely to eat their young, and the newborns are big enough to be able to swim quite strongly. Platies and swordtails fall somewhere in the middle, so deciding on whether to leave the mother and babies together is a bit of a judgment call.

In livebearers, as with some cichlids, water conditions can have an effect on the ratio of males to females. As the water gets harder, more male guppies are produced than females, which can be incredibly irritating to your remaining outnumbered females, although it does provide for a more colorful tank. Some degree of experimentation is required to establish the perfect pH and hardness for your fish, but as a general rule, slightly hard, slightly alkaline water conditions are best for guppies, platies, and swordtails. Fairly to very hard water with a pH above 7.5 is more suitable for mollies.

Although female guppies tend to look very similar, the males of the various breeds differ in color and finnage.

Livebearers

EXAMPLE AQUARIUMS

A SLIGHTLY BRACKISH COMMUNITY AQUARIUM (SPECIFIC GRAVITY 1.002-1.004)

This sort of aquarium is the most appropriate home for platies and swordtails, though it would accomodate guppies and Endler's livebearers nicely as well. Mollies can also do well here, as long as the specific gravity is kept at the top end of the range. Tankmates for these livebearers could include any brackish fish that you find in a "freshwater" tank at a fish store, such as glassfish and bumblebee gobies.

Puffers are probably not a good choice—at best they will eat any fry, and more likely nip at the fins of guppies and mollies. But the more peaceful pufferfish species could be used with swordtails, which are large enough and fast enough to avoid the attentions of these engaging but sometimes unpredictable fish. Dwarf varieties of cichlids are an option as well—take the orange chromides, for example, which are inept predators at best and a threat only to the fry.

The popular small catfish, such as *Corydoras*, cannot be kept in a brackish aquarium, but the sturdier species of *Hypostomus* and *Ancistrus* will do well at the low end of the specific-gravity range suggested here. These fish are truly gentle giants and ignore even the smallest livebearer fry. They also do a good job of cleaning up any algae and leftover food. While pufferfish sometimes take a bite from their fins, these catfish usually handle themselves well in such situations, driving off their persecutors by swishing at them with their heavily armored tails.

Plants for this sort of aquarium include hardy, fast-growing *Hygrophila*, *Elodea*, and hornwort if the salinity is kept at the lower end of the range, while Java fern, Java moss, and *Anubias* usually do well even at the higher end. Some species of *Cryptocoryne* and *Vallisneria* can also be grown in slightly brackish water, although they are fussier about having bright lighting and require additional fertilization beyond simply using whatever waste the fish produce. An iron supplement is particularly important for these plants.

A STRONGLY BRACKISH COMMUNITY AQUARIUM (SPECIFIC GRAVITY 1.008-1.010)

This sort of aquarium is the best environment for shortfin and sailfin mollies, as they will grow quickly and be relatively resistant to fungal infection and other maladies. Guppies and Endler's livebearers also are quite happy with this salinity, although platies and swordtails do not do well in such salty water. Instead, choose peaceful brackish-water fish such as knight gobies, bumblebee gobies, *Brachirus* soles, and wrestling halfbeaks.

If you happen to have orange sailfin mollies, you might want to avoid orange chromides. Their coloration is so similar that an orange chromide in the mood to breed might harass the mollies incessantly if its

> **The Expert Says...**
>
> Most saltwater aquarists use a fishless cycle when starting up a new tank, but for those who prefer to cycle using fish and live rock, or fish only, mollies are an excellent alternative to damsels. They are not only far less aggressive when you eventually put other fish in, but can also be removed from the tank quite easily. Many people have experienced the labor of having to pull out most of the rock, corals, and decorations just to catch and remove one damselfish that has started to attack more expensive and attractive fish!

needs are not being sufficiently met by another chromide. This causes undue stress to the mollies—it does not even matter if the mollies are male or female, as chromides do not seem to be able to tell the difference!

Aside from young shark catfish, no commonly available catfish are happy at this salinity. And although the mollies will eat some algae, they prefer to nibble on strands growing on the edges of plants and ornaments, and don't really clean the glass at all. Freshwater snails are not an option either, because they will die quickly at this salinity. If you happen to live near an estuary, however, wild-caught brackish-water snails are certainly an option—assuming it is legal to collect them. Bear in mind, though, that snails frequently host parasites, which might be passed on to your fish.

Unfortunately, neither mollies nor any other known fishes eat the stag-horn algae that tends to develop in areas of high water flow within strongly brackish aquaria, so it will have to be removed manually. Live plants like Java moss, Java fern, and *Anubias* sometimes adapt to specific gravities as high as 1.008, but not always. In general, plastic plants are a far better choice.

LIVEBEARERS IN THE NANO-REEF

A nano-reef is a small marine aquarium designed specifically to maintain corals and other marine invertebrates along with a few species of small marine fish. Surprisingly to some aquarists, livebearers actually make good residents of such aquaria. Peaceful and clean, they do not damage invertebrates or produce waste the filter cannot deal with quickly. However, livebearers are usually kept as freshwater or brackish-water fish, and must be adapted to full marine conditions slowly. Generally speaking, adapting freshwater fish a couple of points along the specific-gravity scale per day (for example, from 1.000 to 1.002 one day then from 1.002 to 1.004 the next, and so on) is about right, although fish already adapted to a high-salinity brackish-water system (a specific gravity of 1.010 or more) usually can be taken to marine conditions relatively quickly—often within a day or two.

Guppies are ideally suited to very small (5 gallons, or 19 liters, or less) nano-reefs where even a pair of damsels or clownfish might get a bit crowded once rock and coral have been added. Regular-size mollies do well in nano-reefs of 10 gallons (35 liters) or larger, although a fully grown pair of sailfin mollies needs the added space of a 30-gallon (75-liter) reef or larger. Clownfish, green chromis, and most marine gobies make good companions, as do whatever invertebrates (such as small crabs, sea urchins, feather duster worms, and starfish) are appropriate for your saltwater tank. Needless to say, predatory fish and invertebrates should not be kept in such systems.

Gobies and Sleepers
By Naomi Delventhal

Gobies are one of the largest and most diverse groups of fishes, but some generalizations can be made. They are usually bottom-dwelling fishes and so are most characteristic of complex benthic habitats, notably coral reefs. They are also frequent inhabitants of estuaries and other coastal marine, brackish, and freshwater habitats. Ichthyologists have described about 2,000 goby species, and new ones are being discovered every year. As a result, Gobiidae ranks as one of the three largest fish families, rivaled only by the minnows, family Cyprinidae, and possibly the cichlids, family Cichlidae. Larger species are eaten by people, and in some island countries, the young of migrating species are collected in huge numbers as they return to fresh water.

Gobies are one of the few groups of fishes that are popular with both marine and freshwater aquarists. In general, they are small and hardy and often brightly colored. While naturally retiring, often slipping into a burrow or cave at the first sign of danger, in captivity they settle down nicely and become interesting and fun fish to watch. Many will breed in captivity, and it is amusing to watch the males defend territories and spar with one another.

Gobies and Sleepers

Numerous species are suitable for the brackish-water aquarist, with new ones turning up on a fairly regular basis. Several, such as the bumblebee goby and the knight goby, have become firm favorites and can be found in most good tropical fish stores.

Also popular among brackish fishkeepers are the gudgeons, or sleeper gobies, of the family Eleotridae. Sleepers look like typical gobies at first glance, but closer inspection reveals a key difference. Most gobies have their pelvic fins fused into a single round sucker that they use to attach themselves to rocks and plants, but the pelvic fins of sleepers are not fused and look much like those of any other fish. Even so, it is not uncommon to see sleepers prop themselves up on their pelvic fins, using them almost as they might short legs. Generally, sleepers are a bit larger and more piscivorous than the average goby, but a number of small sleepers don't present much of a threat to anything save the smallest fishes. These can make very good community residents.

DIVERSITY

Even though they are among the biggest groups of fishes (one in ten species of fish is a gobioid), remarkably little is known about most species. Experts recognize as many as nine families within the suborder Gobioidei, but only the Gobiidae and Eleotridae are familiar to most freshwater and brackish aquarists. A third family, the Ptereleotridae, is better known to marine aquarists since it includes the firefish and dart gobies that do very well in reef aquaria. Among the minor groups of little or no interest to aquarists are the Odontobutidae, which resemble sleeper gobies both in appearance and habits; the Rhyacichthyidae, which, unlike most other gobioids, have a complete lateral line and resemble hillstream loaches; and the Schindleriidae, small fishes whose adults are *paedomorphic*—that is, they retain many larval characteristics.

Even concentrating on just the family Gobiidae, you will find a huge diversity in body form, habitat, life history, and behavior. Although a few gobies reach a size of 20 inches (50 cm), most gobies are small, typically less than 4 inches (10 cm) long. In fact, the tiny size of some goby species has earned them a place in *The Guinness Book of World Records*.

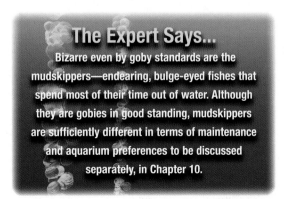

Many marine gobies are known for their associations with larger fishes, burrowing shrimps, stinging anemones, and sea urchins. Some gobies are cleaners, such as the more well-known cleaner wrasses and shrimps. These species set up stations on coral reefs where larger fish come to have external parasites removed. Other gobies are elongated and eel-like. Still others are blind and live in caves.

"TRUE" GOBIES—*GOBIIDAE*

Gobiidae is the largest family of gobioids and includes about 1,800 species. Its members are often referred to

Members of the family Gobiidae are often referred to as the "true gobies," but also may be called "disc gobies."

as the "true gobies," although the other gobioid groups are closely related and all can be considered true gobies.

As noted earlier, one of the easiest ways to tell a goby from another fish is to look at the pelvic fins. Gobies usually have pelvic fins fused into a suction cup, termed the pelvic disc, but the degree of fusion varies among the different groups of gobies. Gobies in the subfamily Sicydiinae have highly developed membranes connecting the pelvic fins; they form such a good suction device that these gobies are capable of climbing up major waterfalls during their upstream migrations! Other gobies, like the *Valenciennea* spp. (sifter gobies) popular with marine aquarists, have pelvic fins that are nearly separate; these fishes can be easily confused with sleeper gobies, whose pelvic fins are always completely separate. Fortunately for aquarists, knowing what family a goby belongs to is far less important than knowing its species when it comes to keeping and breeding it.

SLEEPER GOBIES—*ELEOTRIDAE*

Over 200 species of sleeper goby are known, and most are found in estuarine and freshwater habits. They are widely distributed, but mostly appear in tropical and subtropical waters; they are notably absent from European waters. Many make good aquarium fish but only a few species have become popular. Some are exquisitely beautiful, while others are a drab, mottled brown. Some rest on the bottom, while others swim freely in midwater. Many species have a migratory life cycle, and a number of larger species are a source of food to humans.

The common names "gudgeon" and "sleeper goby" are often used interchangeably for eleotrids, although typically gudgeon is applied to species of Indo-Pacific (especially Australian) origin, while sleeper goby, a more

115

Gobies and Sleepers

Goby Evolution

From the viewpoint of an evolutionary biologist, gobies are a fascinating group and, not surprisingly, goby evolution is currently an active area of study. Systematists, those biologists who study the diversity of life and the evolutionary relationships among different organisms, work to assemble phylogenies, or family trees for different groups. Although the greatest number of living gobies occur in marine environments, the latest family trees suggest that a freshwater adult stage is primitive for the group, because the majority of early diverging gobioid lineages are primarily freshwater, estuarine, or amphidromous. These basal lineages include the families Rhyacichthyidae, Odontobutidae, and Eleotridae. It is not known whether the disc gobies first evolved in a marine or freshwater environment, because basal taxa within the Gobiidae have not yet been identified. In general, the trend in derived gobies is that of reduction; they have smaller adult size, fewer bones, and loss of the lateral line.

general term, is applied to American species as well. In other parts of the world, other common names are used—for example, New Zealand's endemic eleotrids of the genus *Gobiomorphus* are commonly called "bullies."

MYSTERY GOBIES

It's not uncommon to find gobies for sale in an aquarium store that don't appear in the usual books and magazines, as these fish can be very difficult to identify. Sometimes these mystery gobies can be identified to the genus based on knowledge of similar species. At other times, the only way to get a goby identified at all is to preserve a specimen and send it to a goby specialist for identification. Natural history museums often have ichthyologists on staff who will be happy to look at a specimen. Preservation is often necessary for identification, because some species are only distinguishable through microscopic examination of minute details such as the pattern of sensory papillae. Even so, many groups of gobies are notoriously difficult to identify to the species level.

There's an oft-quoted rule in the aquarium hobby: Never buy a fish unless you know what it eats and how big it gets. Fortunately, most gobies stay relatively small (although some sleepers are an exception), and most will take readily available live or even dry food. Most also adapt to a wide range of salinities. If you don't know the ideal specific gravity for a goby (this includes species sold as freshwater, as many are actually best kept in brackish water), it is helpful to start with a specific gravity of about 1.003. This is harmless to freshwater species and acceptable for most brackish-water species.

AQUARIUM CARE

With a few exceptions, gobies are not particularly sensitive or delicate animals. Many are tolerant of wide variations in pH, water hardness, salinity, and temperature, as you would expect from fish that thrive in estuaries and tide pools. Occasionally, clues will indicate that salinity must be adjusted. For example, if a fish is kept in too-high salinity, it may become restless; in too-low salinity, it may show symptoms of disease or be more susceptible to shock. However, few will do well if simply dumped into a generic community tank. Few handle aggressive tankmates well, and many are slow feeders who cannot compete with voracious feeders

Gobies are fairly hardy, but care still should be given to preparing the proper living conditions.

like scats or monos. And if you want your gobies to breed, then it is even more important to get their living conditions right.

TANK SETUP AND SOCIAL REQUIREMENTS

In general, tanks for gobies should be set up to provide cover in the form of rocks and driftwood, in particular making sure that sufficient territories are available for each fish. Small species do well in 5-gallon (20-liter) tanks, while larger species should be housed in larger aquaria, up to 4 feet (120 cm) long. Most species like to burrow or dig, so a fine, sandy substrate should be used. Silica sand is ideal, but inimical to undergravel filters and many motor-driven filters, which is why some aquarists like to use old-fashioned, air-driven corner or box filters. Nearly all gobies are territorial within their species, and they may also behave aggressively toward other gobies (or sometimes any other fishes of similar size and habits). It is often beneficial to provide tall rock structures that reach near the surface; this increases the functional habitat for these fish, as they like to remain close to the substrate or large, solid objects. Tall structures can also provide cover for subordinate individuals, which are often chased near the surface where they cannot intrude on the territories of the dominant fish.

One mistake people frequently make is keeping these fish in pairs. Aquarium stores often sell fish in pairs, and keeping a pair seems very appealing. However, serious problems usually become evident when keeping just two gobies, even if they are a male and female. With only two fish, the dominant individual concentrates all its efforts on the subordinate individual, who might gradually waste away, become battered and more susceptible to opportunistic pathogens, or, on rare occasions, be killed outright. Paradoxical as it may seem, a larger tank is often needed to keep just two fish than to keep four! If you do keep two fish, be prepared to separate them if necessary (a plastic tank divider is often handy). With most species, the ideal arrangement is a small group of four or more individuals of the same species.

DIET

Gobies have a reputation for being difficult to feed, although this is not really fair. True, bumblebee gobies, *Brachygobius* spp., are often reluctant to eat anything but live food, and many newly purchased gobies often require live food during acclimation to regain lost body mass. (Aquarists caring for these fish should always be prepared to offer live food. Blackworms can be purchased from most dealers, and daphnia and brine shrimp are easy to rear in large tubs.)

But most gobies and sleepers are not nearly so picky and will eat all sorts of things. They relish blackworms, chopped earthworms, frozen bloodworms (chironomid midge larvae), and even bits of shrimp frozen for human consumption. Larger species enjoy whole earthworms and shrimp. Many gobies are omnivores that will also take flake and pellet foods, and even algae nibbled from the glass or plants in the aquaria. Smaller species

The Expert Says...

One of the very best foods for all but the most finicky gobies is homemade gel diet. It can be frozen until fed, chopped to fit the mouth of any species, and holds its shape well in water. It can be modified to fit the requirements of a particular species, and medications such as de-wormer or antibiotics may be added as needed.

appreciate newly hatched brine shrimp. Many sleeper gobies are lie-and-wait predators, capable of consuming fish as much as half their own size. Fortunately few, if any, species must be maintained on live fishes, and most sleepers will eat the same sorts of foods as other gobies.

Aquarists often ask whether it's important to thaw frozen food before feeding to fishes, but there is no general agreement among experts. When feeding fish such as the bigger sleeper gobies that like to engulf large chunks of food, I recommend thawing the food first. However, when feeding a tank of small tropical fishes a cube of frozen brine shrimp, dropping the food into the tank and letting the fishes pick it apart as it thaws seems to cause no problems.

Bloodworms make a good diet staple for gobies and sleepers.

HEALTH

Most gobies are relatively resistant to disease, although they are subject to the usual aquarium diseases, such as fin rot and ich. Gobies are sensitive to some commercial medications, so when introducing medications, add half-doses initially and observe for stress. After many years of keeping gobies, my aquarium medicine cabinet became significantly emptier as I found that most curable diseases could be treated with just a few medications. Flake food or gel diet prepared with antibiotics or de-wormer are also useful, since they treat the fish itself rather than the water.

As with many brackish-water fish, one of the best ways to deal with ich is simply to elevate the salinity of the tank; a specific gravity of 1.005 or more will fix mild cases fairly quickly. More severe infections, in which the fish appears noticeably uncomfortable, can be alleviated by dipping the fish

Gobies attach their eggs to substrate or other items in the tank.

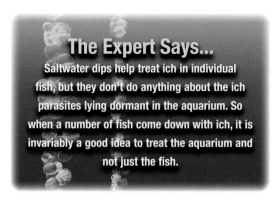

into full-strength seawater for 30 to 60 seconds (or until the fish shows severe stress) once or twice a day until the fish appears more comfortable.

BREEDING GOBIES

PREPARATION AND SPAWNING

The sex of many gobies can be distinguished on the basis of coloration. The shape of the urogenital papilla, a small structure located behind the vent through which eggs or sperm are deposited, can be used effectively to sex nearly all gobies. In males it is typically pointed, but in females it is blunt. In most species, the difference becomes more evident at breeding time. If conditions are to their liking, most gobies will spawn in their regular tank and do not need to be removed to a special breeding aquarium. The best way to encourage spawning is to feed the fish very well, perform frequent and large partial water changes, and ensure that suitable spawning sites are available.

Depending on the species, courtship usually begins the day before spawning. This is often associated with lateral displays, chasing, nudging, and light nipping. In most species, the female becomes bulky prior

You might want to let the male goby hatch the eggs and then move the larvae to another tank.

Gobies and Sleepers

to spawning; in some species, the ripe eggs can be seen. Gobies lay eggs that are attached to substrate (as opposed to scattered or free-floating eggs). After spawning is completed, the male chases the female away and assumes the responsibility of the brood until the eggs hatch. At that point, the larvae are on their own.

HATCHING

Most gobies have larvae that swim freely throughout the tank. Many hobbyists new to gobies are surprised to see that the tiny, almost transparent larvae drift throughout the midwater of the tank rather than hide among the gravel. With some exceptions (desert gobies, round gobies, and others), gobies have a free-swimming (planktonic) larval period during which they drift in the water column and feed on small, free-floating organisms.

It's often easiest to let the father hatch the eggs and afterward use a siphon to collect some larvae. To hatch the eggs artificially, remove the nest about a day before the eggs are expected to hatch and place it in a small tank (with a capacity of about 1 gallon, or 3.75 liters) with heavy aeration. Do not let air touch the eggs when you are moving the nest. Although air does not directly damage the eggs of most freshwater gobies, it will cause some of the eggs to become dislodged from the nest, making them difficult to hatch. When the eggs are due to hatch, usually in the evening, observe the nest. If not all the eggs have hatched by the next morning, try gently rubbing them with your fingers, as the father goby would have fanned them, to stimulate hatching. The larvae should soon start to hatch. If this does not work, wedge the nest of eggs in a plastic cup full of clean water and swirl the water around in the cup. This usually causes most of the larvae to hatch quite quickly. Pour out the larvae, a few at a time, and repeat until all the eggs are hatched.

REARING THE FRY

Aeration must be gentle once the larvae have hatched. The larvae of some species hatch with a small yolk

Be careful—if there is too much food in the water, water quality will plummet and the larvae will die.

sac remaining, but other species must be fed right away. It's often easy to raise young gobies in a small, 1-gallon tank for the first week or so, because the food is nearer to the larvae. At least 10 percent of the water must be changed each day.

Free-swimming larvae need food that is available in the midwater level they inhabit. With smaller species, marine rotifers are the best food choice, as they will survive in brackish water. They can be raised in large tubs on micro-algae. Strained, hard-boiled egg yolk can sometimes work for a day or two if the aeration is adjusted to keep it lightly suspended, but it causes too much waste build-up in the tank to be very practical for the long term. When raising larvae, keep in mind that the amount of food you provide is important. If food is scarce, larvae spend more energy chasing it than they gain from nutrition. If the food is too abundant, the water quickly becomes polluted and the larvae suffocate.

To determine whether larvae are large enough for brine shrimp, add a very small number of newly hatched brine shrimp. If the larvae are able to eat them, you will soon see their guts full of pink-orange shrimp. If they are not large enough, siphon out the uneaten shrimp and try them again the next day. Be sure to use newly hatched brine shrimp, because older ones are too large and powerful for small goby larvae. Also, some brands of brine shrimp are smaller than others, so it pays to try several brands. Once all the larvae are eating brine shrimp, they can be transferred into a larger rearing tank.

Eventually, the larvae become pigmented and undergo metamorphosis. After metamorphosis, they hop around at the bottom of the tank, behaving like miniature adults. At this time, the larvae are usually easy to feed on baby brine shrimp, microworms, and, depending on the species, flakes.

The advice given so far is applicable to gobies that have relatively large larvae, such as bumblebee gobies. However, many brackish and freshwater gobies are migratory. In the wild these species hatch larvae in rivers or streams, which are swept out into the ocean to develop for several weeks or months in the plankton before returning to fresh waters, where they remain throughout the rest of their lives. This lifecycle strategy is termed *amphidromy*, and the larvae of amphidromous gobies are typically very small and delicate—very few species have ever been reared successfully. Nonetheless, plenty of opportunity is here for the adventuresome aquarist. Rearing experiments for these gobies must be done using salt water and the tiniest of live food, such as newly hatched rotifers.

COMMONLY KEPT SLEEPERS AND GOBIES

FAT SLEEPER—*DORMITATOR MACULATUS*

Fat sleepers are large, sturdy fish that are among the most adaptable brackish-water fishes, tolerant not just of a wide range of salinities but able to do well at a wider range of temperatures than most other tropical fish—they do fine even in unheated tanks. As adults they are distinctly omnivorous, and will happily eat smaller tankmates. Otherwise, they are peaceful and can be combined with robust species of fish from similar brackish-water habitats.

Fat sleepers do best in larger aquaria decorated with plants that provide them with shade and cover. They do, however, enjoy digging, so the plants should be sturdy and either unrooted (like Java fern) or with their roots protected using stones. These fish spend much more time swimming in midwater than do typical gobies.

Gobies and Sleepers

Dormitator maculatus

Although not brightly colored, they do have an attractive pattern of light and dark spots along the flanks, in particular a shiny patch on the gill covers behind the eyes. And they are big fish—although they rarely exceed 10 inches (25 cm) in captivity, they still make for a pretty large animal that needs an appropriately large aquarium with good filtration.

Fat sleepers will spawn in captivity, but rearing the larvae has not been successful. Eggs are laid in large caves and on stones. The extremely tiny larvae hatch in about 12 hours. Salt water is recommended for rearing experiments.

Fat sleeper

Name	*Dormitator maculatus*
Other names	Fat sleeper, jade goby
Origin	Atlantic side of North America
Size	28 inches (70 cm); smaller in captivity
Water conditions	Fresh to fully marine; happy at subtropical or tropical temperatures
Diet	Omnivore; greedily consumes most foods available, including plant matter
Temperament	Usually peaceful midwater swimmer; should not be kept with fishes small enough to swallow
Availability	Fairly widely traded and inexpensive
Ease of maintenance	Easy
Specific problems	Large size; predatory

The genus *Dormitator* is widespread, and other species besides the fat sleeper turn up from time to time in aquarium stores. One of these is *D. lebretonis*, sometimes called *Batanga lebretonis*, from West Africa. It is a much smaller fish, often called the clay or mud goby by aquarists, and is more handsome than pretty. It has a nice row of dark spots running along its flanks, and the fins bear an attractive reticulated pattern as well. Being relatively small—barely over 4 inches (10 cm) when mature—it is eminently suitable for inclusion in a fresh to weakly brackish community tank with not-too-small companions. Because of its cheerful disposition and healthy appetite, it is a highly desirable dither fish for bringing out shyer gobies, such as medium-size river gobies like *Awaous*. It will eat a variety of foods, including algae, but particularly relishes mosquito larvae and bloodworms.

EMPIRE GUDGEON—*HYPSELEOTRIS COMPRESSA*

The empire gudgeon is popular with people who keep rainbowfish and may be housed with them in medium-size tanks furnished with rocks and plants. They will spawn in captivity, and the extremely tiny eggs hatch within 24 hours. The larvae should be reared in brackish or salt water on the smallest of foods. Other

Hypseleotris compressa

125

Gobies and Sleepers

Empire Gudgeon

Name	*Hypseleotris compressa*
Other names	Empire gudgeon
Origin	Australia and New Guinea
Size	4 inches (10 cm)
Water conditions	Fresh or slightly brackish (specific gravity <1.005) for adults
Diet	Small live and prepared foods
Temperament	Generally quiet, peaceful midwater swimmer
Availability	Rare
Ease of maintenance	Easy
Specific problems	None

Hypseleotris species are suitable for the aquarium; some live solely in fresh water, while others are migratory.

CRAZYFISH—*BUTIS BUTIS*

Crazyfish are one of the few regularly traded sleeper gobies. They have become quite popular as oddball fish for community aquaria. There are a few problems with this, though. For one thing, these fish grow fairly large, and they are also highly predatory and will eat any small fish they can swallow. Because they have very large (and expandable) mouths, it is not wise to keep them with fish less than half their size—slim fishes such as minnows and livebearers are at particular risk. Spiny fishes, such as cichlids and catfish, will be ignored, as will anything too large to be swallowed whole. They do well with larger, stouter gobies, such as knight gobies.

These fish do best in a relatively large aquarium; a 36-inch (90-cm) aquarium is about the minimum size for adults. The common name "crazyfish" comes from their habit of swimming sideways and upside down. They

Crazyfish

Name	*Butis butis*
Other names	Crazyfish, flathead gudgeon, bony-snout gudgeon
Origin	Indo-Pacific
Size	6 inches (15 cm)
Water conditions	Tolerates fresh to fully marine water, but best kept at about 1.002 to 1.012 specific gravity
Diet	Carnivore; consumes small fish, earthworms, and other live foods; can be trained to take shrimp pellets
Temperament	Predatory, but generally ignores similarly sized fish
Availability	Available sporadically; relatively inexpensive
Ease of maintenance	Fairly easy
Specific problems	Predatory

Butis butis

are also very fond of perching on the underside of rocks, so it is important to provide large rocks with caves and overhangs for the fish to hide in. Big pieces of bogwood or artificial roots can be used too, as live plants are only viable at the lower end of the salinity range. Although tolerant of variations in salinity, crazyfish like warm water, so keep the temperature of the aquarium between 72° and 82°F (22° and 28°C). Crazyfish can be kept with large mudskippers if the tank is large enough and they are provided with sufficiently deep water—at least 4 inches (10 cm). Other *Butis* species, while not generally imported, require similar care. Breeding has not been reported in captivity.

Dwarf Neon Goby—*Amoya* sp.

Dwarf neon gobies have recently been imported in increasing numbers, but little seems to be known about them. They should be kept in an aquarium at least 30 inches (75 cm) long, with rocks to offer hiding places. They seem to do poorly in crowded freshwater tanks (as found in pet shops), but can be brought back to health under good conditions. These gobies are easy to feed, readily accepting flake food from the tank bottom and

Redigobius balteatus

127

Gobies and Sleepers

Dwarf neon goby

Name	*Amoya* sp.
Other names	Dwarf neon goby, Indian goby
Origin	India
Size	At least 3 inches (8 cm)
Water conditions	Brackish water; specific gravity about 1.006
Diet	Flake foods, small live foods
Temperament	Territorial with its own species, but can be kept in small groups if enough hiding places are available
Availability	Available sporadically
Ease of maintenance	Not recommended for beginners
Specific problems	Apparently sensitive to shock and bacterial infection in fresh water

midwater. Breeding in captivity has not been reported. Other species of *Amoya*, as well as *Acentrogobius* and their relatives, are usually small- to medium-size gobies. Typically, they have rows of blue or green iridescent spots and often inhabit brackish water.

Naked Goby—*Gobiosoma bosc*

Naked gobies, so named because they lack scales, can be collected in traps throughout their native range and are among the best bets for aquarists wanting to try out one of the temperate species of goby. They will not tolerate tropical temperatures and need an aquarium kept between 58° and 72°F (14° and 22°C). In summer, this may require the use of an aquarium chiller, or at least placing the aquarium somewhere cool and

Naked goby

Name	*Gobiosoma bosc*
Other names	Naked goby
Origin	Atlantic North America, New York to Texas
Size	2.5 inches (6 cm)
Water conditions	Brackish to marine; specific gravity 1.015 to 1.024
Diet	Small pieces of frozen seafood, flake food, brine shrimp
Temperament	Lively and territorial; a male may be kept with two females; peaceful with other species
Availability	Not likely to be available commercially
Ease of maintenance	Easy
Specific problems	None

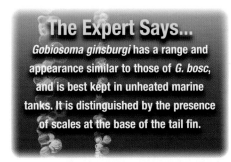

out of direct sunlight, such as in a basement.

These gobies do not need much space. An aquarium around 20 inches (50 cm) long is suitable for a trio, which will feel right at home if the tank is decorated with some combination of small caves, PVC pipes, and seashells. Males court females in typical goby fashion, and eggs are laid in seashells, under stones, or in PVC pipes. The small larvae can be reared on marine rotifers until they are large enough to take brine shrimp.

FLATHEAD GOBIES—*GLOSSOGOBIUS* SPP.

With a long lower jaw and flattened body shape, the various *Glossogobius* species resemble many sleeper gobies, although they are easily distinguished by their fused pelvic fins. Also like many sleepers, they are relatively large and predatory, but they can be kept without problems with medium-size brackish-water fish.

Identification to the species level is difficult without looking at the papillae patterns on the head, so it is just as well to treat them all as *Glossogobius* species and assume they will grow into fairly large, predatory fish. They must be kept in the same general way as crazyfish, sharing the same need for caves

Awaous sp.

Flathead goby

Name	*Glossogobius* spp.
Other names	Flathead goby
Origin	Indo-Pacific
Size	About 6 inches (15 cm), depending on the species
Water conditions	About 1.002 to 1.008 specific gravity recommended
Diet	Carnivore; blackworms, small earthworms, and other live foods; frozen bloodworms and pieces of chopped shrimp
Temperament	Rather secretive; should not be kept with small fishes
Availability	Rarely imported
Ease of maintenance	Relatively easy
Specific problems	Size (some species)

and crevices if they are to settle into the aquarium well, but beyond that, these are adaptable, relatively unaggressive fish.

RIVER GOBY—*AWAOUS FLAVUS*

This tropical goby is generally lively but sometimes shy, so it should not be kept with more aggressive species. River gobies often bury in the substrate and sift through it, as do many marine gobies. For this reason, it is important to use fine sand instead of gravel in their aquarium. They are best kept in groups of at least three, since both males and females are antagonistic toward one another. River gobies perform vigorous side-by-side displays and may even fight by locking jaws, but injuries are rare. Males are more colorful than females and usually have larger mouths.

River goby

Name	*Awaous flavus*
Other names	Striated river goby, candystripe goby, Brazilian pinstripe goby
Origin	Eastern South America
Size	4 inches (10 cm)
Water conditions	May be sold as brackish-water fish, but adults do best in fresh water
Diet	Smallish live food, dry tablets, and flakes
Temperament	Generally peaceful and shy; not predatory
Availability	Imported sporadically
Ease of maintenance	Moderately easy
Specific problems	Needs sandy substrate

Like most gobies, males stake out territories around a cave, inside which the females lay their minute eggs. The larvae hatch after 12 hours and drift in the water column. In nature, these larvae develop in the ocean. Unlike most *Awaous* species, the lifespan of *Awaous flavus* is usually under two years. Rarely, other *Awaous* species are imported; they too have an amphidromous life cycle, and some grow moderately large. Depending on the species, they occur in fresh or sometimes weakly brackish water.

BUMBLEBEE GOBIES—*BRACHYGOBIUS* SPP.

These delightful little black-and-yellow gobies often perch on rocks or hover in midwater. They are undoubtedly the most popular brackish-water goby in the hobby. Although each fish defends a small territory, they are best kept in groups of eight to twelve individuals in an aquarium large enough for each to stake out its own patch. Having said that, they don't need a lot of space per fish—a 5-gallon (18-liter) aquarium containing lots of rocks, plants, and snail shells is perfectly suitable for a group this size. They are happiest in warm water and require it to breed, but they can survive very well for months in temperatures in the mid-60°F (17° to 20°C) range. Under these conditions, bumblebee gobies can be maintained in excellent health even if fed only once a week or less; cooling the water is a good strategy during the winter months, when live food may be scarcer. Despite being small, bumblebee gobies are relatively long lived, with a 5-year lifespan typical of individuals that are cared for properly.

Although widely thought of as a novelty fish for the community aquarium, bumblebee gobies are best kept in a tank to themselves, because most other fishes will gobble up all the food before the bumblebee gobies get any. Males are slimmer and often more orange than females, who lay large eggs that are fanned and cleaned by the male until they hatch in about seven days. Larvae should be fed rotifers as soon as the yolk sac (if present) disappears. Brine shrimp may be offered in five to seven days.

About 10 species of *Brachygobius* are known, but most are not common in the trade. Most often available are those of the *B. doriae* species group, but sometimes *B. nunus* (a smaller species) and others are imported.

Bumblebee gobies

Name	***Brachygobius doriae* is the most commonly traded species**
Other names	**Bumblebee goby**
Origin	**Southeastern Asia**
Size	**1.5 inches (4 cm)**
Water conditions	**Fresh to slightly brackish water, 1.000 to 1.004 specific gravity recommended; prefers warm water, 80° to 85°F (27° to 30°C)**
Diet	**Small live foods; can rarely be trained to eat prepared foods; relishes chopped earthworms**
Temperament	**Peaceful with fishes that swim in the upper portion of the tank; may nip at other bottom-dwellers**
Availability	**Very common and inexpensive**
Ease of maintenance	**Fairly easy**
Specific problems	**Requires live foods**

Gobies and Sleepers

Brachygobius doriae

Brachygobius xanthozona, also known as *Hypogymnogobius xanthozona*, is often referred to as the bumblebee goby in aquarium literature, but it is larger and very rare in nature. It is rarely, if ever, imported.

Desert Goby—*Chlamydogobius eremius*

The desert goby is an active, endearing fish that stays on the bottom of the tank. Males are territorial; one may be kept with two females in smaller tanks. They do well in small tanks—about 20 inches (50 cm) long—furnished with rocks, stones, and plants. The dominant males are yellow, with a bright blue dorsal fin, but females and nondominant males are relatively plain.

Desert goby

Name	*Chlamydogobius eremius*
Other names	Desert goby
Origin	Australian desert
Size	2.5 inches (6 cm)
Water conditions	Can tolerate hypersaline conditions, but best kept at 1.000 to 1.004 specific gravity
Diet	Omnivore; enjoys algae, small live foods, and prepared flakes
Temperament	May be kept with other small fishes; males are territorial
Availability	Available sporadically; easy to breed, so usually can be obtained from other hobbyists
Ease of maintenance	Easy
Specific problems	Relatively short lifespan

Chlamydogobius eremius

Gobies and Sleepers

Evorthodus lyricus

These are among the easiest of all gobies to breed. Very large eggs are laid in caves underneath flat rocks. Hatching time depends on temperature—these fish breed well at anything from 72° to 80°F (22° to 27°C). The fry are very large, and no free-swimming larval stage occurs. Instead, the fry hop around on the substrate like adults. They are easy to rear on brine shrimp, microworms, and crumbled flake foods.

Unlike most brackish fish kept by aquarists, desert gobies do not come from estuarine habitats. Rather, they are native to desert springs, streams, and wells, which often become highly saline. They have a short lifespan, only about one to two years. Other *Chlamydogobius* species require similar care and make excellent aquarium fish, but are unlikely to be seen outside Australia.

LYRE GOBY—*EVORTHODUS LYRICUS*

In nature, lyre gobies are often found in muddy water. In the aquarium, they seem able to tolerate less than ideal conditions. They are not too picky about salinity, and fishkeepers have discovered little difference between brackish and fresh water for their long-term health. While the natural range of this species includes subtropical and tropical regions, it is best to keep them at temperatures close to that of the

Lyre goby

Name	*Evorthodus lyricus*
Other names	Lyre goby
Origin	Western Atlantic
Size	4.75 inches (12 cm)
Water conditions	Tolerates fresh to salt water, but slightly brackish water is best
Diet	Detritivore; finely crumbled flakes, frozen baby brine shrimp, and sinking wafers that dissolve into small particles
Temperament	Peaceful, but territorial with own species
Availability	Not likely to be available commercially, but easy to collect
Ease of maintenance	Moderately easy
Specific problems	Only feeds on small particles on the substrate; likely to starve without proper attention

Gobioides broussonnetii

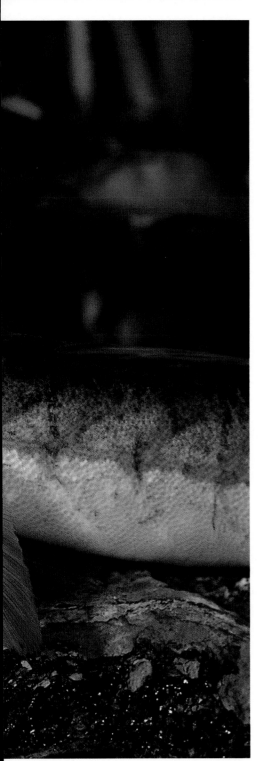

environment from which they were collected.

These small gobies are *detritivores*, adapted to sifting through mud for edible material. Unless fine, sinking food is available, they are likely to starve in captivity,

because they will not take foods on the surface or in the water column. Large males are territorial with their own species, but are likely to be picked on by other, more aggressive species. The aquarium should be at least 20 inches (50 cm) long, with a soft substrate such as silica sand, and a good-size clear area among the rocks and stones for the fish to feed in. Plants or stands of hair algae are appreciated.

Lyre gobies can be bred in captivity, but the larvae are small. After the eggs have hatched (about 20 hours after being laid), the fry are planktonic and require tiny live foods. Rearing attempts should be made in salt water.

Violet goby

Name	*Gobioides broussonnetii*
Other names	Violet goby, dragon goby
Origin	Atlantic coast of North America (Georgia to Brazil)
Size	22 inches (55 cm)
Water conditions	Tolerates fresh water, but best kept at about 1.005 to 1.015 specific gravity
Diet	Requires a varied diet including brine shrimp, blackworms, finely chopped earthworms, algae wafers, and sinking foods that disintegrate; not a piscivore
Temperament	Shy, secretive; fights with its own kind, but peaceful with other species
Availability	Commonly available
Ease of maintenance	Moderately easy
Specific problems	Care must be taken to prevent starvation

Gobies and Sleepers

VIOLET GOBY—*GOBIOIDES BROUSSONNETII*

The violet goby, or dragon goby, is a fairly large, eel-like fish that adapts to a wide variety of water conditions. Even so, many specimens starve to death in captivity because their owners mistake their fierce appearance as an indication that these are aggressive, predatory fish. I have never observed one eat even a small fish, such as a guppy—in fact, they are much more omnivorous and need a balanced diet consisting of invertebrates and algae. They feed by shoveling through the substrate for small worms, scraping their teeth against rocks to remove algae, and gulping large mouthfuls of water to capture plankton. In the aquarium, they need a soft substrate that allows them to sift out frozen bloodworms, broken algae wafers, and catfish pellets. They seem to enjoy periodic offerings of small swimming crustaceans, such as newly hatched brine shrimp, and their gulping behavior is very entertaining to watch.

Because their eyesight is very poor, violet gobies do not compete well with quick feeders in a community tank. However, if fed after dark, they can be kept with other medium-size, docile brackish-water fishes, such as fat sleepers. An aquarium for violet gobies should be at least 48 inches (120 cm) long, with lots of long, narrow hiding places, such as PVC pipes, laid on the substrate. They are highly territorial around these burrows.

SKUNK GOBY—*REDIGOBIUS BALTEATUS*

Skunk gobies are often very shy when young, hovering just above the substrate or hiding in small caves. They do well in a small aquarium 18 inches (45 cm) long, with small caves and overhangs. Tiny eggs are laid in caves; larvae should be offered marine rotifers. Other *Redigobius* species are occasionally kept, although

Skunk goby

Name	*Redigobius balteatus*
Other names	Skunk goby
Origin	Indo-Pacific
Size	1.2 inches (3 cm)
Water conditions	Tolerates fresh to fully marine conditions, but best kept at about 1.002 to 1.008 specific gravity; should not be kept in totally fresh water for extended periods of time
Diet	Small live foods such as whiteworms, blackworms, mosquito larvae, brine shrimp; can be trained to take prepared foods
Temperament	Shy but territorial; should not be kept with aggressive species, but may be kept with other small fishes that swim near the surface
Availability	Imported sporadically
Ease of maintenance	Moderately easy
Specific problems	None

rarely imported.

Knight Goby—*Stigmatogobius sadanundio*

Knight gobies are second only to the bumblebee gobies in popularity, although they are substantially larger and thus require a bigger aquarium. Compared to many other gobies, they spend relatively little time on the substrate, and often are seen hovering or swimming in midwater. They can be a bit retiring when first placed in the aquarium, though as with many shy fish, one of the best ways to encourage them out is to offer them lots of hiding places; if the tank lacks suitable hiding places, knight gobies may become extremely nervous and dash about the tank at the slightest disturbance. They are best kept in groups along with other medium-size species in a larger tank, because the presence of other fishes seems to calm them. The tank should be decorated with many caves, plants, roots, and other hiding places.

Knight goby males can be distinguished from the females by their extended dorsal and anal rays. They seem to be very particular about which females they will spawn with. Eggs are laid in large caves and guarded by the parents. The larvae hatch within 48 hours and should be fed the smallest of foods (such as rotifers) after the yolk sac is gone. Knight gobies do not tolerate polluted water well; in these conditions, they will be

Knight goby

Name	*Stigmatogobius sadanundio*
Other names	Knight goby, fan-dancer goby
Origin	Southeastern Asia
Size	3.5 inches (9 cm)
Water conditions	Fresh or slightly brackish water; best kept at a specific gravity between 1.002 and 1.008
Diet	Chopped earthworms, frozen bloodworms, other frozen and prepared foods
Temperament	Usually peaceful with fishes too large to eat
Availability	Commonly available
Ease of maintenance	Moderately easy
Specific problems	Nervous; sensitive to pollution

sensitive to chronic bacterial infection. *Stigmatogobius pleurostigma* is a similar species that is smaller and has fewer spots.

Stigmatogobius sadanundio

Australian Fishes
By Bruce Hansen

The Australian aquarist interested in maintaining a brackish aquarium is indeed fortunately placed; not only is there ready access to the equipment and technology required, but a wide and varied range of suitable species lives in the waters of the island continent. Aquarists in other parts of the world don't see many of these fishes, but they do see some, and a number of them—including the rainbowfish, some of the gobies and sleepers, and one or two others—have become staples of the hobby.

THE AQUARIUM HOBBY IN AUSTRALIA

The retail aquarium trade in Australia, although generally thriving, is limited by a restrictive list of approved species allowed for import, stringent quarantine and inspection requirements, and very few major importers. These restrictions are aimed at limiting the risk of further environmental damage to aquatic habitats from feral populations of fish from other countries. Australia already has huge problems with pest fishes in the form of

Aquarists worldwide stock their brackish tanks with tidal estuarine inhabitants, like *Monodactylus argenteus*.

carp, mosquitofish, and tilapias, and a whole host of other minor, localized problems with several other exotic species. Though economically useful, there is also the difficult question of the deliberate introduction of exotic species into Australian lakes and rivers for angling purposes, including trout, salmon, and European perch. While appreciated by fishermen, these fishes are a threat to native fish populations.

Species suitable for brackish-aquarium enthusiasts obviously fall into three natural groups based on salinity tolerances—essentially marine species that can tolerate varying degrees of decreased salinity; essentially freshwater species that can tolerate varying degrees of increased salinity; and species that can handle the whole range from marine to fresh water.

This last group, the tidal-estuary inhabitants, are the most adaptable and, consequently, the most suitable for most brackish aquarists. Aquarists around the world regularly keep species from such genera as *Scatophagus*, *Selenotoca*, *Toxotes*, *Arius*, *Monodactylus*, and *Terapon*, and the fish fauna of Australia has representatives from all of these. However, these are just the tip of the iceberg—literally dozens of other species suitable for brackish aquaria abound, simply waiting to be discovered by the discerning aquarist. Although some may be found in the few aquarium shops that specialize in native fish, a better option in many cases is simply to collect them from the wild.

The Expert Says...

It cannot be stressed enough: Whenever collecting specimens of any kind anywhere in the world, check local laws and regulations, and if on private lands, obtain the permission of the owner.

Collecting your own specimens opens up a major new spectrum of satisfaction for the hobbyist—from researching suitable species to developing capture and transport techniques. You can enjoy the satisfaction of maintaining and hopefully breeding those species you collect. And as a bonus, you also get to evaluate the habitat you may wish to recreate in your tank—from substrate, rocks, and plants to associated invertebrates and other fish species. Last but not least, you can directly assess the water parameters your chosen species prefer (using ordinary aquarium test kits) and use this information to adjust the conditions in your aquarium as necessary. Needless to say, the closer you mimic the natural conditions of your fishes, the better they'll look, the healthier they'll be, and the greater the chance you'll have of getting them to breed.

There also is one final advantage: As long as you handle them carefully, animals caught in the wild are almost always in good health!

THE FISHES

With such a wide variety of species available to the collector, the brackish enthusiast must critically assess the available facilities as well as the expertise required to properly maintain the target species. (Rapid growth is one of the consequences of good care for many species, but this might in turn outstrip the aquarist's ability to maintain good water quality.) The following groups are a bit arbitrary, since there are just too many possibilities to cover comprehensively.

THE WHOPPERS

Few of us, with the exception of large public aquaria, have the space or finances to keep potentially huge

Some larger Australian fishes like *Lutjanus argentimaculatus* might be available from aquaculturists.

species such as *Carcharinus leucas* (bull sharks), *Pristis microdon* (sawfish), or *Dasyatis* and *Himantura* spp. (stingrays). Indeed, the avid collector in northern Australia may find himself at risk from these fishes rather than the other way around!

The juveniles of many food fishes make interesting aquarium subjects; however, legal size restrictions may be a potential problem in some states. Because some of these food-fish species are aquacultured—*Lates calcarifer* (barramundi) and *Lutjanus argentimaculatus* (mangrove jack), for example—aquaculturists might be a legal source of juvenile specimens.

THE CLASSIC BRACKISH SPECIES

Two species of scat, *Scatophagus argus* (the spotted scat) and *Selenotoca multifasciata* (the striped scat), can be found along the northern and eastern coastlines of Australia, and both are very popular aquarium fish. Also highly popular is the silver mono, *Monodactylus argenteus*, which occurs in huge schools and is a common bait-stealing pest for coastal anglers. Few aquarists realize that these three species grow to around 1 foot (30 cm) long in the wild. The juveniles of these species are hardy and attractive and adapt well to aquarium life, but adults can be a bit more demanding and require well-filtered, strongly brackish water and plenty of swimming space.

Although Australia boasts four species of archerfishes, only two are suitable for brackish-aquarium purposes.

Scats are among Australia's most popular brackish fishes.

Though hard to find, *Arius graeffei* can make a good addition to an Australian brackish tank.

Australian Fishes

The common archerfish, *Toxotes jaculatrix*, often referred to as the banded archerfish in Australia, is predominantly a denizen of brackish and marine environments. The seven-spot archerfish, *Toxotes chatareus*, is found more frequently in brackish and freshwater habitats. Both these species are common in the northern half of the continent, and juveniles are not difficult to obtain. Most of the time these fish feed on smaller fish and aquatic invertebrates, but they famously supplement their diet by spitting water to shoot down terrestrial insects from overhanging vegetation. The ability of these fishes to calculate the range precisely with their eyes underwater and get to their prey as it hits the water is impressive. It is fascinating to see this behavior in nature, and many aquarists encourage their pets to exhibit these skills in captivity.

Another classic brackish-water group well represented in Australian waters is the sea-catfish family Ariidae, commonly called either fork-tailed catfish or salmon-tailed catfish in Australia. This family includes the popular Colombian shark catfish, *Hexanematichthys seemanni*, from South America. About half of the roughly 80 species found worldwide exist in the general Australia and New Guinea region, but only three of the smaller species of the genus *Arius* are kept in aquaria. They are popular for their constant, actively swimming, schooling behavior, their no-nonsense omnivorous diet, their lack of aggression, their tolerance of a wide range of salinities (from freshwater to marine), and their modest price tag.

The juvenile *Arius* fishes form schools, which are collected for the aquarium trade during the warmer months. Most often available is *A. graeffei*, the blue catfish to some, but in some places called the salmon-tailed catfish (as distinct from another local group, the Plotosidae—the eel-tailed catfishes). Occasionally available is the smaller, darker, more slender northern species *A. berneyi*, as well as the stockier *A. leptaspis*.

Although the Australian region is rich in grunters of the family Teraponidae, most of these are freshwater inhabitants. Only one species, the targetfish or crescent perch, *Terapon jarbua*, is internationally traded as a brackish-aquarium species. This boisterous fish has a very wide geographical distribution (from East Africa to Samoa) and can be found in both shallow coastal seas and estuaries. It is generally as tough as they come, but due to its active, predatory nature is not an ideal community fish when kept with smaller and gentler species. However, it can hold its own against much larger fishes if given a little cover. The related bar-tailed grunter, *Amniataba caudavittata*, is another attractive species, but it is only occasionally available and is even more pugnacious. Reliable reports exist of this species taking on and beating much larger specimens of supposedly aggressive cichlids when kept together in aquaria.

GOBIES

Gobies are extremely diverse and widely distributed. New species are being found faster than the limited number of eminent gobiologists can identify and describe them. Currently around 2,000 species are known worldwide, and Australia has a fair share of them in habitats ranging from the artesian springs of the interior to freshwater streams, estuaries, and coastal seas, and out onto the coral reefs. Most are small—less than 15

inches (30 cm) long—and often colorful, and all make interesting aquarium subjects. Strictly speaking, only the fishes of the family Gobiidae are called gobies, but many aquarists call members of the family Eleotridae gobies as well; in Australia, though, it is more common to hear eleotrids called gudgeons instead. This can be confusing for American and European aquarists more familiar with the coldwater gudgeons, *Gobio* spp., bottom-dwelling cyprinids that closely resemble loaches.

Generally, gobies are carnivores that can handle some vegetable matter as well. They usually take most of the live, frozen, and prepared foods available to the aquarist. Most gobies have similar breeding habits: Males tend to have larger fins and more color, and after display-based selection, pairing results in spawning on a hard surface. Male gobies fan and guard eggs until they hatch after a few days, then the fry are on their own. Raising the fry can be a challenge in some species, because these may be tiny and require the smallest grades of the micro-encapsulated, essential-fatty-acid foods that have been developed for the aquaculture industry. However, with a little trial and error, most species should be able to multiply in captivity and add to the satisfaction of the enthusiast.

Chlamydogobius

The Australian aquarist inquiring after native gobies at the local pet shop or aquarium store usually will be offered limited fare. The desert goby, *Chlamydogobius eremius*, is an exception. This species has adapted

Awaous species occasionally are available in aquarium stores.

to artesian springs around Lake Eyre in the hot, dry center of Australia. This is one of the harshest aquatic habitats in a harsh land, but this fish can survive temperature extremes, salinity extremes, and oxygen depletion. Although listed as a freshwater species, desert gobies will thrive and breed in seawater and do well in a brackish tank. Unlike most other gobies, desert gobies also have evolved the ability to digest algae and seem to need some vegetable matter in their diet even if more meaty fare is offered to them in the aquarium.

The other five species of *Chlamydogobius* that have been described are rarely seen outside of books, and only two are found in habitats beyond artesian springs. One of them is *C. japalpa*, found in the Finke River, reputed to be the oldest flowing river in the world. The other species is the tadpole goby, *C. ranunculus*, which may become more popular among brackish-water aquarists thanks to its natural range, which includes low-salinity environments as well as freshwater rivers and streams.

Glossogobius

Northern streams contain a range of generally larger gobies of the genus *Glossogobius*. These fishes have a marine larval stage but as adults move into freshwater habitats (although they remain tolerant of brackish conditions). Some of these are occasionally available from dealers but usually are self-collected by the enthusiast. *Glossogobius aureus*, *G. concavifrons*, and *G. giurus* can be found in aquarium stores from time to time, as can several other locally common but as yet undescribed species. Because they include small fishes and crustaceans in their diet, they must be kept with peaceful tankmates that are larger than they are. Like all gobies, they are great jumpers, so a secure tank cover is a necessity.

Mugilogobius

The genus *Mugilogobius* provides a wide array of attractive, small, peaceful species eminently suitable for brackish-aquarium purposes. These fish are found in a range of coastal habitats along the east coast of Australia. Look for *M. platynotus*, *M. stigmaticus*, *M. littoralis*, *M. wilsoni*, *M. platystomus*, *M. notospilus*, *M. rivulus,* and perhaps one or two others. Their qualifications for being great aquarium fish start with their small size—at most 2.5 inches (6 cm) long—and willingness to spawn in captivity, as well as tolerance of a wide range of salinities from slightly brackish conditions to full-strength seawater. Some will even adapt to fresh water. They like a mangrove root and a rock or two to pose near, but seem just as happy with a few pieces of PVC pipe.

Redigobius

Redigobius is another genus of small gobies eminently suited to life in aquaria. In Australia, the most commonly available is the bug-eyed goby, *R. bikolanus*, which is widely distributed in the western Pacific in mangroves, estuaries, and the lower reaches of freshwater streams. *Redigobius macrostoma* is similar but has a larger mouth and occurs further south along the eastern coast. Farther north, collectors can find two very attractive species—the rhino-horn goby, *R. balteatus*, and the spot-fin or gold-spot goby, *R. chrysosoma*. Aquarists are fond of all four species because of their peaceful nature, interesting behavior, hardiness, and longevity in aquaria. As a bonus, breeding is possible, and even when fully grown they do not exceed 1.5 inches (4 cm) in length.

The rhino-horn goby, *R. balteatus*, is among the more attractive varieties of *Redigobius*.

Schooling Gobies

At least two species of small schooling gobies may be considered. The glass goby, *Gobiopterus semivestitus*, only grows to around 1 inch (2.5 cm) in length and is rather prone to injury during capture. Even when settled into an aquarium, it can easily become lunch for larger species of fish, including other gobies. The second is the delightful little *Pandaka lidwilli*, which rarely exceeds 0.8 inches (2 cm) in length and buzz around the tank in groups, a particularly charming sight given its handsome checkered body and its tendency to keep its yellow-and-black first dorsal fin well spread. Both of these species, unlike most other gobies, are midwater swimmers. In addition to these species, collectors will regularly find gobies that they have extreme difficulty identifying; doing so requires the help of experts. Even then, sometimes a definite decision cannot be reached because published taxonomy often lags well behind surveys and collections.

Other Gobies

Many other species of small, attractive coastal gobies have been successfully kept in aquaria by Australian hobbyists. *Pseudogobius olorum* and a few other as yet unidentified species in that genus head the list. Southern hobbyists also keep two species of *Afurcagobius*—*A. suppositus* and *A. tamarensis*—as well as two species of bridled gobies—*Arenigobius bifrenatus* and *A. frenatus*—and the crested mud goby, *Cryptocentrus cristatus*. Farther north, species favored include the shadow goby, *Yongeichthys nebulosus*, and the puntang goby, *Exyrias puntang*. Mudskippers also are well represented in Australia; the two most commonly

The Expert Says...

Empire gobies are known for having extremely tiny eggs.

Australian Fishes

Mudskippers are big in Australia and beyond.

available species are *Periopthalmus argentilineatus* and *P. novaeguineaensis*. Mudskippers are covered in depth in Chapter 10.

GUDGEONS

Numerous gudgeons, or sleeper gobies, can be found in Australia, especially in fresh water. Generally, they are larger and a little more aggressive than the gobies, which makes them a bit easier to adapt to community tanks but also troublesome if they decide to treat the other fish as trespassers on their territory. The two flathead gudgeon species of the genus *Philypnodon* are common and relatively small, and one of the few Australian fishes regularly seen in tropical fish stores around the world is the empire gudgeon, *Hypseleotris compressa*. When in full breeding colors, the male is spectacularly red, with white, black, and blue in the fins. Unfortunately, this display usually takes place in fresh water, and only after this will the resultant tiny fry drift down to the brackish-water estuaries. Also, while empire gudgeons spawn readily in aquaria, the fry need the finest of starter foods to get them off to a good start.

The crazyfish, *Butis butis*, is named after its unusual ability to sit upside down or vertically at will, usually near cover. Both *Butis* and the closely related small-eyed sleeper, *Prionobutis microps*, are ambush predators with surprisingly big gapes and an appetite to match. Another attractive, large tropical representative of this group is the spangled gudgeon, *Ophiocara porocephala*, which features attractive dark and light blotches when juvenile and develops blue spangles on the sides and yellowish edges to the fins in adult males. A large male, which can reach 1 foot (30 cm) in length, is an impressive sight.

The king of freshwater and brackish sleepers is undoubtedly the snakehead gudgeon, *Giurus margaritacea*, formerly known as *Ophieleotris aporos*. Widely distributed in the Indo-West Pacific region as well as Australia, this large and colorful species moves well into freshwater reaches after the pelagic marine larval stage matures. Several local color forms have been noted, perhaps akin to the stream-specific geographical populations of some species of rainbowfishes, *Melanotaenia* spp. At a maximum size of 16 inches (40 cm) and displaying colors to rival even koi, this is a serious aquarium fish. Be warned: the snakehead gudgeon needs a heavy cover on the tank. There are no records of its breeding in captivity so far.

Another very attractive species is *Bostrichthys zonatus*, alternately known as the barred or sunset gudgeon.

Melanotaenia species don't make the best brackish-tank occupants.

This species moves up into freshwater drains and rivulets in the northern wet season and only grows to around 6 inches (15 cm). Another big, silvery-gray gudgeon with similar habits is the sinuous gudgeon, *Odonteleotris macrodon*, which quickly becomes tame enough that it will eat from the aquarist's fingers. It grows to around 1 foot (30 cm) long. The brown gudgeon, *Eleotris fusca*, and the ebony gudgeon, *E. melanosoma*, are also occasionally available from the northeast coastal areas.

SCHOOLING FISH

While many brackish fishes are found in large schools in nature, because of their competitive nature in the aquarium situation, they often must be kept as solitary specimens. To reduce the persecution of individuals, if the aquarist wishes to keep more than one, it is necessary to maintain a group of five or more. Naturally, this requires more tank space.

Glassfish

A large aquarium featuring a school of monos is a wonderful sight as they wheel and turn with the light reflecting off their mirrored sides—but many aquarists simply do not have the space for such an aquarium. Fortunately, a similar effect can be obtained on a smaller scale using schools of the various available species of glassfish, or glass perches, of the genus *Ambassis*. Although many of the Australian species are freshwater inhabitants, look for *A. marianus*, *A. interruptus*, *A. vachelli*, and perhaps *A. miops* as good residents of slightly brackish water. The giant glassfish, *Parambassis gulliveri*, although not generally considered a brackish denizen, is often found in hard, alkaline waters and will tolerate significant salinity in the aquarium. All these glassfish must be kept in reasonably large groups, preferably at least five, and away from aggressive tankmates.

Glassfish can be somewhat reticent at feeding time. They prefer live foods, so it is best to house them with slower-moving fishes that will not compete for food too strongly.

Rainbowfish

Traditionally the group of Australian fishes that most people around the world think of as good aquarium fish, the rainbowfishes boast bright colors, hardiness, and a willingness to spawn in captivity. Rainbowfish

Australian Fishes

are often suggested as being good fish for brackish-water aquaria, but this is not strictly true. Although a few dozen species in several genera from both Australia and New Guinea are commercially available worldwide, not one species seems to have evolved into a permanent inhabitant of brackish situations. Unlike their close relatives the Atherinidae (including fish like the blue-eyes and the hardyheads), which both have brackish and even marine representation, the rainbowfish family, Melanotaeniidae, appears to be completely confined to freshwater habitats.

Most species will tolerate brackish water with a salinity one-tenth that of normal seawater (a specific gravity of 1.002), and the hardier species will take up to one-fifth seawater (a specific gravity of 1.005), but none will thrive in such conditions. However, the lacustrine New Guinea species have evolved to handle very hard water and have been used successfully as dither fish in aquaria for African Rift Valley Lake cichlids. Of all

Bleher's rainbowfish is one of the New Guinea species that tolerate slightly brackish water.

the rainbowfish, the New Guinea species are the ones most likely to do well in slightly brackish water.

One such rainbowfish is Bleher's rainbowfish, *Chilatherina bleheri*, which features whitish fins on a body shaded pink at the head and red at the tail. Another of these New Guinea species that has become especially popular among aquarists is Boeseman's rainbowfish, *Melanotaenia boesemani*. These fish have a blue-gray front half and a yellow or orange back half. In the males, these colors intensify at spawning times to indigo and bright orange. It is no wonder that aquarists around the world have made this species a firm favorite in the hobby.

Yet another rainbowfish from New Guinea that is regularly traded in Europe and North America is the red rainbowfish, *Glossolepis incisus*. Although the females are simply plain, silver fish, the males develop a tremendously vivid, uniform red color when mature, as well as an impressively arched back, making them very dramatic animals that will bring color and movement to your aquarium.

Blue-eyes

Blue-eyes are atherines, members of a group that includes more well-known species like the Madagascar rainbowfish, *Bedotia geayi*, and the Celebes rainbowfish, *Telmatherina ladigesi*, both freshwater rather than brackish-water fishes. Blue-eyes lay a few relatively large eggs daily in plants or artificial spawning mops. These hatch in seven to ten days, and fry are easily raised on fine dry and live foods in a similar fashion to killifish.

Australia has three species of blue-eye, *Pseudomugil*, that are suitable for the brackish aquarium. The Pacific blue-eye, *P. signifier*, is widespread down the eastern coast, and although some populations have adapted to fresh water entirely, many thrive in marine and brackish situations. These are small, peaceful, and attractive schooling fish that are easily bred in captivity and thrive under standard aquarium management. Populations from differing locations vary in color, fin length, and size, and responsible aquarists will not interbreed these different strains.

Even more colorful is the blue-back blue-eye, *P. cyanodorsalis*, a species with a more northern distribution. This is a smaller fish than the Pacific blue-eye and more consistently found in brackish water. A school of these spawning in the morning sun is spectacular to see. The males become transformed—the lower half of the body assumes a golden glow, the neon blue stripes shine brightly, and the tiny fish spread their bright yellow, black-edged fins and perform rapid barrel rolls around each other to attract the females. The other brackish species in this group is the rarely available and aptly named *P. inconspicuus*.

Miscellaneous Schooling Fish

Closely related to the blue-eyes are the hardyheads, of which the small-mouthed hardyhead, *Atherinosoma microstoma*, is a particularly attractive and easy-to-keep schooling fish for the medium-size aquarium. It will do well in fresh, brackish, and marine conditions, but being relatively large (up to 4 inches, or 10 cm, long when

155

fully grown), it needs plenty of space. Also, it is a very active fish and appreciates a strong water current to swim into.

Another atherine that looks great in a school is the blackmast, *Craterocephalus stramineus*. Although naturally an inhabitant of hard, alkaline streams in the north of Australia, it will adapt well to slightly brackish waters up to a specific gravity of 1.005. The males have a prominent black stripe (the "mast") in their first dorsal fins.

Schools of the common jollytail, *Galaxias maculatus*, can be maintained without too much difficulty, although like other galaxiids these fish require well-filtered, relatively cool water. This fish has a marine larval stage and is one of the most widely distributed freshwater fishes in the world, being found across the southern Pacific from Australia to South America and all the islands in between. It also is found along the Atlantic coast of South America, including the Falkland Islands. It is commonly found in fresh waters not far from the sea, and it will tolerate fresh, brackish, and marine conditions—it can even tolerate hypersaline conditions for extended periods.

Sweeping a fine scoop net in an estuarine area often will produce an interesting mixture of various juveniles that will tend to school well in the aquarium. However as they mature and their identity becomes obvious, these specimens must be critically evaluated. Quite a few will turn out to be wolves in sheep's clothing and begin to devour their former schoolmates!

THE ODDITIES

For the real brackish enthusiast, Australia is home to a host of oddities that can be searched out with some difficulty and are worth a mention here: *Arramphus sclerolepis* and *Zenarchopterus novaeguineae* (garfish); *Strongylura kreffii* (a needlefish known as the long tom); *Aseraggodes klunzingeri* (a small sole); *Tetractenos hamiltoni* and *Chelonodon patoca* (puffers); *Gymnothorax polyuranodon* (a brackish-water moray eel); *Hippichthys heptagonu* and *H. penicillus* (brackish pipefish); *Neopomacentrus taeniurus* (a brackish damselfish); *Apogon hyalosoma* (the buccal-brooding mangrove cardinalfish); *Notesthes robusta* (the bullrout, a relative of the stonefish that also has venomous, if less dangerous, spines); and last but not least, *Kurtus gulliveri* (the nurseryfish), famous for a particularly unusual reproductive strategy. Males of this species carry around a loop of eggs attached to a structure known as the nuchal hook, which extends forward from the "forehead" of the fish.

Many of these interesting species venture into the lower reaches of freshwater streams and can also be considered freshwater fishes. For aquarists outside Australia, this might seem like something of an unattainable wish list, but *Chelonodon patoca*, *Gymnothorax polyuranodon*, *Neopomacentrus taeniurus*, and *Notesthes robusta* are fairly regularly traded—and they are described in detail elsewhere in this book.

AUSTRALIA-THEMED AQUARIA

Because of the diversity of species to draw from, the brackish tank with an Australian theme can take many forms. Traditionally, the brackish enthusiast decides on a preferred salinity range, then chooses species from the available list that will do well in those conditions. By choosing truly estuarine species that are adaptable to

a wide range of salinities, rather than freshwater species that can handle some salinity or marine species that will tolerate some reduction in salinity, the hobbyist can feel comfortable that the conditions provided are not stressful to the residents of the aquarium. As with all aquarium maintenance, water quality is paramount, of course, and the appropriate temperature range must be maintained as well.

The natural behavior of each species also should be accommodated. Obviously tank size is important, since overcrowding always brings conflict. And furnishing your aquarium is not simply a matter of decoration; some planning is required to provide for the needs of each species. Plants, driftwood, rock, and even depth and texture of substrate must be considered. If the salinity is low, then live plants can be used—otherwise, plastic plants make a good alternative, especially once algae has grown over them.

When performing water changes, try alternating and varying the salinity of the new water and observe the behavior of your fish. In nature, the fish are subject to regular tidal movements and irregular rainfall that changes the local conditions—and if conditions don't suit them, the fish will simply swim upstream or downstream until they find water conditions closer to what they prefer. When you put that glass box around them, the fish can no longer do this, so you must work hard to create optimal conditions.

A LARGE AUSTRALIA-THEMED AQUARIUM

Start with the largest aquarium you can afford that will fit the available space; an aquarium 72×24×24 inches (180×60×60 cm) large is ideal. Because so many of these fish like to jump, install covers of glass or transparent plastic panels that rest on top of the tank below the lights. If you want to see the archer spit for his dinner as described in Chapter 4, then plan on keeping the water level around 4 inches (10 cm) below the covers. Provide plenty of hiding places and visual appeal with several well-soaked mangrove roots, and ensure that some protrude above the water line. Allow plenty of swimming space in the front and center. Then arrange rocks and substrate to provide varying levels as well as horizontal cover. Once the tank has cycled, fish can be added on a regular basis, as long as the nitrogen cycle stays under control.

With the specific gravity maintained around 1.010, consider a combination of an archerfish, several scats, a few monos, one crescent perch (targetfish), a fork-tailed catfish, a male snakehead gudgeon, and a male spangled gudgeon. Start with smallish specimens, and try to get scats and monos of roughly equal size to reduce bullying. If you have arranged the rocks and roots properly, you will find that the gudgeons will tend to establish a territory of their own at each end, and the perch will select a favorite cave to dash out from. Archerfish invariably have a preferred thicket of roots to lurk near, while the others will swim around, continuously looking for food.

Most of these fish tend to grow quite quickly and establish a pecking order, especially at feeding times. The aquarist must spend some time ensuring that each specimen gets enough to eat. The archer can practice his shooting and supplement his diet with insects introduced under the cover.

Once these fish are all settled in, adding new fish will usually be disastrous, with the

newcomers either being mercilessly bullied by the territorial fishes or, if small, eaten by the more piscivorous fishes, such as the archer.

A SMALL AUSTRALIA-THEMED AQUARIUM

My favorite low-salinity brackish-water aquarium was created using a tank 48×18×18 inches (120×45×45 cm) large, decorated with mangrove roots, rocks, and salt-tolerant plants including *Vallisneria*, Java fern, *Hydrilla*, and *Bacopa monnieri*, plus some algae-covered rocks from a nearby tidal river. Strong fluorescent lighting for twelve hours daily helped maintain good plant growth.

The top 4 inches (10 cm) of the aquarium were patrolled by a school of blue-backed blue-eyes, and beneath them was a school of Pacific blue-eyes. The rest of the tank was populated with a collection of small gobies that varied with my excursions and skills. Because of the fishes' interesting behavior, watching this tank was a constant source of interest. The gobies spawned regularly, and the occasional blue-eye survivor from the fry they produced almost continuously helped maintain the interest. Although none of the inhabitants was over 2 inches (5 cm) in length, this was always a very attractive display.

Cheldonodon patoca is a nice addition to a brackish tank, but some specimens are persistent fin nippers, so choose tankmates with care.

Common and popular though they are, monos are just one of many attractions among Austrailian brackish fish.

Brackish-Water Cichlids

By Neale Monks

The family Cichlidae is one of the more well-known groups of secondary freshwater fishes. Because their ancestors evolved in the sea, members of this family are much more tolerant of salty water than are primary freshwater fish such as characins and cyprinids. Having said this, some cichlids do not like brackish water at all, most notably the popular discus, *Symphysodon* species, and angelfish from the soft, acidic waters of South America, *Pterophyllum* species. It isn't a good idea to keep the hard-water species from the African Rift Valley lakes in brackish water either. Like the South American species, the cichlids from lakes Malawi and Tanganyika have become highly specialized to a particular kind of water chemistry and lack the adaptability to deal with the quite different mineral composition of brackish water.

But on the whole, most of the hardier cichlids that do well in a variety of freshwater habitats will do well in a brackish-water aquarium where the specific gravity is kept below 1.005. Among the species worth trying out are the riverine *Haplochromis* from Africa, the Central American hard-water cichlids, and the South American "*Aequidens*".

Brackish-Water Cichlids

Any of the South American "*Aequidens*," like *A. pulcher*, is worth a try in a brackish tank.

Cichlids have always been popular with aquarists, and most need little excuse to introduce a few specimens into their community tanks. Fortunately for brackish-water-aquarium keepers, numerous species naturally inhabit brackish, even marine, waters in the wild. Some of these are rarely imported, such as *Paretroplus damii* from Madagascar and the Near East genus *Iranocichla*, but many others are regularly seen in tropical fish stores. Of all the brackish-water cichlids, the orange chromide, *Etroplus maculatus*, has become far and away the most popular, not least because of its good nature and the ease with which it spawns in captivity. (Consequently, this species has the next chapter of this book all to itself.)

Lots of other brackish-water cichlids are seen from time to time as well, and these cichlids are the focus of this chapter. We begin with one that is more well-known as a freshwater fish than a brackish-water one, the West African dwarf cichlid, commonly known as the krib.

KRIBENSIS—*PELVICACHROMIS PULCHER*

Pelvicachromis pulcher is one of the nicest of all the dwarf cichlids, combining exquisite colors with a generally tolerant personality and an ability to adapt to a wide variety of water conditions. In the wild it inhabits overgrown streams, and feels most comfortable living close to the bottom, under vegetation or close to a cave in which it can hide when threatened. Like most dwarf cichlids, individuals stake out small territories and drive off any other fishes that come too close. Generally speaking, they ignore fishes that swim in the upper levels of the aquarium, so livebearers will be ignored. Anything that stays close to the bottom, however, is more of a problem. The territory that a pair of kribs will hold is small, though, and in a 36-inch (90-cm) aquarium, it is possible to combine them with other bottom-dwellers, such as medium-size sleepers and gobies, as long as each fish has its own cave to call home. In a smaller aquarium, it is safest to avoid keeping any other bottom-dwelling fish with kribs.

Kribs readily form pairs even in community tanks and generally prove to be excellent parents. They lay

Pelvicachromis pulcher can vary widely in coloration, but all types are beautiful fish.

approximately 100 eggs inside a cave, and both parents protect them. The fry are no less adaptable than their parents, and in a mature aquarium will find plenty to eat just pecking around on the gravel and at any algae they find. Indeed, many aquarists never even know that their kribs have spawned until they see the pair shepherding their brood around the aquarium in search of food. The only problem with spawning kribs is a tendency for a preponderance of one sex over the other in any given brood. The critical factor is pH: In alkaline conditions, more males are hatched, while in acidic conditions, there are more females. A neutral pH

Kribensis

Name	*Pelvicachromis pulcher*
Other names	*Pelmatochromis kribensis*, krib, kribensis, rainbow krib, common krib
Origin	West Africa
Size	Males up to 10 cm, females quite a bit smaller
Water conditions	Slightly acidic fresh water to slightly brackish water (specific gravity <1.005)
Diet	Invertebrates; prepared fish foods
Temperament	Territorial, but otherwise good community fish
Availability	Commonly traded, inexpensive
Ease of maintenance	Easy
Specific problems	None

Brackish-Water Cichlids

Unlike other *Pelvicachromis* species, *P. taeniatus* should be kept only in fresh water.

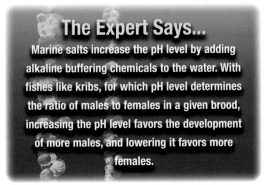

The Expert Says...

Marine salts increase the pH level by adding alkaline buffering chemicals to the water. With fishes like kribs, for which pH level determines the ratio of males to females in a given brood, increasing the pH level favors the development of more males, and lowering it favors more females.

is ideal, ensuring an approximately equal number of each sex. Bear in mind that while aquarium stores are usually happy to take any excess stock you have, they do prefer equal numbers of males and females so they can sell them as pairs.

Occasionally other species of *Pelvicachromis* are offered for sale. *P. ocellatus* is a species that is naturally found in slightly brackish as well as fresh waters, so it can be included in aquaria similar to those suited for kribs. In most regards, it is a very similar animal, although a bit smaller and less tolerant of the hurly-burly of community-aquarium life. If you want to spawn this species, a quiet tank is necessary. Another species, *P. taeniatus*, is also seen from time to time, but it should only be kept in freshwater aquaria.

JEWEL CICHLID—*HEMICHROMIS BIMACULATUS*

Jewel cichlids, *Hemichromis bimaculatus*, are among the best-looking of all the cichlids. Good specimens are basically brick red in color, but when in spawning condition they turn a brilliant red quite unlike anything else kept by freshwater aquarists. At all times they are further enhanced with a pattern of electric-blue spots on the gill covers, flanks, and fins, but these spots only really become bright when the fish are in spawning condition. Big dark spots also are present on each flank, with one other on the gill cover and one about midway along the body. The spots on the gill covers are edged with gold, making them look a lot like eyes. Indeed, when threatening one another, these fish raise the gill covers to display these false eyes in the same way as the well-known firemouth cichlid, *Thorichthys meeki*.

However, *Hemichromis bimaculatus* has never become really popular because of its extremely waspish behavior. Some specimens are merely a bit rough and can be combined with comparably sized fish in a large community tank. Mated pairs, however, are particularly single-minded and hold their territories with a remarkable ferocity for such beautiful animals. The best advice with these fishes is to keep them in a species tank. They can, however, be combined in a large aquarium with fishes that are able to handle themselves well in any aggressive encounters. The various tilapias are obvious examples, and many of them inhabit the same sorts of conditions as *H. bimaculatus*, but alternatives include the bigger sleeper gobies, such as *Dormitator maculatus,* and the schooling predator *Terapon jarbua*.

In all other regards, these fish are easy to keep. They are predatory but do not need live fish (although they will eat small fish given the chance). Invertebrates such as frozen bloodworms and krill make an ideal staple when combined with a good-quality flake or pellet food. Occasional feedings of earthworms and small insects will bring out their more predatory instincts. Color-enhancing foods can be used as well, but these aren't really necessary if you offer a good variety of unprocessed invertebrates. Jewel cichlids are easy to breed and, like the kribs, generally make outstanding parents.

A similar *Hemichromis* species regularly offered for sale is the red jewel cichlid, *H. lifalili*. This isn't a

Jewel Cichlid

Name	*Hemichromis bimaculatus*
Other names	**Jewel cichlid**
Origin	**West Africa**
Size	**From 5 to 8 inches (12 to 20 cm); captive-bred specimens tend to be smaller than wild ones**
Water conditions	**Soft, acidic water to slightly brackish (specific gravity <1.005)**
Diet	**Predatory; prefers invertebrates but will also eat flake and pellet foods**
Temperament	**Varies, but generally territorial and aggressive, especially when spawning**
Availability	**Widely traded and fairly inexpensive**
Ease of maintenance	**Fairly easy**
Specific problems	**Aggressively territorial**

Hemichromis bimaculatus is not all that popular because it has a very waspish personality.

brackish-water species and shouldn't be kept in an aquarium containing salty water. Neither should the smaller *Hemichromis* species, such as *H. cristatus*.

TILAPIAS—*OREOCHROMIS, SAROTHERODON,* AND *TILAPIA* SPP.

The tilapias have received bad press as aquarium fish, and it is certainly true that almost all of them are large animals that demand a big tank with powerful filtration. Because most are inveterate excavators, undergravel filters are not ideal, and instead a high-capacity, external canister filter should used. Plants will be eaten and so should be left out, with the exception of the tough and unpalatable Java fern. Otherwise, opt for plastic plants, bogwood, and large stones for your decorations, but be sure to leave plenty of swimming space, because these active fishes like to hang out in open spaces where they can display to one another.

These fish are generalists when it comes to diet. They eat both plant and animal matter, but it is wise to keep the vegetable part of their diet in the majority. Vegetarian flake and pellet foods are an ideal staple, with frozen bloodworms, shrimps, and other meaty foods given regularly to add variety. Try not to overfeed these fish—they pollute the water heavily, and while they are somewhat tolerant of ammonium and nitrites, any other fishes kept with them most likely will not be.

The other major problem with tilapias as aquarium fish is that they tend to become sexually mature long

Tilapias

Names	*Oreochromis aureus, Oreochromis mossambicus, Oreochromis niloticus, Sarotherodon galilaeus, Sarotherodon melanotheron, Tilapia rendalli,* and *Tilapia zillii,* among others. The taxonomy of these fishes is under major revision, and *Tilapia* may wind up monotypic.
Other names	Tilapia; numerous varieties and local names
Origin	Africa; widely introduced elsewhere
Size	Most species 8 to 16 inches (20 to 40 cm); rarely smaller, often larger
Water conditions	Variable, but many species will tolerate half- to full-strength seawater
Diet	Omnivorous; prepared fish foods as staple, with some vegetable matter regularly supplied as well
Temperament	Some variation, but most are belligerent, boisterous fishes only for communities with similarly robust fish
Availability	Not widely traded, but inexpensive
Ease of maintenance	Fairly easy
Specific problems	Large size; require powerful filtration; difficult to dispose of unwanted juveniles

Brackish-Water Cichlids

Tilapias, like *Oreochromis aureus* are usually hardy and easily tamed, but many are aggressive and need a large tank with sturdy tankmates.

before they have reached full size. Most breed readily in captivity, and the mouthbrooders in particular are especially suited to raising their offspring in the crowded conditions of the home aquarium. Just remember that tilapias are very much fish for the advanced aquarist and disposing of unwanted juveniles can be difficult. Breeding habits vary among species, but as a rule, the species in the genus *Tilapia* are substrate spawners, and the pair holds a territory and shares the responsibility of looking after the eggs and fry. Typically, they are only slightly sexually dimorphic, the male being larger and perhaps colored differently. *Oreochromis* and *Sarotherodon* are mouthbrooders, and depending on the species, either one parent will assume all responsibility for looking after the eggs and fry or they will share these duties between them. *Sarotherodon galilaeus* is one of the biparental mouthbrooders, and strong bonds exist between the parents. *Sarotherodon melanotheron*, on the other hand, is a paternal mouthbrooder, with the male looking after the offspring and the female showing no interest in them at all. And species of *Oreochromis* tend to be maternal mouthbrooders, with males playing no part in brood care. Instead, the males display at "leks," or arenas, which they create by digging in the sand or gravel. In the wild, these leks are commonly more than 20 inches (50 cm) in diameter. Thus, within the confines of the aquarium, expect some serious disruption of the substrate and decor should the male

> ## The Expert Says...
> Dimorphism is profound between the two sexes of *Oreochromis*—the male is far larger and more intensely colored than the female.

170

decide it is time to display!

One other issue with male *Oreochromis* is that in their anxiety to mate, they might harass a female brooding her eggs. And if the female is stressed, she may swallow them. Even after the fry are mobile and she is able to feed, it is essential that she be kept apart from the male for a few weeks so she can feed freely and regain lost weight and condition. The best thing to do is to separate the fish after the eggs are fertilized, preferably by removing the male so as not to stress the female.

Having described the problems with the tilapias, we must recognize that these hardy and often very handsome fish are able to tolerate a wide variety of salinities, making them very useful fishes for the advanced aquarist who desires something unusual. Of the species likely to be encountered by aquarists, three will tolerate full-strength seawater: *Oreochromis mossambicus*, *Sarotherodon melanotheron*, and *Tilapia zillii*. The remainder will do well in anything up to half-strength seawater (specific gravity less than 1.010): namely, *Oreochromis aureus*, *Oreochromis niloticus*, *Sarotherodon galilaeus*, and *Tilapia rendalli*.

Note that at least two other tilapias are occasionally offered for sale, *Tilapia buttikoferi* and *T. mariae*, but neither of these species naturally occurs in brackish water, although they may adapt to a slightly brackish-water system with a specific gravity less than 1.005. Hybrids between tilapias are common, but of little interest to the fishkeeper looking for breeding stock. Without knowing the parentage, it is difficult to predict these hybrids' tolerance of brackish water. *Oreochromis* hybrids are particularly common, a by-product of the aquaculture industry.

While they can be a bit boisterous, the tilapias are inept predators and ignore any fish much larger than

In their impatience to mate, male *Oreochromis* species often harass females brooding their eggs, who might in turn swallow them.

Brackish-Water Cichlids

Some types of tilapia, including
T. buttikoferi, can be adapted only to
slightly brackish tanks.

172

a swordtail, making them better community fish than *Lutjanus argentimaculatus* or a Siamese tigerfish. They combine well with large schooling fish such as Colombian sharks, scats, and monos, and since they have the usual cichlid traits of boldness and intelligence, and become tame very quickly, they can be counted on as the personality fish for a community aquarium.

As far as looks go, *Sarotherodon melanotheron* and *Tilapia rendalli* are probably the species most desired by aquarists. *Sarotherodon melanotheron* is basically silvery gold in color with a bit of pink around the fins, but what attracts many aquarists to this species (besides its interesting breeding behavior) is the bold, black chin stripe beneath the mouth. Most of the time, *Tilapia rendalli* is a pretty ordinary-looking, silvery-green fish, but in breeding condition it develops an intense red coloration across the ventral surface and lower half of the flanks, giving it a most dramatic appearance.

CENTRAL AMERICAN "CICHLASOMA"

Like the tilapias, the fishes of Central America once lumped into the genus *Cichlasoma* are a bit of a mixed bag as far as their usefulness in brackish water goes. Naturally enough, those species adapted to soft-water habitats are intolerant of brackish water, and these fishes, like *Cichlasoma bimaculatum* (the black acara) and *Cichlasoma portalegrense* (port acara), should be left out of the brackish-water aquarium. But this leaves plenty of species that do well in brackish, even marine, conditions. This section describes some of those species that occur naturally in brackish waters and appear frequently enough in the hobby to be worth trying out in a low- to medium-salinity brackish-water system. Species not listed here, but adapted to hard, alkaline waters, can certainly be tried in a low-salinity aquarium, but the specific gravity should be kept at 1.005 or less.

Cichlasoma

Names	*"Cichlasoma" urophthalmus, Herichthys carpintis, Nandopsis haitiensis, Nandopsis tetracanthus,* and *Vieja maculicauda,* among others
Other names	Various
Origin	Central America; Caribbean islands including Cuba and Hispaniola
Size	Most species 6 to 12 inches (15 to 30 cm)
Water conditions	Most Central American cichlids are freshwater fish, but some will thrive in brackish, even marine, conditions
Diet	Prepared flakes and pellets generally accepted; augment diet with frozen bloodworms and other invertebrates
Temperament	Some variation, but most are belligerent, boisterous fishes only for communities with similarly robust fish
Availability	Fairly widely available and moderately priced
Ease of maintenance	Easy
Specific problems	Aggressive, territorial fish that need a large aquarium; some species are piscivorous

Brackish-Water Cichlids

'Cichlasoma' bimaculatum

One problem with many of these fish is their tendency to dig. In the wild, this behavior is part of the advanced brood care these cichlids offer their young—the open depressions they create are easier to defend, since they allow better visibility of potential threats. But in captivity, this behavior can be a nuisance. The best solution is simply to take this into consideration when creating the aquarium by removing anything fragile (like an aquarium heater) to a place where the fish cannot get to it (such as inside the filter). Certainly do not expect an undergravel filter to be left undisturbed. Decorate the aquarium with things you want the fish to play with, such as fine sand or gravel, and things physically too large for it to move, like bogwood and artificial rockwork. Avoid creating any sort of structure that could collapse if the fish moves the sand around; these could trap the fish, or worse, smash the aquarium glass.

The other major problem with these fish is the need for space. A 210-gallon (800-liter) aquarium is an ideal size if you want a community of these fishes, and it will provide enough space for half a dozen or so mature specimens, along with some companions such as shark catfish and garpikes. Be warned, though, that a mated pair could easily commandeer most of that aquarium should they decide to spawn, with unfortunate consequences for any fish too slow or too stupid to get out of the way. If the aquarist intends to breed these fishes, it is far better to keep a mated pair in its own aquarium, which will need to be 50 gallons (200 liters) in size at the very least, depending on the species.

"Cichlasoma" urophthalmus is a handsome but rather large cichlid, up to 15 inches (40 cm) long, and is particularly common in mangrove habitats along the Atlantic coastline of Central America. A mated pair makes an ideal centerpiece to a large community tank when kept with other robust fishes such as garpike or shark catfish. It is truly euryhaline, and although it will live and breed under marine conditions, it is equally happy in moderately hard fresh water. This makes it an even more adaptable fish than many of the other classically euryhaline aquarium fishes, such as mollies and scats, which need at least a little salt in the water to do well.

Like most of the more robust Central American cichlids, this fish is somewhat piscivorous in habit and will readily eat small fish given the opportunity. In captivity, it thrives on a mixed diet of flakes, pellets, and frozen invertebrates such as bloodworms. Although territorial and sometimes aggressive, it mixes well with other Central American cichlids of a similar temperament, as well as with gars and Colombian shark catfish.

Herichthys carpintis is not quite such a big cichlid, rarely exceeding 6 inches (15 cm) in captivity. While decidedly waspish in temperament, it can be kept with other robust fishes with success, provided that each fish has plenty of room. This is an attractive fish, with a deep, laterally compressed body that is basically silvery blue in color but patterned with bright blue blotches and spots.

Also, *H. carpintis* is less piscivorous than the other cichlids described here, but still should not be trusted with very small fish. It prefers benthic invertebrates, such as insect larvae and small worms, and it will sift the sand in much the same way as firemouth cichlids. Even when not feeding, this species is a notorious burrower, moving around huge quantities of sand or gravel to clear itself a space to call home. While this species

'Cichlasoma' uropthalmus is attractive, but reaching 15 inches in length, it definitely requires a large tank.

175

Brackish-Water Cichlids

Herichthys carpintis is an attractive choice for some tanks, but it can be a bit temperamental.

occasionally has been seen in marine conditions, it isn't commonly seen in the sea and is a much better bet for low- to medium-salinity systems (specific gravity <1.010).

More typically associated with marine conditions are *Nandopsis haitiensis* and *N. tetracanthus*. Neither species is particularly common in the aquarium trade, which is a shame, because they are quite desirable fish. The Cuban cichlid, *N. tetracanthus*, is, as the name suggests, endemic to Cuba, although it is closely related to the more well-known *N. managuensis* from the Central American mainland. *Nandopsis tetracanthus* also rather similar in shape and coloration, but is considerably smaller (both *N. haitiensis* and *N. tetracanthus* are about 8 inches, or 20 cm, in length when fully grown). The basic color of the body is silvery gold, with dark, chocolate-brown to black markings on the flanks, making it altogether a most handsome fish.

Not quite as aggressive as some of the other fishes described here, *N. tetracanthus* can kept with other robust fish, in particular top-dwelling fishes that will keep out of its way, such as monos and scats. The Haitian cichlid, *N. haitiensis*, is similar, and both species live up to the reputation of *Nandopsis* for being accomplished piscivores. In the wild, they readily take small livebearers and killifish, but in captivity, there

The vegetarian *Vieja maculicauda* can reach up to 10 inches in length.

is no need to feed them live fish. Instead, offer them a mixed diet of prepared foods along with frozen invertebrates such as bloodworms. Live earthworms and river shrimps will be eaten with gusto. Small pieces of squid and even whole lancefish can also be used, but with chunky foods like these, take care to avoid overfeeding and putting a strain on the filter.

Vieja maculicauda is a much more well-known cichlid and is seen reasonably frequently in aquarium stores. Commonly known as the black-belt cichlid, this distinctly omnivorous cichlid requires a sizeable component of its diet to be made up of plant foods such as cucumber, algae, blanched lettuce, and other soft greens. Vegetarian flake and standard cichlid pellets make an excellent staple diet, with frozen invertebrates offered for variety. When fully grown, males can reach lengths of up to 10 inches (25 cm), with the females being a bit smaller.

Like *Herichthys carpintis*, this isn't a fish for the high-salinity system, but at low and moderate salinities (specific gravity <1.010), this fish makes a reasonably good community fish. Outside of breeding time, it isn't at all aggressive and mixes well with other robust fish. As with the other Central American cichlids, it is more

Brackish-Water Cichlids

aggressive toward conspecifics and closely related cichlids and less aggressive toward dissimilar fish that it does not see as rivals, such as gar. Of course, when defending eggs or fry, these fish are less tolerant and will treat *any* fish in their territory as a potential threat.

The Asian chromides are believed to be among the most primitive cichlids alive in the world, and they closely resemble the marine ancestors of the family Cichlidae.

GREEN CHROMIDE— *ETROPLUS SURATENSIS*

The green chromide, *Etroplus suratensis*, is closely related to the more well-known orange chromide, *E. maculatus*, but is much larger and more herbivorous. It is a hardy fish and relatively easy to spawn, and it likes the same sort of habitat as the orange chromide—the two species are often found together in the wild. One interesting aspect of this is the behavior of the smaller orange chromides toward the much larger green chromides: The former act as a cleaner fish, picking off dead skin and ectoparasites from the latter. They do this in captivity as well, and the two species can easily be kept together. While both species are well known as the definitive brackish-water cichlid, neither actually likes high salinities, and neither will tolerate seawater. They will survive in half-strength seawater, but they much prefer only slightly brackish water with a specific gravity around 1.005. On the other hand, the green chromide does differ from the orange chromide in that if it is kept in completely fresh water, it becomes sickly, whereas the orange chromide will live and breed in hard, alkaline fresh water.

For many aquarists keen on cichlids, species of the genus *Etroplus* are most interesting because they are among the most primitive cichlids alive today. Their brackish-water habitats are strongly reminiscent of the environments the marine ancestors of the cichlids must have passed through, and the anatomy of the orange and green chromides is in some ways a blend of both cichlid characters and those of their ancestors.

Green Chromide

Name	*Etroplus suratensis*
Other names	Green chromide, silver chromide
Origin	Southern India and Sri Lanka
Size	Up to 10 inches (25 cm)
Water conditions	Slightly brackish water (specific gravity 1.003 to 1.005)
Diet	Primarily herbivorous; vegetable-based, prepared fish foods should be used as a staple
Temperament	Peaceful, schooling fish; only territorial and aggressive toward conspecifics or when spawning
Availability	Rarely traded
Ease of maintenance	Fairly easy
Specific problems	Large size; poor health when kept in fresh water; will eat soft-leafed plants

Etroplus suratensis is a large, schooling herbivore that gets along well with scats, monos, and archerfish.

The Orange Chromide
By Bob Edwards

The orange chromide, *Etroplus maculatus,* is one of three cichlids found in southern Asia and the only one regularly traded as an aquarium fish. The green chromide, *Etroplus suratensis*, is rarely imported, although sometimes it does appear within batches of orange chromides. It isn't a particularly good aquarium fish, in part due to its large size and waspish attitude toward tankmates. A third species, *Etroplus canarensis*, is known as the pearl-spot chromide; it is about the same size as the orange chromide, but is very seldom seen.

The chromides are very interesting cichlids in many ways. For a start, they are the only group of cichlids in Asia, except for a few tilapia-type cichlids in the Near East that are basically outliers of the African groups. All three species of chromide are from the southern coastline of India and Sri Lanka. They are considered to be rather primitive, resembling in some ways the common ancestors of both the cichlids and their close relatives, the marine damselfish so beloved by marine aquarists. Next time you visit a fish store stocking marine fish, check out the green chromis, *Chromis viridis*, and you

The Orange Chromide

Etroplus canarensis, also known as the pearl-spot chromide, is extremely rare.

will see quite a similarity in shape and form. Chromides are normally found in estuarine and brackish waters, again pointing to a close relationship with the marine ancestors of the cichlids.

Orange and green chromides can occur in mixed groups, with juvenile orange chromides behaving as cleaner fish, pecking off fungi, parasites, and dead skin from the much larger green chromides. Both species are euryhaline fishes that must be kept in brackish waters. Green chromides in particular require salty water—a specific gravity of 1.010 is about right. Living their entire lives in brackish-water habitats makes them rather different from the salt-tolerant cichlids like kribs, *Pelvicachromis pulcher,* which will put up with a bit of salt rather than actually needing it.

The orange chromide is available in two color forms, or morphs: a selectively bred bright amber-orange form and the wild form, which is a paler yellow green with distinctive dark blotches on the flanks. The orange form is by far the most commonly seen and is particularly attractive, with small red dots on the scales along the flanks. The intensity of the red dots' color varies, being more obvious in some fish than others. A small patch of shiny scales is usually located immediately under the eye, as well. When the fish are displaying or spawning, both sexes develop black markings on the flanks.

The wild form is very variable, with the basic color of the fish varying from a yellow green to almost orange. Unlike with the artificial morph, the wild type's flanks are patterned with dark-green to black blotches. A small but relatively dark spot is usually located in the middle of the flank above the pelvic fins, and another spot lies ahead of that one, just above the pectoral fin. Also, one or two fainter spots lead back toward the tail. In some fish these spots are all relatively circular, but in others the spots are elongated and rather more like stripes. When breeding, these fish can change color dramatically, with the spots becoming much darker and larger, and the bottom half of the flank especially becoming a very dark green, even black. The species name of this fish, *maculatus*, simply means "spotted" in Latin and refers to this pattern. Both color forms become more vibrant as they age and settle into their tank.

The wild-type orange chromides can reach a length of 3 inches (8 cm). The artificial morphs are usually a little smaller, but either way these can be comfortably thought of as dwarf cichlids. Orange chromides are hardy in the right aquarium, and between their typical cichlid alertness and their readiness to spawn, they will give you a very interesting tank to watch for many hours. If you keep them well, they should last for several years.

In the past, orange chromides have not been the easiest cichlids to acquire, since relatively few dealers regularly keep brackish-water fishes of any sort. In recent years, however, the amber variety of orange chromide has become a staple, and can usually be found along with other brackish-water species in larger tropical fish stores. If your local dealer doesn't carry them, he might be able to order them especially for you. Normally, dealers are only willing to do this if you are taking a whole batch of fish rather than just one or two, but it's certainly worth asking.

CHOOSING YOUR ORANGE CHROMIDES

Once you have located a store with these cichlids in stock, you must inspect the batch in the dealer's tank to check that they are strong, full-bodied, colorful, parasite- and disease-free, and roaming the tank actively. With cichlids in general, perky, inquisitive behavior is a key trait of happy, healthy fish—it really should be a question of who's watching whom. If they appear dull and don't seem interested in you or each other, then these are not the fish for you. Come back in a week or two; perhaps they will have settled down, or the dealer will have some new stock in.

If an orange chromide is perky and its colors are bright, chances are it's a healthy specimen.

The Orange Chromide

It's a good idea to keep orange chromides in pairs rather than schools, since they squabble with each other when in larger groups.

Regardless, always check that the fish are feeding well and have been properly quarantined.

Males and females can appear very similar, especially when they are juveniles or not in prime breeding condition. The easiest way to differentiate between the sexes at this stage is by color, but this can still be hit and miss. The brighter, more strongly colored individuals are normally the males, and the slightly paler fish are the females. This applies to both the artificial amber form and the wild type.

Never place two males in one tank; they will never accept each other, unless the tank is big enough for several mated pairs to set up their own territories. If you do buy a pair, it is worth asking the store if you can exchange one of them for another fish in case you do happen to take home two males. The better fish dealers will allow you to do this, especially if you're a regular customer. If you end up with two females, don't worry too much—they'll get along fine with each other—but you still might want to swap a female for a male to make a pair. (Occasionally a female might turn into a male; such sex changes aren't common in fish, but they do happen in some species, including orange chromides.) Finally, once you've found your fish, don't forget to ask the dealer what water conditions they're being kept in, particularly the salinity. As with introducing any freshwater or brackish-water fish, you want to introduce them to the water conditions in your tank gradually.

Once you have purchased your pair of orange chromides, get them home as quickly and safely as possible. Acclimate them in the same way you would any other tropical fish, equalizing the water slowly so the fishes are not shocked. After you release the fish and they've had a few minutes to adjust to their surroundings, they will begin to explore their new habitat and start defining territories. Within the first two to four hours, you should find out if you have returned with two males: Aggressive behavior and fighting will begin. It is fair to say this is general aggression and not mating interaction—it usually takes several days for a pair of fishes to be comfortable enough in their new home for the latter to happen. The next 24 hours will back up any suspicions of having two males, because they will continue to fight for territory. Eventually one will give in. The loser may die if not removed, since the dominant male will continue to give the loser grief, even if the loser does not fight back. In the wild, the loser could swim away, but in an aquarium he normally ends up cowering in a corner.

I think the ideal size for new orange chromides is around 1 inch (2 to 3 cm) in length, because they settle in more easily and adapt readily to whatever foods you offer them.

The details that follow concentrate on keeping pairs, since most people trying to keep schools of orange chromides in the confined space of an aquarium have stated that they constantly squabble with each other. Although they may be gregarious in the wild, it requires quite a large aquarium to keep them peacefully, allowing each pair the chance to maintain its own territory.

MAINTAINING YOUR ORANGE CHROMIDES

Orange chromides can be kept in relatively small tanks, from a minimum of about 26 gallons (100 liters), with plenty of rockwork, driftwood, and swimming space. Like most dwarf cichlids, orange chromides only settle down in an aquarium in which they feel secure. This is best achieved by giving each fish a lair to call home, such as a cave, a piece of wood to hide behind, or some sort of ornament

The Orange Chromide

Orange chromides need very clean water, so make sure your filter is up to the task.

into which the fish can retreat. Although small, these fish enjoy swimming in the open, particularly when breeding and displaying to one another.

You can keep orange chromides in a near-freshwater system or in a saltier, moderately brackish system. Orange chromides like fine gravel or sand best, because they enjoy digging, especially around breeding time. Fine coral sand can be used in saltier systems that require high pH and hardness levels, but take care that the grains are not large enough to choke the fish if they swallow some.

As far as water is concerned, orange chromides are best thought of as fishes of slightly to moderately brackish waters, rather than strongly brackish waters (unlike the green chromides mentioned earlier). They like waters with a specific gravity of between 1.002 and 1.006, which works well for many other species of fish, such as gobies and rainbowfish. In the wild, they can venture into saltier waters and even fresh water temporarily, but they do not do well in such conditions indefinitely. They will die if the salinity is maintained much above 1.006 for long periods, so these are not fish to mix with species that like near-marine conditions,

When choosing tankmates for orange chromides, consider a figure-eight puffer.

like scats and Malayan angels (monos). And in fresh water, they are particularly susceptible to fungus. Besides getting the salt concentration right, the water also must be moderately hard, with a pH between 7 and 8, and kept at a temperature of around 77°F (25°C). In aquaria with fine substrates, canister filters provide the best way to clean the water, and an ultraviolet filter will help keep the water clear and remove any parasites, algae, bacteria, and free-floating organisms. These fish do need clean water, so water changes of at least 10 to 25 percent on a weekly basis are in order, as well.

Although they do some digging, these are not particularly destructive cichlids, and as long as you give any plants a chance to get established (for example, by placing the roots within pots), these small cichlids will not be able to uproot them. Java fern is particularly useful, being a species that naturally occurs in brackish waters and often comes on pieces of bogwood ready to place in an aquarium. Established plants

The Orange Chromide

The female will attach her eggs to a sheltered area, which is cleaned beforehand.

can be prolific even under moderate lighting, quickly sending out daughter plants that can be cut away and tied onto other bits of wood and rockwork. Orange chromides will completely ignore the foliage of plants and actually do very well in planted aquaria, something that cannot be said for cichlids in general.

ORANGE CHROMIDE BEHAVIOR

Orange chromides are active, intelligent, territorial, colorful fish. They can be mixed with a variety of other brackish fish in a community aquarium. These may include figure-eight and green puffers, *Tetraodon biocellatus* and *T. nigroviridis*; bumblebee and knight gobies, *Brachygobius* spp. and *Stigmatogobius sadanundio*; glassfish, *Parambassis* spp.; and mollies, *Poecilia* spp. Orange chromides also can be kept with young archerfish, *Toxotes* spp.; scats, *Scatophagus* and *Selenotoca* spp.; and monos, *Monodactylus* spp. But as adults, these fish grow rather large and require a more saline water than orange chromides enjoy.

Orange chromides are on the whole peaceful and hardy fish, as long as the aquarium is not overstocked and good water quality is maintained. They aren't aggressive or persistent enough to bother larger fish, and they normally ignore smaller fish. About the worst thing an orange chromide might do to another fish is give it a small push, as if to say "Go away!" If you are adding orange chromides to an existing aquarium, though, you must be watchful of how the orange chromides pick territories; you may find that your favorite puffer gets evicted if its home is classed as a good spawning site. Orange chromides will choose a lair that is easy to defend; in a community aquarium, this desire can be satisfied by offering them caves and niches. In addition to being defensible, the enclosed walls of these retreats will serve as a place to attach their eggs, which they stick to the walls.

BREEDING YOUR ORANGE CHROMIDES

Breeding orange chromides is straightforward in a species-only tank, where the pair are the only inhabitants and there aren't any predators to worry about. It does happen that cichlids eat their own eggs or fry, but it is not common unless the parents are overly disturbed. In a community tank you are unlikely to have much success in raising the fry, although it does occasionally happen.

To get your orange chromides to breed, you must first have the tank running at optimum water-quality levels. You can raise the temperature fractionally to help them along, too. The orange chromides require conditioning on a diet of live foods if available; if not, frozen will have to do. This diet must be varied: bloodworms, glass worms, white river shrimp, and so on are ideal. This allows the fishes to build up their energy reserves for the arduous duties of spawning and raising the young. Maybe the presence of fresh food even gives the fishes the impression that this is a good time to breed.

Soon the fishes will initiate a series of sparring matches, circling each other, making fast dashes at each other, and finally engaging in some serious mouth wrestling. This is all quite a shock to watch at first—their aggression toward each other can be surprising, but it serves to demonstrate each fish's strength and suitability as a mate.

The Orange Chromide

Orange chromide fry can swim freely within a week of hatching.

After the fish have selected an acceptable site (normally a slightly sheltered retreat that receives some, but not too much, water movement and is easily defended), they will begin to clean the area. This is also where some digging comes into play. They will begin excavating the groomed breeding site an inch or so deep (unless they have chosen somewhere with no substrate), building up the entrance with the substrate in a similar fashion to kribs. They will at times dig similar, smaller pits randomly around the tank, where they will in time transport their fry on little excursions.

Finally, the female will begin to attach her eggs to the prepared site. The eggs are oval, light green, and 1 to 1.5 mm in size. They may number as many as 300. The male takes turns passing over the site, shedding his milt to fertilize them. During mating, the fishes' colors become enhanced somewhat, and the black markings on the flanks intensify dramatically. The male's fins may have a red tinge to the tips, too. Also, the pair might continue to spar occasionally. Once spawning is finished, the female cares for the batch of eggs, while the male defends the territory against intruders. She will fan the eggs to prevent particles from settling on the eggs and to keep them aerated. She will also mouth them to clean them. It takes about four to six days for the eggs to hatch.

Once hatched, the fry may be moved to one of the pits. Within a week the fry can swim freely, and the parents will begin taking the swarm of youngsters on little tours of the territory. The fry are very small by cichlid standards, and will need infusorians or newly hatched brine shrimp for at least the first few days. This contrasts with kribensis fry, for example, which are larger and will feed on algae and aquarium detritus quite happily without any need for help from the aquarist. Like discus, orange chromides produce extra mucus on their flanks, which they allow their fry to eat. This is the fish equivalent of milk production by mammals, and it is found in several species of cichlids.

Orange chromides are colorful, display all kinds of fascinating behaviors, and are small and easy to maintain. So it is surprising that they are relatively poorly known in the hobby, and that few people have experience keeping and breeding them. In fact, the hardest thing about keeping orange chromides and other brackish fish often seems to be trying to find information about them!

Mudskippers

By Richard Mleczko

Mudskippers have fascinated aquarists for a long time due to their funny antics in the aquarium. But they remain something of a mystery. In hobbyist literature, the earliest article on mudskippers that I could find dates back to 1968. Since then, I have found about 20 articles in aquarium and nature magazines, many of which had numerous factual errors, such as the wrong species names and incorrect accounts of where certain species were found. After about 10 years of collecting information and photographs, mainly from the scientific literature, I am now in a position to present this chapter based on scientific fact.

Mudskippers are gobies, and they belong to a subfamily within the Gobiidae known as the Oxudercinae. About 40 species are included within this subfamily, which is scattered among 10 genera, four of which are highly amphibious—these are the mudskippers. *Periophthalmus* and *Periophthalmodon* are the two genera most frequently kept by home aquarists; individuals of these two genera spend the most time on land. *Boleophthalmus* and *Scartelaos*, which are much less commonly seen in aquaria, are the other two mudskipper genera. The mudskipper is known as *schlammspringer* in German and *mutsugoro* in Japanese.

Mudskippers

GEOGRAPHIC DISTRIBUTION AND HABITAT

Mudskippers are tropical fish that can be found throughout the equatorial regions of Africa, Madagascar, the Arabian Peninsula, southern and southeastern Asia from Pakistan to Japan, Australia, and the Indo-Pacific oceanic islands as far east as Tonga. They are absent from the Americas. Wherever they occur, mudskippers favor habitats that are hot and humid, with air and water temperatures in the range of 75° to 86°F (24° to 30°C) and air humidity at 60 to 80 percent. Getting both the water and above-water conditions right in the mudskipper aquarium is absolutely essential to their long-term health (which is discussed later in this chapter), but as with many brackish-water fishes, mudskippers are fairly tolerant of environmental fluctuations.

In Kuwait, for example, the temperature can vary from 46°F (8°C) in winter to 113°F (45°C) in summer, although the mudskippers themselves are usually only active when air temperatures are between 55° and 104°F (13° and 40°C). Similarly, some species are quite tolerant of changes in salinity, with those adapted to life in estuarine and brackish-water habitats able to tolerate salinities from 10 to 90 percent that of seawater. Other species stick to normal marine habitats and need full-strength seawater.

MANGROVES

In many parts of the world, mudskippers and mangrove plants are inextricably linked—most mudskippers sold for aquaria are collected from the wild and are accustomed to mangrove habitats.

Worldwide there are about 65 species of mangroves. They are a group of salt-tolerant plants that grow in both tropical and temperate zones, from the Americas (including Florida) to Africa, Asia, and Australia. Mangroves can grow in water that is fresh all the way to marine, but seem to grow best in brackish water, so they are ideally suited to a brackish terrarium. Mangroves grow in zones that are parallel to the shoreline or the banks of tidal creeks or rivers. The seaward side is likely to be dominated by the gray mangrove, *Avicennia marina* (sometimes known as the black mangrove), which is a tough species with the ability to tolerate low temperatures and a variety of intertidal conditions. The mangrove apple, *Sonneratia alba,* also can be found in this zone. Behind the seaward zone grows the red mangrove, *Rhyzophora stylosa,* also known as the stilt or

Fish Out of Water!

The most remarkable adaptation of mudskippers is their ability to live as fish out of water. How do they achieve this amazing feat? Mudskippers have evolved to extract oxygen directly from the air using different parts of their bodies. Recent research indicates that some species don't use their gill filaments in oxygen exchange, instead using them only to excrete ammonia. They actually use their skin for as much as 40 to 70 percent of their oxygen exchange, and they use other parts of their gill chambers and mouth as well. When they use their mouths to breathe, they gulp a mouthful of water, which they swirl around to mix with air. When more oxygen is required they may gulp more mouthfuls of air or water. The mudskipper must always keep its mouth and skin moist, because oxygen must diffuse into the layer of water on the skin or in the mouth before the body can absorb it.

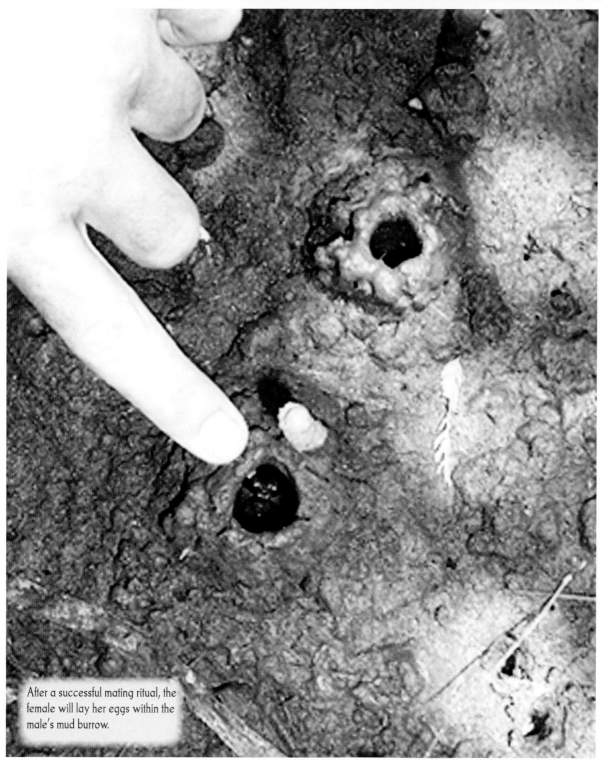

After a successful mating ritual, the female will lay her eggs within the male's mud burrow.

spider mangrove. The next zone farther from the water may only be inundated by periodic spring tides, and the soil is firmer and more saline due to evaporation. The yellow mangroves, *Ceriops* spp., can be found here. In soils that are still less saline, orange mangroves, *Bruguiera* spp., will grow.

Mangroves can survive in salty water because they have developed specialized ways of coping with salt. Some species, called salt excluders, prevent salt from entering the roots by filtering out as much as 90 percent of the salt in water. These include *Rhyzophora, Ceriops, Bruguiera,* and *Osbornia* species. Other species, like *Avicennia, Sonneratia,* and *Acanthus*, are salt secretors. Their leaves have specialized salt glands which excrete the salt taken in by their roots, and salt crystals become visible on the leaves. The salt drops off or is washed off by rain. Also, the leaves of mangroves are thick and waxy, preventing excess evaporation, which in turn helps keep the plant's internal salt concentration low.

Each species of mangrove is specially adapted to its particular environment. The red mangrove, for example, lives close to the sea and is constantly beaten by the waves, so it develops a system of stilt or prop roots that help anchor the tree firmly. They also absorb oxygen, which helps compensate for the fact that soil in mangrove swamps is usually dense, stagnant, and very deficient in oxygen.

Gray mangroves solve this problem in a different way. They have roots called pneumatophores that act as "snorkels," growing vertically out of the soil and carrying oxygen down into the root system. Orange mangroves are different still—their roots loop out of the mud and then back in again.

BEHAVIOR AND REPRODUCTION IN NATURE

The entertainment value of the mudskipper is hard to beat because of its unique behavioral and social interactions, especially during the breeding season. The male's colors and markings become more intense, and he becomes more active—doing what appear to be pushups, leaping into the air, and standing on his tail are among the ways male mudskippers attract females. The male also becomes more aggressive toward other males, warding off intruders through mouth gaping, biting, and raising its dorsal fins.

The changes in the female are subtle, although, as with many other fishes, the swelling of the ovaries makes her appear more rounded around the pelvic fins than usual. When she has been attracted to a mate, she engages in a mating ritual that includes very distinctive body movements. If the ritual fails, the frustrated male may attack her and drive her off, but if all goes well, she descends into the male's burrow, where she lays her eggs on the roof of the spawning chamber, a special part of the burrow the male builds for the occasion. The male then fertilizes the eggs and, as with other gobies, takes over full responsibility of the eggs. To oxygenate the burrow, the male may gulp air at the water's surface and then descend to the burrow and release the fresh air.

LOCOMOTION

Mudskippers employ various modes of locomotion. In deeper water, they swim just like any other goby, with side-to-side movements of the body and tail. They can also skim across the water's surface at high speed. However, they are most famous for their ability to walk on land. They have two main gaits when on

Mudskippers "walk" on mud by propping themselves up on their pectoral fins.

land: a slow "crutching" movement and a faster skipping motion consisting of a series of jumps. Crutching is a type of walking gait that uses the pectoral fins as crutches. This is different from the method employed by the walking catfish, *Clarias* sp., which uses its pectoral fins primarily as anchors while it rocks its body forward using the tail. Instead, mudskippers move their pectoral fins forward, then pull their body forward. The weight is then transferred to the pelvic fins and the underside of the tail; the pectoral fins are thrown forward again to begin the next stroke.

The second terrestrial mode of locomotion is skipping or jumping, which is of course the method of movement that has given these fish their common name. To perform the jump, the fish bends its tail forward and to one side, with the caudal fin anchored in the mud. Then it rapidly straightens its body, projecting itself forward and upward into the air. Jumping forward is obviously a useful way to escape predators, but the most dramatic jumps are the vertical ones that the males perform during the breeding season to attract a female.

Besides walking and jumping, mudskippers also can briefly stand on their tails—again, this is done primarily during the breeding season to attract mates or threaten rivals. Also, mudskippers have the fused pelvic fins typical of gobies, and they use them as a sort of suction cup to help them climb. They can be seen climbing straight up mangrove roots, riverbanks, rocks, and, in the aquarium, the glass walls of the tank.

KEEPING MUDSKIPPERS

Mudskippers are adaptable fishes and will thrive in an aquarium setup that resembles the environment from which they have been taken. The ideal sort of setup is a terrarium (or vivarium). Because many species of mudskipper spend over 90 percent of their time out of water, the aquarist must make sure the dry land part of the tank is sufficiently spacious for these relatively large and active fish. If a mudskipper is forced to remain

199

Mudskippers

When they do spend time in water, mudskippers require brackish conditions.

submerged too long, it may not survive. This is especially important for those species that prefer to feed on land.

AQUARIUM CONDITIONS

As with many brackish fishes, mudskippers in the wild must be able to withstand a wide range of environmental conditions, particularly low and high temperatures and salinities greater than that of normal seawater. These high salinities are produced by the evaporation of water from saltwater pools and lagoons.

Mudskippers will not tolerate unheated aquaria in temperate environments, and so must be kept in heated aquaria. Below 59°F (15°C), mudskippers become lethargic; at 50°F (10°C), they become completely inactive. If kept this cold for too long, they will die. Neither will mudskippers do well in excessively hot conditions; prolonged exposure to water temperatures above 93°F (34° C) will lead to death. A lid on the aquarium is absolutely essential to produce the warm, humid air these fish need, and it must have a temperature close to that of the water. Aim for a water temperature range of 79° F to 90°F (26° to 32° C), and stick a liquid-crystal thermometer onto the glass above the water level to keep an eye on this.

Mudskippers are definitely brackish-water fish, and laboratory experiments have shown that they generally avoid fresh water in favor of water with some salt content. They do well in water that has a specific gravity of 1.005 to 1.015, and fluctuations within this range are fine. The water should be hard (not less than about 120 parts per million of calcium carbonate) and have a pH of about 8. Unfortunately, many aquarium stores sell mudskippers as freshwater fish and do not tell the purchaser they need brackish water. In some cases, this may be due to sheer ignorance, but at other times they do so because it is much easier to sell fish that do not require special care from the buyer. Either way, you cannot expect mudskippers that have been kept in fresh water for weeks or months to be in particularly good health.

TANK SETUP

One habitat that can be created quickly and with minimum effort is an aquarium half-filled with water.

200

Mudskippers hail from smelly swamps and are very resistant to ammonia, so heavy filtration usually isn't necessary in their aquarium.

Mudskippers

Place gravel or sand on the floor of the tank, and add a few rocks large enough to give the mudskippers a place to rest outside the water. Also, driftwood, tree roots, or small branches can be glued into place in the aquarium to give the mudskippers more objects to climb.

While this simple setup can work, many aquarists prefer the sloping aquarium design rather than a few props sticking out of the water. This design has deep water at one end and shallow water (or land) at the opposite end. To create a slope, build up the depth of substrate at one end of the tank, and add driftwood or rocks to that area. You can insert a small sheet of glass or plastic into the substrate where it meets the water so it stands vertically and acts as a retaining wall, mitigating the slippage of substrate into the deep end of the tank. Use silicone sealer to glue the partition to the sides of the tank.

If you use sand or mud as a substrate, you can plant mangrove seedlings (or any other plants that grow in brackish water). Also, in nature mudskippers make their homes in burrows which they dig themselves. In an aquarium, these burrows or tunnels will only hold their shape if the mud is the right consistency and not too sloppy, which is difficult to achieve. Instead, create artificial burrows by partially burying anything that can introduce an open space underground—PVC pipes, hollow ceramic objects, or large shells make good hiding places for mudskippers.

Mangroves

If you are lucky enough to obtain a mangrove seedling by collecting them yourself or by buying them through mail-order or over the Internet, they should be grown in a small pot or an old ice cream container before being added to an aquarium.

Fill the container with mangrove mud or other sand. Then fully saturate it with brackish water. Plant the seedling in the substrate with the root end facing downward, then leave it outside (if in a warm climate) or keep it inside by a window. The idea is to expose it to plenty of light, so a lamp also may be used in temperate zones during winter when daylight alone might not be sufficient. Always keep the substrate water-logged. When the plant is mature enough, carefully remove it from its container, being careful not to damage the roots, then replant it in your terrarium.

Mangroves grow very slowly, so don't expect to be ready to plant your mangrove plant in the terrarium for at least three months. The plant will be ready when it has grown a few of its own leaves and has sunk some roots into the substrate.

To maintain the mangroves, add aquarium-safe plant fertilizer from time to time, which will provide the plants with essential nutrients like iron. And remember to outfit the aquarium with lighting sufficient for live plants.

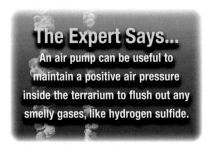

The Expert Says...
An air pump can be useful to maintain a positive air pressure inside the terrarium to flush out any smelly gases, like hydrogen sulfide.

Filtration

Don't be too worried about filtration; after all, mudskippers naturally inhabit very smelly mangrove swamps! Plus, mudskippers are the most ammonia-tolerant fish alive—ammonia levels that will kill most fish in two hours can be tolerated by mudskippers for two weeks. They also have a higher tolerance for hydrogen sulfide and cyanide.

Mangrove plants will do a great job of filtering out waste products.

Aquarists who use mangroves report dramatic decreases in nitrates and phosphates.

If you find that you have cloudy water (which especially happens with a muddy substrate), then any filter system is suitable, except for an undergravel filter, which would not fit in with the landscaping of your terrarium. You can try a corner or box filter, a trickle filter system, or an external filter. Or if you use an over-the-side hanging filter, you can place it so it forms a little waterfall and a stream flowing over the land area into the water.

Partial water changes are still recommended, especially if no filter system is used. Every two weeks, remove one-quarter of the water and replace it with either pure fresh water or marine-strength salt water. This will create a fluctuation in salinity for your brackish fishes.

> **The Expert Says...**
> You also can drain your terrarium with a gravity feed, instead of using a pump. Just connect a tap near the bottom end of the hose to adjust and control the flow of water.

Aeration

Aeration also is not that critical, since mudskippers get most of their oxygen from the air and not from water. Aeration can work to circulate the tank water in the absence of filtration, though. Or if you use a corner or box filter, then an air pump is part of this system anyway.

Tide Control

The final addition that will make your terrarium truly reminiscent of a mudflat is a system of tide control. Tide control can be achieved in a number of ways, including off-the-shelf tide-making systems. The dedicated mudskipper keeper who wants his mangrove aquarium to match the natural habitat as closely as possible could employ any of these.

Another option is to create your own system. For this you will need two aquarium pumps, a sump, and two timers. Mark where the high and low water marks will be on the glass of the terrarium, then fill the terrarium with water until it reaches the high water mark. Since there are four tide changes each day (two high tides and two low tides), set the timer so it pumps water out of the terrarium into a sump for six hours so it hits the low mark. The exit hose can be mounted out of sight at the base of the terrarium or fed in over the side. In the sump, place another pump on a timer, so that it takes six hours to refill the terrarium up to the high water mark. The rate of draining and filling will depend on the capacity of the pump and the diameter of the hoses, and will take some experimentation to get right, since you don't want the water to drain too quickly.

Using a sump has many benefits: it can hold the heater, which frees up aquarium space, and you can remove water from the sump when doing water changes so you don't have to open the lid of the terrarium and disturb the fish. It is also very easy to take water samples from the sump to test water chemistry.

> **The Expert Says...**
> In nature, the four tides are not all exactly equal, and can be very different in many parts of the world. To be as realistic as possible, you might want to set up your tide system so it mimics the tides of West Africa, northern Australia, or wherever your mudskippers were collected.

Other Species

The simplest way to keep mudskippers is in their own tank without any other fish. This avoids the problem of needing sufficiently deep water for the companion fishes while keeping a large enough portion of the tank above the water level for the mudskippers. However, possible

Mudskippers

Name	***Periophthalmus argentilineatus***
Other names	Barred mudskipper, silver-lined mudskipper, big-fin mudskipper
Origin	Brackish mangrove and nipa palm areas from the southern Red Sea and eastern coast of Africa. Also Madagascar, Seychelles, Pakistan, Sri Lanka, Malaysia, Japan (southern islands), Indonesia, Borneo, Philippines, New Guinea, Australia, and Oceania as far east as Tonga and the Solomon Islands
Size	To 7.5 inches (19 cm)
Sexual Dimorphism	None, other than genitalia
Water conditions	Brackish, specific gravity above 1.005
Diet	Live foods such as insects, worms, brine shrimp; will accept prepared fish foods including dried shrimp and bloodworms
Temperament	Territorial and can be aggressive
Availability	The most commonly traded mudskipper, this species is widely sold and inexpensive
Ease of maintenance	Some work to set up the aquarium properly; otherwise easy to feed and care for
Specific problems	Avoid overfeeding; be aware of bullying by larger mudskippers
Special Notes	It is the most widely distributed of any mudskipper species. It has nice red and white colors in the dorsal fins

Name	***Periophthalmus barbarus***
Other names	Atlantic mudskipper, butterfly mudskipper
Origin	Known only from West Africa: Gambia, Senegal, Benin, Nigeria, Angola, and the Gulf of Guinea Islands
Size	4 to 8 inches (10 to 20 cm)
Sexual Dimorphism	See *P. argentilineatus*
Water conditions	See *P. argentilineatus*
Diet	See *P. argentilineatus*
Temperament	See *P. argentilineatus*
Availability	Fairly common and inexpensive
Ease of maintenance	See *P. argentilineatus*
Specific problems	See *P. argentilineatus*
Special Notes	Beautiful, strong blue in the dorsal fins

Name	***Periophthalmus kalolo***
Other names	Common mudskipper
Origin	Brackish mangrove areas from East Africa to Samoa: Madagascar, Seychelles, Sri Lanka, Malaysia, Indonesia, Philippines, New Guinea, and Oceania; recently turning up in Australia
Size	1.5 to 4 inches (4 to 10 cm)
Sexual Dimorphism	See *P. argentilineatus*
Water conditions	See *P. argentilineatus*
Diet	See *P. argentilineatus*
Temperament	Territorial and can be aggressive
Availability	Fairly common
Ease of maintenance	See *P. argentilineatus*
Specific problems	See *P. argentilineatus*
Special Notes	Nice stripes in the dorsal fins

Name	*Periophthalmus* sp. (probably described by Hamilton in 1822 as *Gobius novemradiatus*; needs clarification)
Other names	Indian mudskipper
Origin	Only known from southern Thailand, but common name suggests India as well
Size	Up to about 2.5 inches (7 cm)
Sexual Dimorphism	Female lacks first long spine in first dorsal fin
Water conditions	See *P. argentilineatus*
Diet	See *P. argentilineatus*
Temperament	See *P. argentilineatus*
Availability	Variable, but currently fairly commonly traded
Ease of maintenance	See *P. argentilineatus*
Specific problems	See *P. argentilineatus*
Special Notes	Very strong red in the dorsal fins

Name	*Periophthalmodon septemradiatus*
Other names	None
Origin	Brackish mangrove areas from eastern India, Myanmar (Burma), Thailand, Vietnam, Malaysia, Indonesia, and Borneo
Size	1.5 to 3 inches (4 to 8 cm)
Sexual Dimorphism	Male has a long first spine in the first dorsal fin; first and second dorsal fins almost joined; females have very small dorsal fins
Water conditions	Brackish, specific gravity above 1.005
Diet	See *Periophthalmus argentilineatus*
Temperament	See *Periophthalmus argentilineatus*
Availability	Common
Ease of maintenance	See *Periophthalmus argentilineatus*
Specific problems	See *Periophthalmus argentilineatus*
Special Notes	When in full mating colors, this mudskipper has the most beautiful combination of colors of any mudskipper species

tankmates can include sailfin mollies and knight gobies, which both do well in the warm, brackish water mudskippers enjoy.

In a really large aquarium, it may be possible to use larger brackish-water fishes such as archerfish and scats, but adult specimens of these fish will need a water depth of at least 1 foot (30 cm) to feel comfortable. Also, archerfish are predatory and will eat any very small fish they can catch, so it would be unwise to mix adult archers with baby mudskippers. If the two species are of similar size, however, they get along well, and the vivarium-type tank that mudskippers like is also useful for getting archers to shoot for their dinner (see Chapter 4). Even with nonpredatory fishes such as scats or monos, it is a good idea to make sure they are about the same size as the mudskippers—it is often the case that placing large, active fishes in the watery part of their home frightens the mudskippers somewhat, and they become very nervous about going into the water to swim.

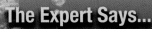

The Expert Says...

Because they require saline conditions, mudskippers do not make good tankmates for newts, frogs, or turtles, despite their similar need for a mix of aquatic and terrestrial environments.

Diet

Mudskippers like live foods such as flies and other small insects, spiders, live brine shrimp, worms, mosquito larvae, and

Mudskippers

Try to purchase mudskippers that keep their pectoral and caudal fins spread out—that is a sign of good health.

small shrimp such as ghost shrimp. They will also eat dry fish food, such as freeze-dried shrimp or krill, freeze-dried worms, frozen brine shrimp, sinking shrimp pellets, and flake food. Large mudskippers will also eat small fish, including smaller mudskippers.

As with many fish, it is better to err on the side of caution when feeding and give them less than they will readily eat. Mudskippers don't need to be fed every day; every other day is enough. Overfeeding leads to problems with digestion, in particular acute constipation: In this case, the anal area appears reddish and stretched, and the mudskipper experiences a painful death. Mudskippers especially experience digestive problems if overfed on dry food, which expands in the stomach after it has been eaten. Confining their staple diet to the live or frozen foods they would encounter in nature (in other words, no crickets or mealworms) should help prevent these problems. Prepared foods, like flake and pellets, should be used to augment the diet, but only once or twice a week.

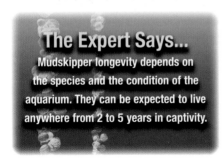

The Expert Says...

Mudskipper longevity depends on the species and the condition of the aquarium. They can be expected to live anywhere from 2 to 5 years in captivity.

HEALTH

Besides the dangers of overfeeding, little is known about mudskipper health problems compared to other aquarium fish. But in general, they seem to suffer less from the usual infections than do freshwater aquarium fish—which is typical of most fish kept in brackish water. However, wounds and ulcers can cause problems if not promptly treated. Bacterial gill infections in particular can cause serious health problems because they fuse the gill filaments, making gaseous exchange less efficient.

As with any wild-caught fish, it is entirely possible that newly purchased or collected mudskippers carry a variety of parasites. Among the more common parasites are protozoa in the gall bladder and gills, and copepods (crustaceans) and trematodes (flatworms) adhering to the buccal cavity, gill arches, and gill filaments. Acanthocephalans (spiny-headed worms) make their homes in the intestines.

The ghost goby, *Apocryptes bato,* is extremely rare.

When your mudskipper fails to hold open its pectoral and caudal fins, which it normally keeps partially or fully spread out, the fish is in discomfort and could be unhealthy. This change in behavior does not tell you what the problem is, but it serves as a warning sign to check the aquarium conditions and see how the tank community is getting along.

Bullying can be a major problem when more than one mudskipper is kept in the same tank. Bigger mudskippers may bully smaller ones to the point of stressing the victim so severely that it dies. Do not imagine that this is a characteristic of adult fishes only: I have had this happen even when the two mudskippers involved were only about 1 inch (3 cm) long! Also, while physical attacks on one another that result in mortal wounds are rare, they do occur.

REPRODUCTION

In the wild, mudskippers breed under a complicated set of conditions, and unless this can be replicated in the aquarium, they will never breed in captivity. For one thing, the male mudskipper must dig a burrow underground, where the female will lay her eggs. Failing to provide the mudskippers with substrate that is sufficiently soft and sticky for this burrow is probably the main reason aquarists have not been successful at spawning mudskippers. On its own, sand isn't sticky enough to form a stable burrow, so in the wild, mudskippers make their burrows in mud instead. However, mud isn't a popular choice for use in aquaria because it tends to make the water cloudy. The best compromise is a mixture of mud and sand that is stable enough for the mudskippers to burrow into, but not so messy that it makes the water completely turbid.

Besides having the right sort of aquarium setup, to start a home-breeding program the aquarist obviously

The Expert Says...

When on land, mudskippers often roll onto their sides, apparently to remoisten their skin. I thought they sensed when their skin was becoming too dry and only rolled over then, but I have observed that they do this when submerged in deep water as well, so what prompts this behavior isn't clear.

Mudskippers

Name	*Apocryptes bato*
Other names	Ghost goby
Origin	Brackish mangrove areas from eastern India to Myanmar (Burma)
Size	Up to 5.5 inches (14 cm)
Sexual Dimorphism	Males have a much longer caudal fin
Water conditions	Brackish, specific gravity above 1.005
Diet	Live foods such as insects, worms, brine shrimp; will accept prepared fish foods including dried shrimp and bloodworms
Temperament	Peaceful
Availability	Rare
Ease of maintenance	Relatively easy to keep; not particularly amphibious but should be given a shallow water bank or ledge as well as a normal, deep area for swimming
Specific problems	Avoid overfeeding
Special Notes	A plain-looking goby

Name	*Parapocryptes serperaster*
Other names	Mud-rill skipper
Origin	Brackish mangrove areas from eastern India, Myanmar (Burma), Thailand, Malaysia, Indonesia, and China
Size	1.5 to 5.5 inches (4 to 14 cm)
Sexual Dimorphism	None, other than genitalia
Water conditions	Brackish, specific gravity above 1.005
Diet	See *Apocryptes bato*
Temperament	Peaceful fish
Availability	Formerly rather rare, but now seen with some regularity
Ease of maintenance	See *Apocryptes bato*
Specific problems	Avoid overfeeding
Special Notes	More like a goby than a mudskipper

Name	*Pseudapocryptes elongatus*
Other names	Asian dragon goby
Origin	Brackish mangrove areas from eastern India, Myanmar (Burma), Thailand, Malaysia, Indonesia, Vietnam, and China
Size	1.5 to 7 inches (3 to 18 cm)
Sexual Dimorphism	None, other than genitalia
Water conditions	Brackish, specific gravity above 1.005
Diet	Herbivorous; try flake food like *Spirulina*; known to eat *Tubifex* and sinking pellets; could experiment with live brine shrimp or worms
Temperament	Territorial and can be aggressive
Availability	Formerly rather rare, but now seen with some regularity
Ease of maintenance	This species appreciates a shallow water area and some sort of sand bank; it is also an obligate air breather and must have access to air or it will drown
Specific problems	Avoid overfeeding
Special Notes	More like a goby than a mudskipper; a good aquarium algae eater

Mudskippers kept in groups may raise and lower their dorsal fins like flags in response to a threat.

must also have at least one male and one female. This is not easy to achieve, since the gender of most species is very difficult to determine. Recently, a German aquarist reported that his mudskippers were spawning in his aquarium and that he had 10-day-old fry. Unfortunately they died soon after, but this does at least indicate that breeding mudskippers is possible, and it is an obvious focus for the efforts of dedicated aquarists.

BEHAVIOR

Why do people keep mudskippers in aquaria? The reason is simple: They are very entertaining to watch. That's probably why many public aquariums around the world exhibit mudskippers. Mudskippers make very good pets. They do some silly things like leap into the air or the water from a piece of driftwood. The funniest thing that I have seen one do is try to float vertically underwater, only to sink backward. I once tamed a mudskipper, and it often climbed onto my finger if I happened to put my hand into the tank for some reason, or onto the palm of my hand to eat food.

Their activity at feeding time is one of the most entertaining aspects of keeping mudskippers. Mudskippers are skilled and ferocious hunters with excellent eyesight. Drop the tiniest worm into the aquarium, and they will find it. Throw in a live moth or fly, and you will have at least half an hour of entertainment as you watch your pets battle each other and try to outsmart their prey.

Mudskippers are sometimes aggressive toward each other. If a large land area is available in the tank, they become very territorial, and the biggest one will try to control the best position. However, when space is limited, they are more tolerant of each other, sharing the same branch or piece of driftwood. A bit of one-upmanship,

Mudskippers

Periophthalmus argentilineatus is among those mudskippers that spend the most time on land.

however, will continue as the fish work out their pecking order; they are amusing to watch as they chase each other around. Fortunately, they rarely cause serious injury to one another, although one morning I noticed that one of my specimens had an eye hanging by a thread of tissue, possibly pulled off by a rival in a fight. The eye eventually fell off, the scar healed over, and the fish remained healthy and lived a long life as a one-eyed 'skipper.

One of the most interesting things that you will ever see your mudskipper do is flagging. This is the raising and lowering of the first and second dorsal fins in response to a threat. A mudskipper kept on its own will rarely flag, so keep at least two. Many species display nice colors in their dorsal fins, such as spots or stripes that may contain blue, red, orange, black, and white. This flash of bright color is all the more enchanting because it is set against the rather somber colors of the rest of this fish.

As much fun as mudskippers can be, remember that you must have a tight-fitting, gapless lid on the aquarium. Gaps for power leads and air hoses must be sealed. Mudskippers will escape from your aquarium given a chance—I found one dried up like a pretzel a few days after I noticed it was missing. In addition to being good at jumping, the suction-cup pelvic fin makes the mudskipper an excellent climber, able to scale not just wires and pipes, but even the glass sides of the aquarium as well.

COMMONLY TRADED MUDSKIPPERS

Numerous species of mudskipper are imported, and tropical fish stores often have no idea which species they are selling. Even aquarium books and magazines commonly misidentify them. The following section will help you understand what distinguishes each species.

The species of mudskipper sold in your local tropical fish store will depend greatly on where you live.

The mudskipper's frog-like eyes add to the illusion that this fish is an amphibian scampering around the mudflats.

Mudskippers

In Europe, mudskippers are often imported from West African countries such as Gambia and Nigeria. Because only one mudskipper, *Periophthalmus barbarus*, is found in West Africa, it is highly probable that this is the species that will be offered by European tropical fish dealers. An Indian species of mudskipper, the mud-rill skipper, *Parapocryptes serperaster*, is the only other mudskipper imported into Europe with any frequency, and it is quite easy to distinguish from *Periophthalmus barbarus*.

Within the last two years, a new, undescribed species of *Periophthalmus*, referred to as the Indian mudskipper, has found its way into American and Japanese markets. Actually, it is most likely *P. novemradiatus* as described by Hamliton (*Gobius novemradiatus*, 1822). The current *Pradiatus novemradiatus* (after Murdy, 1989) probably needs to be renamed.

North America receives both *Periophthalmus barbarus* from West Africa and various species from southeastern Asia, most commonly *P. argentilineatus*. Both European and North American aquarists sometimes come across *Periophthalmodon septemradiatus*, which is becoming a popular import from southeastern Asia.

Australia is home to more species of mudskipper than any other continent, but not all of them are suitable for the home aquarium. The most frequently seen Australian mudskippers offered for sale include *Periophthalmus argentilineatus*, which is probably the one most commonly sold; *P. novaeguineaensis*, an attractive species with nice orange spots; and probably the small mudskippers *P. gracilis* and *P. minutus*. Occasionally *Periophthalmodon freycineti* is seen, although it is really too large for the home aquarium—it can grow to 1 foot (30 cm) in length.

AMPHIBIOUS MUDSKIPPERS—*PERIOPHTHALMUS* AND *PERIOPHTHALMODON*

These mudskippers are the types that spend the most time out of the water and include those species that have become the most popular among aquarists. Generally speaking, they share the same tidal mudflat habitats, although some variation occurs: Species of *Scartelaos* are found closest to the sea, and *Boleophthalmus* and *Periophthalmodon* occur successively farther upshore. *Periophthalmus* species in particular can be found climbing rocks and trees and resting on land that is never covered by the tide, making them by far the most terrestrial of all the mudskippers. They dig burrows that extend more than 3 feet (1 meter) underground,

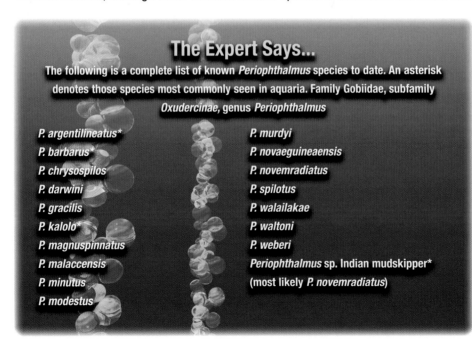

The Expert Says...

The following is a complete list of known *Periophthalmus* species to date. An asterisk denotes those species most commonly seen in aquaria. Family Gobiidae, subfamily Oxudercinae, genus *Periophthalmus*

*P. argentilineatus**	*P. murdyi*
*P. barbarus**	*P. novaeguineaensis*
P. chrysospilos	*P. novemradiatus*
P. darwini	*P. spilotus*
P. gracilis	*P. walailakae*
*P. kalolo**	*P. waltoni*
P. magnuspinnatus	*P. weberi*
P. malaccensis	*Periophthalmus* sp. Indian mudskipper*
P. minutus	(most likely *P. novemradiatus*)
P. modestus	

Periophthalmus barbarus is the only mudskipper found in West Africa and is sold in aquarium stores in Europe and North America.

and provided that these burrows are flooded by the tide at some point, they can be as much as 330 feet (100 m) away from any permanent water. The burrows have turrets that stick above the level of the mud, and the deeper chambers are permanently filled with water.

Periophthalmus is also noted for being one of the genera best able to breathe out of water, the other genus being *Periophthalmodon;* this is reflected in their alert, active behavior when on land. Unlike many other mudskippers, these fish are vigorous hunters that will eat a wide variety of terrestrial arthropods, including flies, moths, beetles, and worms. They will also take small crabs, shrimps, and fish (including smaller mudskippers). *Periophthalmus* will also eat algae, and in captivity it is important to offer them a balanced diet of meaty and vegetarian foods.

Periophthalmus are easily the most widely distributed mudskippers and the most suitable for aquaria. These 18 species are the most amphibious and have a natural range that spans West Africa, Asia, and Oceania. The most recent species was discovered in Darwin Harbor in 2001. *Periophthalmus* are quite variable, with species ranging from 1.5 to 8 inches (3 to 20 cm) in length. The body is generally slender (but not eel-like) and rather stocky at the front, and has some sort of colorful markings, such as spots or stripes, on the body and dorsal

Mudskippers

Periophthalmodon septemradiatus is recognizable for its nearly joined pair of dorsal fins.

fins. Usually the first dorsal fin is more colorful than the second, and in the males of a few species, the first dorsal fin is a bit more elongated as well. The eyes are notably positioned at the top of the head on short stalks, almost like periscopes. (The scientific name of the genus actually refers to this, coming from the Greek *peri* meaning "around" and *ophthalmos* meaning "eye.")

Periophthalmodon are only a bit less terrestrial than *Periophthalmus*, and they can still be found climbing rocks and riverbanks, if not quite as expertly. They prefer to hunt for food in or close to the water, however, and feed extensively on crabs and smaller mudskippers (including *Periophthalmus*). They also dig deep burrows, but instead of a turret, the burrow opens out into a large, shallow bowl as much as 3 feet (1 m) across. The burrow is permanently filled with water, but this water is often lacking in oxygen. During the mating season, the male shares his burrow with the female. After the eggs have been laid, he oxygenates them by gulping air at the surface of the burrow and then releasing it underground in the chamber containing the eggs. *Periophthalmodon* don't range as far from their burrows as *Periophthalmus*, but they have been seen swimming freely in nearby rivers, holding their heads above the water.

Superficially at least, *Periophthalmodon* species look a lot like species of *Periophthalmus*, being sturdily built gobies with colorful dorsal fins and frog-like eyes sticking out above the head. *Periophthalmodon* are generally

quite a bit larger than *Periophthalmus* though, with *Periophthalmodon schlosseri* reaching 1 foot (30 cm) in length, compared to the 3 to 6 inches (8 to 15 cm) typical of most *Periophthalmus*. It is not a surprise then that *Periophthalmodon schlosseri* and the similarly sized *Periophthalmodon freycineti* are widely known as giant mudskippers in the aquarium trade.

Less Amphibious Mudskippers—*Apocryptes, Parapocryptes,* and *Pseudapocryptes* spp.

For the most part, none of these mudskippers is important to aquarists and all are traded only rarely. *Apocryptes bato* is one of the few seen with any frequency, but because it looks rather more like a regular goby than a mudskipper, lacking the buggy eyes typical of mudskippers, it is usually thought of as a fully aquatic goby. *Apocryptes bato* makes burrows within the tidal limits of rivers, but beyond that, not much else is known about its behavior and ecology. *Parapocryptes* is another genus about which little is known. It looks a bit more like a proper mudskipper but is still mostly—perhaps entirely—aquatic. At least one species, *P. serperaster*, is traded from time to time.

Mudskippers of the genus *Pseudapocryptes* are found in mangroves and mudflats. One species, *P. elongatus*, is sometimes seen in aquarium stores, where it is known as the Asian dragon goby. It gets this name from its

Mudskippers

Parapocryptes serperaster is rare, and relatively little is known about it.

Mudskippers

Despite some specific and complicated needs, mudskippers make nice, friendly pets.

rather elongated shape, similar to the more well-known dragon (or violet) goby, *Gobioides broussonnetii*, which is especially widely traded in the United States. *Pseudapocryptes* species prefer to stay submerged in shallow pools but can flip themselves from one pool to another using their tails, or else walk using their pectoral fins in a way similar to that of the more terrestrial mudskippers. They also are obligate air breathers and will suffocate if they cannot gulp air at the surface. They appear to be mostly vegetarian, grazing on algae and photosynthetic bacteria they extract from the mud. They will also eat small crustaceans and in aquaria adapt well to a mixed diet including vegetarian and prepared fish foods (such as sinking pellets).

RARELY TRADED MUDSKIPPERS—*SCARTELAOS, BOLEOPHTHALMUS, APOCRYPTODON, OXUDERCES,* AND *ZAPPA* SPP.

Scartelaos make burrows similar to those of *Periophthalmodon*, and they do not stray far from them. Like *Periophthalmodon*, *Scartelaos* is known to gulp air and take it into its burrow to increase the amount of oxygen there. At least one species of *Scartelaos* is believed to hibernate in its burrow during the winter months, allowing these fish to tolerate cooler winters than other mudskippers. They are omnivorous and will eat algae and small crabs. The genus *Scartelaos* contains four species, but only one is even occasionally traded, *S. histophorus*, known as the blue mudhopper, the eel-skipper, or the bearded goby. This last name is thanks to the barbels on its chin, something not seen on any of the other mudskippers. The other names refer to its long, eel-like body, which is bluish gray in color and patterned with blue spots on the face and body. The dorsal fins lack the colorful patches seen among *Periophthalmus* and *Periophthalmodon* species.

Boleophthalmus also make their homes in deep burrows, around which they build impressive pentagonal walls that define their territories and which they defend vigorously—they are so busy defending their burrows that they won't stray far from them. Known for jostling, mouth gaping, and biting intruders, they are possibly the most aggressive mudskipper genus.

Unlike the other genera mentioned so far, species of *Boleophthalmus* are distinctly herbivorous, feeding on microscopic algae and diatoms they skim off the surface of mud. This diet makes *Boleophthalmus* unsuitable for the home aquarium, because unless the aquarist can provide this microscopic foodstuff on a continual basis at home, the animal may not survive.

Five species of *Boleophthalmus* are known, but only a single species has been traded—the comb-toothed or blue-spotted mudskipper, *B. pectinirostris*. The second name comes from the blue spots that cover its otherwise yellowish brown body and fins; some saddle-like brown blotches might occur on the body as well. Both *Scartelaos* and *Boleophthalmus* are especially keen on tail standing, which the males do to attract females.

The gobies *Apocryptodon, Oxuderces,* and *Zappa* are hard to find in the wild and therefore are very unlikely to ever be available in the aquarium trade. For example, *Zappa confluentus* is only known from the Fly River in New Guinea, where it has been observed flipping around in the mud. Not much is known about the natural history of these gobies.

Freshwater Morays and Other Eel-like Fishes

By Neale Monks

The fishes included in this section are grouped together not because they are closely related but because they all look similar and have much the same requirements. Moray and freshwater eels belong to two families, the Muraenidae and Anguillidae respectively, which both fall within the single order of "true eels," the Anguilliformes. Perhaps surprisingly, this order is closely related to tarpons and ten-pounders—big, herring-like fishes that are popular with sport fishermen because of the fierce fights they put up once hooked. What they share with the Anguilliformes is a distinctive leptocephalus larval form that resembles a transparent leaf.

The third group of eels commonly kept by aquarists consists of the spiny eels of the family Mastacembelidae. This group belongs to a huge order of fishes, the Perciformes, which includes types as diverse as swordfishes, gobies, cichlids, and anabantids. In fact, more than 8,000 species of perciform fishes are known, making them the most diverse order of vertebrates. In many ways, they are also the most advanced of all living fishes, including such specialists as the huge, warm-blooded tunas and the behaviorally complex cichlids, with their sophisticated brood care and mating rituals.

Freshwater Eels and Eel-like Fishes

The long, thin body shape of eels is common among fishes that do a lot of burrowing.

In complete contrast is the fourth important brackish-water eel-like fish, *Erpetoichthys calabaricus* (the ropefish or reedfish). This fish is plated with armor and looks distinctly primitive, belonging to an archaic order, Polypteriformes, that also includes the various bichirs, *Polypterus* spp., which have become quite popular with advanced freshwater aquarists in recent years. Like the bichirs, the reedfish has a pair of lungs instead of a swim bladder and can breathe air, a useful adaptation in the swampy habitats this fish prefers.

A fifth family of eel-like fishes that make their way into brackish waters from time to time is the Synbranchidae. Fish in this family are members of their own order, the Synbranchiformes, and are real tankbusters without much to attract the home aquarist. Only a single species, the marbled swamp eel, *Synbranchus marmoratus*, is offered for sale in tropical fish stores—in general, it should be passed over. It becomes a big, highly predatory animal with a distinctly waspish personality not really suitable for maintenance with any other fishes.

A SHAPE WITH A PURPOSE

The eel shape does seem to be popular with fishes that spend their time burrowing through mud or sand at the bottoms of rivers, lakes, and seas. In addition to the fish mentioned here, numerous others exist, including strictly freshwater fish such as the various loaches and the electric eel, as well as marine fishes like the sand lances and hagfishes. Again, while all these fishes are eel-like, none is particularly closely related to the true eels, which indicates the extent to which this eel-like body plan has evolved again and again. All these fishes burrow into the substrate to hunt for food or escape from predators.

A clue to why all these fishes have this elongated shape comes from the way they swim—by throwing their entire bodies into a series of broad, undulating waves so that, from overhead, these fish look distinctly S-shaped when swimming. In most other fishes, the body does not move from side to side so strongly. In the fastest fishes, the body is held completely stiff and only the tail moves, as is the case with tunas and lamnid sharks like the great white. The less the body wiggles from side to side with each stroke of the tail, the less energy is wasted pushing water to the left and right, and the more energy is available to move the fish forward. So why do all these eel-like fishes keep a design that is intrinsically inefficient? The value of the eel shape is that it works as well for swimming through sand or mud as through water. Being long and narrow is the ideal shape for an animal that wants to wind its way into narrow crevices or through dense stands of water plants or seaweeds.

The Expert Says...
These eel-like fish seem to be among the species of aquarium fish most prone to lymphocystis, a condition in which benign but ugly tumors appear on the outer surface of the fish, most commonly on the fins.

Understanding why these fishes have an eel-like shape gives us some very useful clues as to how they should be maintained in aquaria. For a start, all these fishes need a soft substrate into which they can burrow. Regular aquarium gravel is the worst substrate to use with these fishes because they will have great difficulty burrowing into it, and in many cases, it will damage their skin as they do so, making them prone to infections. Spiny eels in particular often develop mysterious, bloody lesions on the skin and fins, which can be very difficult to treat and may lead to a loss of

Freshwater Eels and Eel-like Fishes

Eels enjoy wood and other crevice-filled decorations, and do best with a fine, smooth substrate like silica sand.

vigor and eventual death. Even if digging into coarse gravel does not physically damage them, it certainly inhibits their natural behavior, something the caring fishkeeper wants to avoid. While very fine gravels are available and could be used in a pinch, better by far is silica sand.

Silica sand (sometimes called quartz sand or silver sand) is fine, smooth, and completely nontoxic, making it the ideal substrate for use with burrowing fishes. It is equally good with fishes like cichlids that take in mouthfuls of sand that they sift for food, and it doesn't abrade the whiskers of catfish as gravel does. It is also a chemically inert substrate that will not alter your tank's water chemistry, unlike lime-rich beach or coral sands, which makes it ideal for use with fishes that prefer neutral or slightly acidic water conditions, such as spiny eels and ropefish.

You probably won't find silica sand in the aquarium supplies section of your local pet store; instead, try the reptile section. Silica sand is often used with reptiles as an alternative to calcium-rich sand. It is also available in garden centers, where it is sold for use with desert plants such as cacti. Before you buy, make sure the sand is smooth rather than sharp; this won't be a problem if you get the sand from a reptile supply store, but the horticulture grades can be a bit rough for use with fish and is likely to irritate or even scratch the skin of any fish that burrow into it.

Sandy substrates are incompatible with undergravel filtration. Sandy substrates aren't porous enough for water to flow through them adequately, and if there isn't enough water movement, then the bacteria cannot remove the nitrogenous wastes quickly enough to keep the water clean. Worse still, sand tends to become compacted over time, which slows the water flow so much that bacteria use up the oxygen inside the sand before it can be replenished from the water. The result is anaerobic decay and the production of potentially harmful gases, such as hydrogen sulfide. To prevent this, remove uneaten food, keep the sand less than 2 inches (5 cm) deep, and stir the sand thoroughly once a week while performing water changes.

Be aware that these fishes can work their way through pipes and cracks just as well as they can dig through sand. Many eel-like fish are to some degree amphibious, able to move from one body of water to another by slithering through wet grass or swampy mud. Usually they do this at night or after heavy rain, when the ambient humidity is high. In the aquarium, expect them to explore every possible way of getting out of the tank. These fish will swim into filters if they can, but more usually slither through gaps between the tank and the hood, and from there, onto the floor below. More often than not you are likely to find these fishes dried up and dead, but if you are lucky, they might just survive their adventures. The true eels, ropefish, and swamp eels in particular are very hardy, after all, provided that their bodies don't dry out completely, although each of these fish manages to breathe air in completely different ways: true eels respire through their skins, ropefish have lungs much like ours, and swamp eels have lung-like pouches alongside the gills. Obviously, it is essential that the aquarium lid fit securely, and you might even want to weight it down so the fish cannot force their way out (the bigger species, particularly among the Synbranchidae, have a well-earned reputation as escape artists).

Although these fishes normally won't get inside a filter with narrow grilles across the water inlets, they are more than able to make their way across a chute and into the return outlet, or through an overflow into a wet-and-dry filter. On the plus side, such a runaway fish is unlikely to meet a premature death quickly inside an unpressurized filter, but on the down side, taking the filter apart to get the fish out and back into the aquarium can be a real hassle. Instead, use plastic mesh and build a fence around any such aperture.

In addition to being great escape artists and having distinctive requirements as far as aquarium decor and filtration are concerned, these fishes also tend to be secretive and frequently nocturnal. Compared to active fish, like cichlids, eels can seem rather boring.

None of these species is easy to spawn, and aquarium specimens are almost always collected from the wild.

Feeding can be problematic, and since eels are predatory, the prospective owner needs a regular supply of meaty live foods, at least until the fish can be weaned onto

Earthworms are a safer live food choice then feeder fish.

frozen or dry foods. Live feeder fish usually aren't necessary (though they will be readily taken) and could carry parasites and other diseases. Suitable alternatives include earthworms, clean *Tubifex*, insect larvae such as bloodworms, and live river shrimp, which all make excellent foods for these fish. Once settled in, some of these fishes will become very tame (the spiny eels in particular are admired for this quality) and can be trained to feed from the hand. Frozen and freeze-dried foods offer the widest and safest range of staple foods for these fishes. Invertebrates including *Mysis* and bloodworms work well for the smaller species, while the larger ones prefer lancefish, krill, clams (without the shells), and even strips of squid.

ROPEFISH—*ERPETOICHTHYS CALABARICUS*

There is but a single species of ropefish—*Erpetoichthys calabaricus*, sometimes known by an older name, *Calamoichthys calabaricus*—but it is a widespread animal, found in fresh and slightly brackish waters throughout West Africa from Nigeria to Congo. Ropefish resemble their close relatives the bichirs in most ways, but are notably much more elongated, have rather small pectoral fins, and lack pelvic fins. Where bichirs are rather pike-like in overall build and habits, ropefish are much more eel-like. Whereas bichirs tend to swim by sculling with their front fins and gently swishing their bodies, ropefish undulate their entire bodies and wind their way up the water column in broad, S-shaped bends, looking for all the world like a sea snake. Another difference between ropefish and bichirs is that they don't prop themselves up on their pectoral fins as bichirs commonly do, because ropefish have pectoral fins that are so much smaller than those of bichirs.

Regardless of their habits, both bichirs and ropefish qualify as living fossils, strikingly similar in many ways to fishes that thrived alongside the dinosaurs during the Mesozoic Era. As living fishes go, they are probably an older group than even those more well-known ancients, the sturgeons, although fish taxonomists continue to debate exactly where they fit into the great scheme of things. Like lungfish, they have paired lungs, but like

Ropefish

Name	***Erpetoichthys calabaricus***
Other names	**Ropefish, reedfish, *Calamoichthys calabaricus***
Origin	**West Africa**
Size	**Up to 40 inches (100 cm) in the wild; typically 18 to 24 inches (45 to 60 cm) in captivity**
Water conditions	**Fresh or slightly brackish (specific gravity <1.005)**
Diet	**Invertebrates, small fish, prepared fish foods**
Temperament	**Peaceful, sociable fish**
Availability	**Commonly traded; inexpensive**
Ease of maintenance	**Fairly easy**
Specific problems	**Needs soft substrate; good at escaping from aquaria; must be kept in groups of three or more; will eat very small fishes**

Erpetoichthys calabaricus

sturgeons, they have a shark-like, asymmetrical caudal fin and a spiral intestine. Most curious of all are their pectoral and pelvic fins, which have distinctive, arm-like lobes strikingly similar to those of the coelacanth.

Even given all these similarities, ropefish have plenty that is unique as well: unusual scales, a whole series of dorsal fins (each with its own set of spines and rays), and juveniles with external gills like those of a larval amphibian. All in all, bichirs and ropefish are veritable museums of unique and primitive bony-fish characteristics, and are among the most bizarre and rewarding animals any aquarist can keep.

Although closely related, ropefish are very distinct from the bichirs in terms of ecology and behavior, and any aquarium in which they are kept needs to reflect this. In addition to the usual precautions that must be taken with burrowing fishes, ropefish are sociable fishes that appreciate caves and plants under which they can hide together. In contrast, most bichirs are distinctly territorial, at least toward conspecifics, and sometimes toward other bichirs too. Certainly, ropefish should not be kept singly if you want them to be at all comfortable; three seems to be the minimum number if you want them to settle down well. They don't really school as such, but seem to like hanging out in groups inside caves with just their heads poking out.

Ropefish are rather more nocturnal than bichirs, which tend to settle into a daytime routine in captivity quite readily, but if the aquarium is quiet and has plenty of shade, then ropefish can become much less shy, particularly at feeding time. Although just as predatory as bichirs, ropefish have smaller mouths and so tend to favor worms and other invertebrates over fishes or meat. Occasionally, they will eat snails as well. Once settled in, they will

Ropefish are happy to chow down on small tankmates like neon tetras.

happily take chunky foods, including strips of squid and clam meat. Ropefish will eat small pieces of cooked chicken and lean, raw beef, although, as with any predatory fish, such rich foods should be used very sparingly.

Nonetheless, they can be piscivorous, and the average-size juveniles seen in the trade will easily take neon tetras, danios, and guppies if the opportunity presents itself; adult ropefish can manage larger prey, up to something the size of a platy, swordtail, or small goldfish. On the other hand, ropefish are perfectly safe with fish too big to swallow, such as midwater cichlids, upside-down catfish, and mormyrids. And although ropefish can be trusted with bottom-dwelling cichlids too, territorial cichlids like the *Pelvicachromis pulcher* might pose a distinct threat to these peaceable animals, and a careful eye must be kept on such a community for signs of aggression. Even relatively small cichlids are capable of nipping the fins or damaging the eyes of these inoffensive animals.

Otherwise, like their relatives the bichirs, ropefish are very hardy and resistant to disease. Unfortunately, ropefish have not been bred in captivity.

Ropefish are suitable for a general community aquarium with medium-size, peaceful fish, provided that there are plenty of caves and a soft substrate for them to burrow into. They aren't deep diggers in the same way as spiny eels, so potted plants or even plants with a sturdy root system, such as *Vallisneria* and *Cryptocoryne*, should be fine.

What is more debatable is their inclusion in brackish-water aquaria. In the wild, these fish are primarily found in swampy fresh waters with neutral or slightly acidic conditions, alongside a variety of other freshwater fish. But, like kribensis, they can sometimes be found in river deltas as well, and this has led to their being described as brackish-water fish. While the waters in these places may be salty to the taste, the specific gravity will be very low, less than 1.005. In this regard, ropefish are better thought of as salt-tolerant rather than truly euryhaline brackish-water fishes, and so resemble kribensis, spiny eels, and certain other fishes sometimes recommended for brackish-water tanks.

Two conclusions can be drawn from this. First, ropefish do not need salt and can be kept just fine in a regular freshwater aquarium. And second, they cannot be kept in true brackish aquaria for euryhaline fish like scats or monos. If you are looking for an eel for such a system, look elsewhere.

TRUE EELS—*FAMILY ANGUILLIDAE*

True eels are much more advanced members of the bony-fish lineage than the ropefish, slotting into the family tree somewhere between the archaic teleosts like the arowanas and mormyrids on the one hand, and the advanced perciform fishes on the other. They are physically very distinctive, lacking pelvic fins and having only very small pectorals. Their bodies completely lack scales, instead being covered in a thick layer of mucus (making them practically impossible to hold). True eels are catadromous, spawning at sea but swimming into rivers as juveniles to spend their lives in streams and lakes before returning back to the sea to spawn and then die. Eels from Europe and the eastern coast of the Americas all seem to migrate to the same part of the Atlantic Ocean—an area known as the Sargasso Sea—a journey that may cover several thousand miles, depending on where the fishes spent the freshwater part of their lives.

Their eggs hatch into leptocephalus larvae that are flattened from side to side and distinctly transparent. This larval form will drift for one year on deepwater currents to get to the American coastline or three years to get to Europe. By this time, the larvae have turned into small eels called *elvers,* which swim up rivers to wherever they choose to live. Some remain in estuaries for most of their lives, but many ascend beyond rivers into artificial canals, streams, and seemingly landlocked ditches and lakes.

Several species of *Anguilla* exist, but the two most likely to be seen are the European eel, *Anguilla anguilla,* and the very similar American eel, *A. rostrata.* Both are large, dark, gray-green fishes in their freshwater phase (known as the "yellow eel" stage), and both turn silvery when migrating back downstream and into the sea to spawn (the "silver eel" stage). Neither of these is traded as an ornamental fish, but they are common enough exhibits in public aquaria, and some fishkeepers may be tempted to try them out at home. In fact, they are rather easy fish to obtain, since they're common in all kinds of freshwater bodies, including ponds and canals in suburban areas.

While they are certainly very hardy and tolerant of practically all water conditions, including fresh and brackish waters, they are not really suitable fishes for the home aquarium for many reasons. One is the sheer size of these animals: Although not much longer than a ropefish, true eels are far chunkier and much

Freshwater Eel

Names	Various *Anguilla* spp.
Other names	Freshwater eel, American eel
Origin	Worldwide
Size	Typically in excess of 40 inches (100 cm)
Water conditions	Fresh or brackish water (specific gravity up to 1.010)
Diet	Large invertebrates, fish, chunks of meat, prepared fish foods
Temperament	Solitary, robust carnivore
Availability	Not usually traded but easily collected from the wild
Ease of maintenance	Difficult
Specific problems	Large size and predatory nature; good at escaping from aquaria

Freshwater Eels and Eel-like Fishes

Anguilla rostrata

more powerful. These predators will easily overpower ornamental fish such as goldfish, and even large and robust fish like gar, *Ictalurus* (channel catfish), and carp should only be combined with eels if there is enough space for all the fishes to feel comfortable. And above all else, eels appreciate plenty of cover. They also are largely nocturnal in the wild and remain very nervous if kept in a strongly illuminated aquarium.

As with all the eel-like fishes mentioned elsewhere in this chapter, a soft substrate is important too. Filtration is of secondary importance; while they appreciate clean water, eels are remarkably tolerant animals and seem to do well regardless of the mode of filtration used. The water must be kept reasonably cool, and although a chiller isn't essential, these are not fish to combine with tropical species like cichlids.

The Expert Says...

The arrival of eels in landlocked bodies of water used to be a great mystery to many people, who supposed eels spontaneously generated from worms or rotting vegetation. In fact, elvers are able to travel over land, particularly at night and after heavy rain, slithering like tiny snakes through wet grass and across roads. When the time comes to return to the sea to spawn, the adult eels do the same thing, but not before the fish have grown from a few centimeters to well over a meter (40 inches) in length and become powerful predators of not just invertebrates and fish but even small water birds, frogs, and other creatures, such as earthworms, which they captured during their terrestrial excursions. Eels are in turn eaten by large water birds like herons, predatory mammals including mink and otters, and by humans, some of whom consider eel to be a particularly fine-flavored fish. (In England, jellied eels are a delicacy enjoyed by the London Cockneys in particular, while the Japanese love smoked eel filets.)

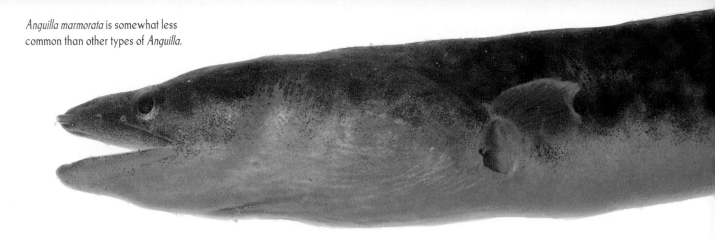

Anguilla marmorata is somewhat less common than other types of *Anguilla.*

Should true eels be kept in a brackish-water aquarium? The short answer is no. Despite being hardy and fairly easy to obtain as native fish go, they don't have much else going for them as pets. As a short-term proposition, small elvers and brackish-water yellow eels might be a possibility, but after a few months or years they are likely to outgrow their quarters and need to move on. In fact, the entire life cycle of the eel can easily span several decades, and cannot be completed if the eel does no return to the sea.

But of course, releasing fish into the wild cannot be recommended for two reasons. First, fishes that haven't experienced the natural environment are likely to be at a disadvantage when it comes to evading predators or tolerating extreme weather conditions. Secondly, it is possible for them to transmit parasites and pathogens from ornamental fish into wild populations. All things considered, if you want a manageable eel for a brackish system, it is probably best to eschew the true eels in favor of their close relatives, the moray eels.

In part because they're large and boring, eels really don't make the best pets for the average aquarist.

FRESHWATER MORAY EELS—*FAMILY MURAENIDAE*

The moray eels are close relatives of the true eels and share the same leptocephalus larval form. They also are equally predatory, although they do tend to be a bit more specialized: The genus *Echidna* has flat, crushing teeth for handling its favored crustacean and molluscan prey, whereas *Muraena* and *Gymnothorax* have more needle-like teeth for catching the small fish and octopus they like to eat.

Various morays are offered for sale to freshwater, brackish, and marine aquarists, but only two species are regularly sold as "freshwater morays" and come close to justifying that name. These are *Echidna rhodochilus* and *Gymnothorax tile*. A third species, *G. polyuranodon*, may be seen occasionally but is more often than not confused with *G. tile*.

Moray eels have earned a reputation for being among the hardiest marine fishes kept in captivity, a trait the brackish-water species share. Since all morays are predatory, it goes without saying that they are not fish to mix with small fish like livebearers or gobies. On the whole, however, these animals are easily maintained, provided that their predatory nature is taken into account. They can be expected to combine well with other individuals of their own species as well as with other fish of comparable size.

In fact, the main problem isn't so much their temperament, which is decidedly mellow, but getting them to feed. Most morays will adapt to dead foods, but they need coaxing. One solution is to stick to live foods: Feeder fish aren't necessary—instead, use chunky invertebrates such as earthworms, *Gammarus* amphipods, and brackish-water river shrimps if you can get them. These last are quite widely traded as food for marine fish and will live indefinitely in a brackish-water aquarium, acting as algae eaters and general scavengers. Small moray eels might take bloodworms, but for the most part they simply will ignore these and other similarly sized invertebrates.

If you don't have a ready supply of live foods, the alternative is to use frozen foods. These can be kept in

Freshwater Moray Eel

Names	*Echidna rhodochilus, Gymnothorax tile*; sometimes other species as well
Other names	Freshwater moray eel
Origin	Tropics, particularly Asia
Size	12 to 24 inches (30 to 60 cm)
Water conditions	Fresh, brackish, and marine
Diet	Large invertebrates, particularly mollusks and crustaceans, and small fish
Temperament	Sociable but predatory
Availability	Rare
Ease of maintenance	Fairly easy
Specific problems	Large size and predatory nature; reluctance to eat dead or prepared foods; sensitivity to some medications and fertilizers; good at escaping from aquaria

Gymnothorax tile

your freezer at home until you need to use them and so are a very handy way to feed species like morays, which need to be fed well but not necessarily every single day. The invertebrate feeders do well with krill and small pieces of clam meat, while the more piscivorous species need varieties that contain whole, small fish. Both kinds of eel usually relish strips of squid and large prawns.

It is also important to note that, while traded as freshwater fishes, morays are really brackish-water fishes, so some salt is appreciated. They will do well at low salt concentrations though, with a specific gravity of 1.005 being acceptable for general maintenance if you want to combine them with hardy plants and salt-tolerant freshwater fish, such as the more placid cichlids. Otherwise, morays can be combined freely with euryhaline brackish-water fishes such as monos, scats, and archerfish, and the salinity can be allowed to change with each water change to more closely mimic their estuarine habitat. Regardless of the aquarium used, it isn't a good idea to mix them with fish that spend most of their time on the bottom of the tank and might fight over hiding spaces, such as catfish or territorial cichlids.

Echidna rhodochilus is the smallest and hardiest of these species, though it's a plain-looking animal. Growing to no more than 1 foot (30 cm) in length, it is basically pink-gray in color with a light peppering of small, cream-colored spots. But being widely traded, inexpensive, and a manageable size, it has much to recommend it to brackish-water aquarists. And while it does need live foods, it will eat invertebrates like shrimps and earthworms. It is a little unpredictable as far as sociability goes, though; some aquarists find they work well in groups, while others have found them to be waspish toward one another. The key is to ensure that each moray has plenty of room, including a cave of its own, and that the fish are brought into the aquarium as youngsters and grow up together.

The chief difficulty in keeping freshwater morays is getting them to feed—while the eels often will adapt to dead foods, they won't take the food without being coaxed.

The second commonly seen species, *Gymnothorax tile*, is generally a lot more amicable—indeed, it is best kept in groups of three or more—but it is significantly larger. It is also a much more attractive fish, with a dramatic patterning of black blotches and spots on a lemon-yellow body with a pale, cream underside. Growing up to 2 feet (60 cm) long in captivity, it is a bigger fish than *Echidna rhodochilus*, but this potential disadvantage is offset by its agreeable nature and the readiness with which it will take to both live and dead foods, making it one of the easiest morays to acclimate to captivity.

The Expert Says...

As with the true eels, moray eels have a complex life cycle that cannot be accommodated in home aquaria, and even the brackish and freshwater species appear to return to the sea to spawn.

All the freshwater moray eels are notably intolerant of the copper-based medications routinely used to treat whitespot and other external parasites of freshwater fish. The obvious workaround is to expose these morays to marine conditions in a quarantine aquarium for a few days (adapting them over the course of 24 hours so as not to shock them). Invariably, this will zap any freshwater parasites on the moray eels while giving you time to use the medications on the main community tank. Naturally, do a full water change afterward to rinse the medication from the system before reintroducing the morays. (If you have the moray eels in a tank with fishes that can tolerate full-strength seawater, then the aquarium salinity can be adjusted as required until the parasites are eliminated.)

Some aquarists believe that all copper-based compounds harm moray eels, perhaps for the same reason that many marine fish and invertebrates react badly to copper-based medicines. For this reason, it is best to avoid using plant fertilizers with copper in them, instead relying on those that contain only iron, such as those designed for use in marine reef aquaria.

SPINY EEL—*FAMILY MASTACEMBELIDAE*

With the exception perhaps of the more serpentine loaches, such as the kuhli loaches, *Pangio* spp., spiny eels are probably the most popular "eels" sold to tropical-fish hobbyists, and they include some very attractive fish that can do well in home aquaria. Coloration ranges from bold black-and-white banding in some of the African species to the red and orange stripes along a gray-black body of the spectacular fire eel, *Mastacembelus erythrotaenia*, from southeastern Asia. Most species are some variety of brown with interesting spots and markings, so even if they don't immediately catch the eye, they are nonetheless attractive fishes.

As their family name suggests, spiny eels bear sharp spines within the dorsal fin, and these can inflict painful wounds and can be equally damaging to nets. Although they are not venomous, it is best to take extra care when handling these fishes. Spiny eels also have mobile snouts that are apparently used to locate prey buried in sand or mud, rather like the whiskers on a catfish.

All spiny eels are a bit more flattened from side to side than true eels or morays, and the females are more deep bodied than the males, so telling the sexes apart is generally pretty straightforward. Despite this, spiny eels have been bred in aquaria only very rarely, and then only with the smaller, more companionable species. And when breeding does occur, it seems to be more by luck than good judgment. The key seems to be getting the water conditions and temperature just right and feeding the eels very well beforehand to bring them into breeding condition. Eggs are laid rather haphazardly around plant stems or floating leaves, and neither parent shows much interest in them afterward. Once the eggs hatch, the fry need very small food to begin with, such as *Artemia* and *Cyclops nauplii*, moving on to tiny worms and insect larvae as they mature.

Maintaining spiny eels is pretty consistent among the species: They need good water quality, soft substrates to burrow into (often completely except for poking their heads out of the sand), plenty of floating plants for shade, and a regular supply of live foods, including insect larvae, small earthworms, and live river shrimp. Some will also adapt to frozen foods, including the small prawns sold for human consumption, but this is by no means guaranteed.

Spiny eels are all predatory toward smaller fishes to some degree, and a foot-long (30-cm) specimen will

Mastacembelus erythrotaenia, the fire eel, is popular, but few aquarists are prepared for its ultimate length of over 3 feet.

Freshwater Eels and Eel-like Fishes

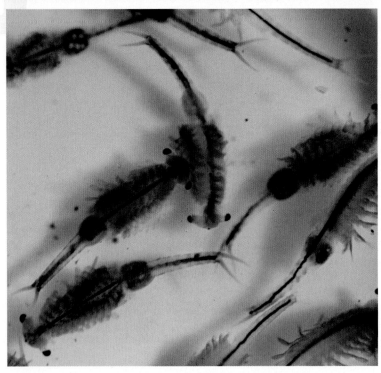

Newborn spiny eels need small fare like *Artemia* or *Cyclops nauplii.*

easily take a fish as large as an adult platy, so it is essential to choose tankmates too large for them to swallow. Most species are peaceful toward dissimilar fish, but can be aggressive toward one another if not given enough space; if you want to keep more than one, introduce them all at the same time and as juveniles, give them each a cave to call their own, and be ready to remove any that are being picked on at the first sign of trouble. In the case of the larger *Mastacembelus* species, such as *M. armatus*, the home aquarist rarely has the luxury of a tank big enough for two or more of these fish, and so they are usually considered to be loner showpiece fish for large community tanks.

All spiny eels are keen on burrowing, and given the chance will spend a great deal of time completely hidden from view. Floating plants help, since these fish will happily burrow upward into the roots and tangled leaves of dense clumps of vegetation, where they will hang out, looking for the small invertebrates they

Spiny Eel

Names	*Mastacembelus* spp. and *Macrognathus* spp.; other genera only very rarely
Other names	Spiny eel
Origin	Tropical Asia and Africa
Size	6 to 36 inches (15 to 90 cm)
Water conditions	Fresh to slightly brackish water
Diet	Invertebrates and small fish
Temperament	Variable; some solitary, others sociable
Availability	Some species quite common
Ease of maintenance	Fairly easy
Specific problems	Rarely adapt to dry foods; need good oxygenation; suicidal in attempts to escape from aquaria; large size; prone to skin infections; intolerant of some medications

The Expert Says...

It is possible to breed the smaller *Macrognathus* species, at least in a generously sized aquarium, although this is rarely done.

particularly like to eat. In fact, this is the best approach to take if you want to see the fishes by day, since a spiny eel not given a soft substrate to burrow into is an unhappy spiny eel indeed. This isn't just from a psychological point of view: They can succumb very rapidly to mysterious skin infections apparently brought about when they scratch themselves while trying to dig into coarse gravel.

As with the other eel-like fishes described in this chapter, these fishes are good at escaping from aquaria. Spiny eels are particularly good at jumping as well as slithering through small cracks between the tank and the hood. A tight-fitting cover should prevent unpleasant accidents, because these fish do not last long out of water, unlike the true eels, swamp eels, and ropefish. Otherwise, spiny eels are basically hardy, provided that you avoid extremes of pH and hardness. (Ideally, aim for a neutral pH and slightly soft to moderately hard water.) They do not do well if the temperature is too high, either: Around 77°F (25°C) is best, and is notably lower than that enjoyed by many tropical fish. In other regards, they are easy to accommodate in a community tank. They will not harass fish they cannot swallow whole. And if looked after well, these are long-lived, intelligent fishes that will overcome their natural shyness and become tame enough to eat from the hand of their keeper, even by day.

Spiny eels are escape artists, so make sure your tank lid is very secure.

Freshwater Eels and Eel-like Fishes

Like the ropefish, spiny eels are not really brackish-water fishes in the sense of being able to adapt to a wide range of salinities. In fact, the majority of species are normally only ever found in fresh water and need not be discussed further here. However, a few commonly traded species do occur in slightly brackish streams and so can make viable residents for a brackish-water aquarium with a specific gravity of 1.005 or less. Several species are imported and seen in tropical fish stores, but of most interest to us are the various species of *Macrognathus* that can be loosely called dwarf spiny eels, since none grows much bigger than 16 inches (30 to 40 cm), and the much larger tire-track eel, *Mastacembelus armatus*.

Some confusion exists over the identity of the dwarf spiny eels usually seen in tropical fish stores. At least three species of *Macrognathus* have been kept on a regular basis by aquarists: *M. aculeatus*, *M. pancalus*, and *M. siamensis*. Of these, the peacock spiny eel, *M. siamensis*, is by far the most commonly seen. It has a pale brown body with a distinctive cream stripe running from behind the eye. The dorsal surface of the fish is vaguely mottled, and up to half a dozen small but prominent black eyespots are found on the dorsal fin close to the tail. In the wild, these fish can reach lengths of about 1 foot (30 cm), but in captivity they tend to remain smaller. Many aquarium books feature this fish but erroneously refer to it as *M. aculeatus*, a quite different fish.

M. aculeatus, the lesser spiny eel, does look rather similar, to be sure, but it has much darker markings on its body. Rather than the simple mottling of *M. siamensis*, these markings consist of thick stripes that slope backward and run all along the body. While the cream-colored stripe and eyespots that *M. siamensis* has are

The tire-track eel, *Mastacembelus armatus*, should interest brackish aquarists with large tanks.

240

Mastacembelus armatus might be small in the store, but it can grow to 3 feet

present in this species too, they are a bit less obvious, tending to be obscured by the much darker markings. *M. aculeatus* has the potential to get a bit bigger than *M. siamensis*, up to almost 16 inches (40 cm) long in the wild, but few if any get to this size in captivity.

The only other *Macrognathus* that is likely to be seen is the barred spiny eel, *M. pancalus*, a delightful fish that rarely grows to more than 6 inches (15 cm) long in captivity and so is eminently suitable for inclusion in small- and medium-size aquaria. The eyespots present on the dorsal fins of the other species are faint or lacking on this species, but the giveaway characteristic is the barred stripe running along the flanks, which gives the fish its common name. Of the three species described here, it is unfortunate that the two species most commonly found in brackish waters in the wild, *M. aculeatus* and *M. pancalus*, are not those most likely to be found in an aquarium store.

The tire-track eel, *Mastacembelus armatus*, is a much more robust fish, capable of getting much bigger (over 3 feet, or 90 cm, long) in the wild and not much less in captivity. Although not actually destructive, its sheer size means that whenever it burrows, it will dislodge pretty much anything in its way, including plants, potted or otherwise. Heaters are also likely to get knocked off the glass if they are too near the substrate. Tire-track eels are surprisingly effective predators that will lunge at small fish and swallow them whole. Even a half-grown specimen can manage small goldfish and livebearers such as platies without much trouble, although they usually avoid spiny fish like cichlids and catfish. That these eels will become such large, predatory fishes isn't always apparent when the purchaser is offered the delicately marked juveniles, typically around 6 to 8 inches (15 to 20 cm) long.

Mastacembelus armatus will tolerate brackish water, but for long-term health, the specific gravity should be kept at 1.005 or less. In the wild, these are primarily freshwater fishes, and they are in no way suited to the sorts of aquaria in which scats and monos do well.

MARBLED SWAMP EEL—*SYNBRANCHUS MARMORATUS*

The swamp eels are closely related to the spiny eels but are far less easy to keep in aquaria. Most swamp eels are aggressive and extremely predatory, and some will even bite an aquarist's hand if it's placed inside the tank! In short, these fish have very little to recommend them as pets.

They are hardy, to be sure, and able to tolerate even quite fetid water for protracted periods by breathing air that they gulp at the surface. In the wild, they are able to burrow in the mud at the bottom of drying ponds and then enter a dormant state known as aestivation to wait for the return of the rains months later. This method of survival in times of drought is strikingly similar to that employed by African lungfishes.

Swamp eels are known to exist in tropical Africa, Asia, Australia, and the Americas, and all look rather similar, with long, eel-like bodies, no pectoral or pelvic fins, minimal dorsal and anal fins, small caudal fins, and a distinctive single gill opening that seemingly runs across the throat "from ear to ear." Most species are rather

Synbranchus marmoratus

Marbled swamp eels are likely to attack anything else in an aquarium, including other eels.

Freshwater Eels and Eel-like Fishes

Marbled Swamp Eel

Name	Synbranchus marmoratus
Other names	Marbled swamp eel
Origin	Tropical, Africa, Australia, and the Americas
Size	At least 40 inches (100 cm)
Water conditions	Fresh and slightly brackish water
Diet	Fish and invertebrates
Temperament	Aggressive and highly predatory
Availability	Rare
Ease of maintenance	Difficult
Specific problems	Aggressive; good at escaping from aquaria; large size

large, commonly 3 feet (1 m) or so long in the wild, and powerfully built. They will attempt to escape from any aquarium they are placed in, which is facilitated by their ability to perform astonishing feats of strength, including forcing off tank covers and aquarium hoods; aquarists keeping these fish frequently use heavy glass instead of plastic, then weigh it down further with bags of sand or even bricks.

Only one species is offered commercially with any frequency, and that is the marbled spiny eel, *S. marmoratus*, from tropical South and Central America. This fish is very widespread and found in a variety of habitats from slightly brackish coastal streams to swiftly flowing rivers, as well as in artificial water bodies including ponds, rice paddies, and canals. In many places, the marbled spiny eel is viewed as a valuable food fish, as it is large, tastes good, and is able to survive out of water indefinitely if kept moist. Small specimens are attractively marked, with a sort of peppery, brown-and-cream pattern, and occasionally find themselves included in shipments of more orthodox ornamental fishes such as tetras and cichlids.

Synbranchus marmoratus grows very rapidly into a real tankbuster, exceeding 3 feet (1 m) in length, and is liable to attack (if not eat) anything else placed in the aquarium with it, including others of its species. It is primarily a freshwater fish but regularly appears in slightly brackish waters; a specific gravity above 1.005 is neither recommended nor necessary. There aren't very many fishes with which it could be combined, so it is best kept in a species tank, in which case adding salt becomes rather a waste of money.

THEMED AQUARIUM: A SOUTHERN INDIA COASTAL STREAM

Spiny eels are probably the best "eels" to create a community tank around, because they are relatively hardy, generally inoffensive toward similarly sized fish of different types, and predatory only toward much smaller fish. Provided that precautions are taken to keep them from escaping, these fish are reasonably easy to keep; the main prerequisites are a sandy substrate for them to burrow into, plenty of floating vegetation up above for shade and cover, and not too much competition at feeding time. Fortunately, such an aquarium works well with fish other than spiny eels as well.

Aplocheilus lineatus is an excellent candidate for a biotope aquarium modeled after southern India.

Freshwater Eels and Eel-like Fishes

The peacock spiny eel makes a good tankmate for many different fish.

Southern India Tank

Theme	Overgrown coastal stream
Specific gravity	1.005
pH and hardness	Neutral pH, medium hardness
Lighting	High
Filtration	External canister filter
Substrate	Silica sand
Planting	Various floating plants, plus Java ferns on logs
Possible fish	Spiny eels, killifish, catfish, cichlids, gobies, glassfish

SPECIES ROSTER

This aquarium idea is based around southern India, a region somewhat overlooked by aquarists but possessing some very nice brackish-water fishes—chiefly, the orange chromide and two of the hardiest and most commonly seen species of killifish, *Aplocheilus dayi* and *A. lineatus*. Less common but nonetheless desirable are the Kerala catfish, *Mystus armatus*, the giant estuarine catfish, *M. gulio*, and the mullet, *Rhinomugil corsula*, usually traded as the false or silver anableps. Many popular brackish-water or salt-tolerant species that are collected from southeastern Asia occur in India as well, including the common glassfish, *Parambassis ranga;* the knight goby, *Stigmatogobius sadanundio;* the climbing perch, *Anabas testudineus;* and various pufferfish, including *Tetraodon fluviatilis* and *Chelonodon patoca.*

Various spiny eels occur alongside these fishes. Of these species, it is the relatively small peacock spiny eel, *Macrognathus aculeatus,* that has the most going for it as a tankmate to some of these fishes. Really the only problem to deal with is feeding, since the more alert and aggressive bottom-feeders are likely to take the lion's share of the food and leave little for the spiny eels. Because of this, the smaller cichlids, *Etroplus maculatus,* and catfish, *Mystus armatus,* which would otherwise seem well suited in terms of size and temperament, should be used sparingly, if at all. If they are included, you must take great care in making sure all the fish get plenty to eat.

On the other hand, the peacock spiny eel would work especially well with the *Aplocheilus* species. and *Parambassis ranga,* since none of these fish feeds at the same level of the aquarium as the spiny eel. The killifish tend to take food at the surface, and could be easily satiated with dry flakes and small pellets most of the time, with live food such as daphnia and bloodworms given as occasional treats. Glassfish are rather pickier and generally ignore dry foods, but they will take frozen food such as *Mysis,* as well as live *Artemia,* daphnia, and insect larvae. Although they will eat food from the bottom of the tank, they prefer to feed in midwater, but even when feeding, they aren't terribly aggressive or greedy, so they usually will leave plenty of leftovers for the spiny eels to find.

The spiny eels should be given plenty of their favorite foods as well, specifically bloodworms, small earthworms, live river shrimp, and frozen tubifex. Gobies, such as *Stigmatogobius sadanundio,* are a possibility

Anabas testudineus will coexist with *M. armatus* just fine.

Egeria densa is one of the best choices for planting these aquariums.

too, since they tend to be rather reticent feeders and prefer to snap up food from midwater rather than the bottom of the tank. The only problem between gobies and spiny eels is likely to be from competition for caves and shelters, and, if the gobies are too small, predation by the spiny eels.

Mastacembelus armatus is an option too, although it does get rather big and would be a distinct threat to the smaller species suggested here, including the killifish and gobies. But it would work well with robust midwater fish such as *Anabas testudineus* and *Etroplus suratensis*, provided it received enough food. The trick is to not overstock the aquarium and to make sure the climbing perch and cichlids are distracted with floating pellets and flakes while you offer the spiny eel its preferred diet of earthworms and small live or frozen shrimps. Once settled in and tame, *Mastacembelus armatus* is quite a hearty eater and shouldn't present too many problems.

Combining this fish with fish that are aggressive or territorial makes much less sense, and although pufferfish seem an attractive contrast to a spiny eel, they don't get along particularly well. Unless you have a specimen that has proven to be docile and trustworthy toward other slow-moving fish, spiny eels and puffers shouldn't be mixed.

PLANTS AND DECOR

Because the burrowing activities of eels of any sort are inimical to rooted plants, the plants suggested here either float at the top of the water, or are not rooted and instead encrust sturdy rocks or bogwood pieces that the spiny eels cannot damage. Fortunately, the relatively low salinities required by an aquarium designed for the fishes described here will be tolerated by a wide variety of aquarium plants, particularly those that do well in hard-water conditions.

Working from the top down, a good choice to create a floating tangle of leaves and stems would be one of the water sprites, *Ceratopteris* spp. Obviously the Indian water sprite, *C. cornuta*, would be ideal, but the closely related common water sprite, *C. thalictroides*, is equally hardy and just as likely to be found in India. Both these ferns demand plenty of light, but once acclimated to an aquarium, they grow rapidly and need regular feedings of plant food to prevent the leaves from turning pale and chlorotic.

A fair substitute for either of these is the common hornwort, *Ceratophyllum demersum*. Again, this is a forgiving plant that tolerates hard water and a little salt, provided that lighting is top notch and it receives adequate fertilization from time to time. Only slightly less desirable are the common pondweed, *Egeria densa*, and the fanworts, *Cabomba* spp. The former can be relied on to do well in aquaria as long as the temperature does not get above 77°F (25°C); the main problem with this species is that it grows very rapidly and forms a thick, dark blanket that will prevent light from getting down to the bottom of the aquarium. While the fish will love this, it isn't good news for other plants, so regular pruning is essential to keep the rampant growth of this species in check. Another problem with *Egeria densa* is the variety of look-alike species, including the

Spiny eels need plenty of free space so they can dig around in the substrate.

coldwater species *Elodea canadensis*, which will not do well in warm water for long.

Cabomba is a fast-growing but fragile plant, and while it works superbly with quiet fish, it is likely to be pecked at by species that are partially vegetarian, such as cichlids and climbing perch. Whichever floating plants you use, it is important that they create regions of shade for the killifish and spiny eels.

To fill out some of the corners, a few nice pieces of bogwood with the encrusting Java fern, *Microsorium pteropus*, attached would fit the bill nicely. This is a singularly hardy plant that will tolerate the shadiness beneath the floating plants and the saltiness of the water. It is unpalatable to most fish, and, being firmly fixed to bogwood or pieces of stone, it rarely gets seriously disturbed by fish.

A key aspect of this aquarium is that it offers both the open sandy substrate the spiny eels enjoy at the bottom of the tank and a more complex planted environment higher up for those fishes that inhabit the upper levels of the aquarium. And since the included plants don't root themselves into the substrate, the tank needs only enough sand for the spiny eels to burrow into comfortably. Depending on the species and how large it is, anything from 1 to 3 inches (3 to 8 cm) might be in order; I recommend starting off at the shallower end of the range with smaller species and adding more sand as the "eels" grow. Because these fish are burrowers, they will agitate the sand and make sure the deeper layers don't become anoxic.

Besides the bogwood and plants, the bottom should be kept as clear as possible to give the spiny eels plenty of space to root around. It is also important that dead spots don't occur in the sand. These will develop under overly large pieces of bogwood or rocks where the spiny eels can't go and into which oxygen cannot otherwise diffuse easily. To be on the safe side, just before each water change lift up any bogwood or rocks, stir the sand underneath them thoroughly, then siphon off the dirty water. Do this regularly and the sand will remain clean indefinitely.

Brackish-Water Pufferfish

By Neale Monks

Pufferfish are among the most popular brackish-water fish, and along with monos, scats, mollies, and Colombian sharks, they are the species most likely to be found in the typical tropical fish store. Endearing little animals, pufferfish are nicely colored and constantly active, and have very expressive faces with bright, alert eyes—a rarity among fish. Once they settle into their new homes, pufferfish make rewarding pets, in large part because of their remarkable intelligence—many puffers quickly learn to recognize their owners and become tame enough to be fed by hand (though it has to be said that puffers' big teeth and strong jaws can easily inflict nasty wounds if handled carelessly).

Puffers are widely distributed throughout the tropics and subtropics, particularly in shallow marine and estuarine habitats where they hunt for their favorite foods: snails, clams, and large crustaceans. Compared to most other fish, puffers are slow swimmers, relying more on their pectoral, dorsal, and anal fins than their tails for propulsion. In fact, most puffers will only use their tail fin to sprint away from potential danger when alarmed. When hunting for food, they cruise slowly over reefs, oyster beds, and other complex habitats

Brackish-Water Pufferfish

Snails can make a tasty treat for some puffers.

and use their large eyes to search for prey. While their swimming mode may be slow, it is extremely subtle, enabling them to scan and explore their habitat with a remarkable degree of precision. Once located, the puffer uses its strong beak to make quick work of its prey, and then swallows it in smaller morsels.

Many pufferfish bear color patterns that allow them to blend in with their surroundings quite well. Like many other fish, they exhibit countershading, with a darker dorsal surface above and a paler ventral surface below. In addition, many puffers are patterned with stripes, spots, and blotches that break up the outline of the fish and make it difficult to see in the rocky, weedy habitats they prefer. If a pufferfish is attacked, it will quickly inflate itself with water and raise hundreds of tiny spines on its body to turn itself into a large, spiky ball that is almost impossible to swallow.

Although they sometimes inflate themselves spontaneously, perhaps to exercise the relevant muscles, pufferfish will otherwise only ever "puff up" when scared, and scaring your pet is obviously not something to be encouraged. Should they inflate themselves with air instead of water, there is the added complication that they cannot always expel the air afterward. Pufferfish inflated with air cannot swim or breathe properly, so acting quickly to remedy the situation is essential. Holding the fish underwater, head upwards, and shaking it gently will help, but do not try to squeeze the air out, as all this will do is damage the internal organs. Veterinarian surgeons can pierce the body cavity and let out the air using a needle, but this is not something that can be safely done at home. Far better is making sure that your puffer does not inflate itself with air. If in doubt, drive the fish into a glass jar underwater and lift it out using that instead of a net.

Many species of pufferfish are toxic, including the notorious fugu puffers eaten by adventurous diners in Japan and elsewhere. While a few predatory fish and sharks will eat pufferfish, most do not, and it is their relative immunity from predation that probably makes them so bold and outgoing, and consequently so entertaining when kept in aquaria. It should also be noted that the poison is inside the fish's tissues, and under normal circumstances cannot seep out into the aquarium.

PUFFERFISH IN THE AQUARIUM

Simply because puffers are commonly sold does not mean they are easy to keep. The biggest single problem with keeping pufferfish is that they are not noted for being tolerant, peaceful fish. In fact, most species are aggressive toward both their own kind and any other fish kept with them. Behavior can vary, of course, and some aquarists have been successful keeping pufferfish in community tanks, but puffers are notoriously unpredictable. Some specimens may be peaceful for months or years, only to become predatory or aggressive seemingly overnight. Other specimens may be consistently peaceful save for a habit of nipping the fins of large or slow-moving tankmates.

One of the problems people have encountered with pufferfish is keeping them entertained. Puffers naturally inhabit complex, dynamic environments, and the aquarist should try to mimic this at home. In a thickly planted tank, pufferfish can be observed to swim up and down every plant, looking over every leaf for snails or shrimps. In strongly brackish aquaria, live plants may not be an option, but plastic ones will be, and in any case, bogwood and rocks could also be used for much the same purpose.

Some aquarists suggest using toys to amuse a captive pufferfish. A small mirror placed outside the tank for an hour or so will give a territorial species something to investigate for a while, and if the mirror is placed in different places each time, so much the better. Another fun toy for most puffers is a feeding rock—a lump of porous stone, such as lava rock, into which prawn or mussel is smeared. The pufferfish can then use its beak to pull out the food just as it would while hunting on a reef or oyster bed. Remove these feeding rocks after twenty minutes or so, as any uneaten food will pollute the aquarium.

Pufferfish also like to dig, and some species even like to bury themselves into the substrate while sleeping, so using sand instead of gravel would be a good idea as well. Because pufferfish inhabit large rivers rather

Puffing Up Puffers

Never try to make your pufferfish "puff," particularly out of water. These fish only inflate themselves when sufficiently scared, which is obviously not a nice thing to do to your pet. Things get worse if they inflate with air—sometimes they are unable to deflate themselves completely, and the poor fish eventually dies because it cannot swim and get water across its gills properly. If it does puff up while out of water (for example, when you net the fish and remove it to a bucket or another aquarium), there really isn't a sure-fire way to deflate it . Holding the fish head-up underwater and shaking it gently can help, but you should certainly never try to squeeze it, which probably would cause fatal internal bleeding. A veterinarian can use a sterilized needle to pierce the body cavity and let out the air, but this requires some degree of skill not to injure the fish, and it cannot be done at home. The best thing to do is simply to make sure the fish cannot inflate itself with air. Instead of netting the fish, drive it into a glass jar or similar container and lift it out of the aquarium still submerged in water.

The most common marine puffer among brackish tanks is the dog-faced puffer.

than ponds, they also expect a certain amount of water movement; couple this with their hearty appetites and intolerance of nitrite and ammonium, and you have a good argument in favor of overfiltering the pufferfish aquarium.

DIET AND DENTISTRY

After their erratic behavior, the second major problem with pufferfish is that they are carnivores that have adapted to eat invertebrates with tough shells, particularly shrimps, crabs, snails, and clams. While pufferfish will happily eat things like bloodworms and mussel meat in aquaria, these soft foods do nothing to wear down their teeth, which are continually growing. Without the right diet, their teeth can grow so long that they prevent the fish from feeding properly and cause it to starve.

Pufferfish therefore need a very specific diet containing shells. Many aquarists find growing pond snails in a spare aquarium or an outdoor pond the ideal solution. One problem is that pufferfish often become lazy in captivity, and will ignore snails if there are tastier morsels like bloodworms and shelled prawns available. This is one good reason not to mix puffers with other species: kept on their own, you don't need to worry that food

Brackish-Water Pufferfish

provided for the other fish is being eaten by the puffer. Moreover, you can encourage the pufferfish to eat the snails by withholding the alternatives.

Besides snails, unshelled shrimp sold for human consumption are another good option for the large pufferfish species. Small pufferfish can be trickier to feed, since apart from small snails, frozen krill and *Mysis* are perhaps the best staple diet for these fish. Soft foods like mussel meat, squid, brine shrimp, and bloodworms are all good treats, but these should not be given too frequently. Some pufferfish seem to enjoy a

Freshwater species like the Amazon puffer have no place in a brackish aquarium.

bit of greens in their diet as well, so offer your fish frozen peas and algae wafers.

While prevention is better than cure, it is often the case that by the time you have taken your new pufferfish home, it will already have overgrown teeth in need of a trim. This is best done by an appropriately trained veterinary surgeon, but short of that, many aquarists have successfully performed this operation at home using nail clippers or cuticle cutters. It is important to sedate the fish first using clove oil. The fish needs to be placed with some of the aquarium water in a container into which clove oil has been added at a concentration of at least four drops per gallon. You may double this concentration for larger or highly active fish, but be aware that an overdose can be fatal. Once sedated, the teeth can be quickly clipped and then the fish is returned to the aquarium and allowed to recover (this normally takes around ten minutes or so).

If you want to try sedating and trimming your puffer's teeth, it's probably a good idea to do a dry run first, sedating it at the lowest concentration of clove oil that works and then immediately reviving the fish without actually doing any dental work. Also, keep in mind that species with teeth that grow very quickly—most infamously *Colomesus asellus*—may require this treatment as often as two to four times a year, regardless of how carefully you feed them.

Also, it is crucial not to overfeed your puffer. Pufferfish tend to overeat in captivity, partly because aquarists offer them much more nutritious food than they would eat in the wild. It is important to remember that pufferfish naturally graze continuously on relatively low-quality food: snails in their shells, whole clams and shrimps, bits of coral, and so on. Owners provide them with higher-quality foods that

FIGURE II.I PUFFERFISH SALT WATER TOLERANCES

Freshwater SG = 1.000	Slightly Brackish SG 1.003 to 1.005	Moderately Brackish SG 1.010 to 1.015	Near to Fully Marine SG 1.015 to 1.018		
				☐	Unsuitable
Colomesus asellus				▨	Short term only
	Tetraodon biocellatus			▨	Tolerated, but not optimal
		Arothron hispidus		■	Optimal
		Chelonodon patoca			
		Colomesus psittacus			
		Takifugu ocellatus			
		Tetraodon fluvialitis			
		Tetraodon nigroviridis			
		Xenopterus naritus			

are not so filling, and the result is that pufferfish seem to be constantly begging for food. An overfed puffer is prone to digestive-tract problems such as constipation, and overfeeding places an unnecessary strain on the aquarium filter. Ideally, feed adult pufferfish once a day, to the point where its belly is gently rounded but not filled to bursting, and remove any uneaten food at once. Juveniles may be fed a little more frequently.

None of the brackish-water puffers is a dedicated piscivore, but neither should any be trusted with smaller tankmates. Some pufferfish are fin nippers as well, though the degree to which this is a problem varies even between different specimens of the same species. Most *Colomesus* species, for example, nip fins only rarely and generally work well in community tanks with fast-moving tankmates, but some specimens will harass tankmates relentlessly and have to be kept alone.

SALINITY

While many of the pufferfish sold to aquarists enjoy brackish conditions, some do not. Of the freshwater species, neither the *Carinotetraodon* dwarf puffers nor any of the freshwater *Tetraodon* species, such as *Tetraodon mbu,* is recommended for inclusion in brackish-water aquaria. Only one freshwater pufferfish is described in this chapter, the South American freshwater puffer, *Colomesus asellus,* because it tolerates slightly brackish water and is peaceful enough to mix with other fish that inhabit low-end brackish water, such as halfbeaks and glassfish. Likewise, most of the species sold as marine fish cannot be acclimated to brackish-water salinities, and so are not discussed here. Some can be, though—most notable are various species of *Arothron* and the South American estuarine puffer, *Colomesus psittacus.*

Even so, there are several strictly brackish-water species of *Tetraodon,* such as *T. biocellatus* and *T. nigroviridis,* and they deserve particular attention from the aspiring and experienced brackish aquarist alike.

DOG-FACED PUFFERFISH—*AROTHRON HISPIDUS*

The dog-faced puffer is a large, sturdy species usually sold as a marine fish, though once in a while batches of juveniles collected in estuaries and seagrass meadows are traded as freshwater fish. It is as handsome, if less immediately showy, as some of the other pufferfish species—brown on the top and sides, cream underneath, and covered with small white or blue spots. Additional stripes may appear along the sides as well, and there is almost always a ring around the base of the pectoral fin.

Dog-faced pufferfish are not particularly picky about water conditions. Even so, while they can be kept in a freshwater aquarium for months at a time, they really need brackish or marine conditions to do well. They are usually sold in the marine section of any local tropical fish store, so they will need to adapt to brackish water. The best approach is to adjust your aquarium to near-marine conditions (a specific gravity of 1.015 or so) before buying the fish. You can then introduce the dog-faced puffer as you would any other new fish, and use water changes over the next few days or weeks to reduce the salinity to the desired level. If you've found a dog-faced puffer being kept in freshwater conditions, then you will need to reduce the salinity in your brackish tank, add the new fish, and then raise the salinity once more over successive water changes. Keeping the aquarium at a fixed salinity over the long term is unnecessary.

Dog-Faced Pufferfish

Name	*Arothron hispidus*
Other names	Dog-faced pufferfish, stars-and-stripes pufferfish, death pufferfish
Origin	Indo-Pacific
Size	Up to 20 inches (50 cm) in the wild; smaller in captivity
Water conditions	Strongly brackish or marine conditions (specific gravity >1.010)
Diet	Chunky invertebrates, particularly snails, clams, and shrimps
Temperament	Territorial, but otherwise a good community fish
Availability	Commonly traded, but relatively expensive
Ease of maintenance	Difficult at first, but easy once settled in
Specific problems	Large size; requires relatively high salinity and excellent water quality

In fact, regularly varying the salinity between brackish and near-marine conditions (i.e., between 1.010 and 1.018) is probably the best way to look after *Arothron hispidus*.

Like most marine fish, dog-faced puffers are intolerant of low oxygen concentrations, so well-filtered water, perhaps with additional aeration, is essential. Otherwise, they are hardy and easy to look after.

The large dog-faced puffer is of course more than capable of eating very small fish, but it is otherwise quite peaceful and only very rarely nips fins. They are somewhat territorial toward one another, but a single specimen will get along well with equally large but peaceful fish including shark catfish, scats, monos, and archerfish. Remember that even in aquaria, this pufferfish can easily exceed 1 foot (30 cm) in length, so even without other fishes to keep them company, you are going to need a large tank and a big filter.

Another neat behavior is the way they use jets of water to blast pits in the sand, presumably to uncover animals like burrowing shrimps and clams. Make sure your aquarium has a sandy substrate if you want to see this fascinating behavior, and let them play hide-and-seek with bits of food. Pufferfish are intelligent, and really enjoy these sorts of games!

Several other brackish-tolerant species of *Arothron* are offered for sale to marine aquarists. *Arothron immaculatus*, *A. manilensis*, and *A. reticularis* are actually quite common in estuaries, mangroves, and seagrass meadows, particularly as juveniles, and can be kept in exactly the same way as *Arothron hispidus*. They do tend to be a bit more aggressive and predatory, so tankmates, if any, should be selected with care.

The Expert Says...

Dog-faced puffers swim at all levels of the aquarium, but one of their more endearing habits is to rest on the substrate with their tails folded along one side of the body, rather like a cat curled up by the fireplace. They are intelligent, lively fish that soon learn to be hand fed (though fingers should be kept well away from their sharp and very strong beak).

Brackish-Water Pufferfish

Arothron hispidus

Some other fairly common relatives of the dog-faced puffer, including *A. reticularis*, can be adapted to a brackish aquarium.

Arothron enjoy a good mix of sand and rocks in their aquaria.

Brackish-Water Pufferfish

MILK-SPOTTED PUFFERFISH—*CHELONODON PATOCA*

The milk-spotted puffer is a large, generally peaceful marine puffer that has a high tolerance for brackish and freshwater conditions. It is quite an attractive species, with a base color of green or light brown and a cream-colored belly marked with a yellowish streak running back along the side of the fish from just under the pectoral fin. There are also four dark bands across the dorsal surface, one between the eyes, two more on the back, and one more at the base of the tail. The trademark milk-colored spots are scattered all across the back and flanks, but aren't particularly bright and so don't have the same visual impact as the dark black spots typical of many *Tetraodon* species.

In many ways, the milk-spotted pufferfish is very similar to the dog-faced puffer and will do well in water with a specific gravity of 1.005 or more. Being a big fish, it needs to be kept in an appropriately sized aquarium, but otherwise places few maintenance demands on the aquarist. As its marine origins would imply, it appreciates hard, alkaline water with plenty of oxygen, but like the dog-faced puffer, it is a remarkably hardy, tolerant fish that poses no real problems to the experienced aquarist.

However, while essentially a peaceful fish, the milk-spotted puffer is not a perfect community fish. In cramped conditions, they will be aggressive toward one another, and perhaps other species of puffer. While milk-spotted puffers are otherwise peaceful, some specimens do become fin nippers, especially as they grow older. If you want to keep multiple specimens of this fish, budget a volume of around 100 gallons (375 liters) per fish; in smaller tanks, keep just one specimen.

Name	*Chelonodon patoca*
Other names	**Milk-spotted pufferfish**
Origin	**Middle East and Indo-Pacific**
Size	**Up to 1 foot (30 cm); smaller in captivity**
Water conditions	**Brackish or marine conditions (specific gravity >1.005)**
Diet	**Chunky invertebrates, particularly snails, clams, and shrimps**
Temperament	**Territorial, but otherwise a good community fish**
Availability	**Rarely traded**
Ease of maintenance	**Fairly easy**
Specific problems	**Large size; fin nipping**

SOUTH AMERICAN FRESHWATER PUFFERFISH—*COLOMESUS ASELLUS*

The South American puffer (SAP) is one of the nicest pufferfish species and certainly among the easier ones to adapt to the community tank. However, it is only rarely found in brackish water and will only just tolerate very slightly brackish water. It is included in this chapter less as a recommendation and more as a contrast with the next fish, the South American estuarine pufferfish, *Colomesus psittacus*—a truly brackish-water fish routinely confused with *C. asellus* by both retailers and the aquarium literature.

South American puffers are very distinctive in appearance. The dorsal surface is green with thick, black

Chelonodon patoca is great for a large, high-salinity brackish tank, but it is very hard to find.

Brackish-Water Pufferfish

South American Puffer

Name	*Colomesus asellus*
Other names	South American puffer, SAP, Amazon puffer
Origin	Brazil, Colombia, Peru
Size	Not usually seen more than 3 inches (8 cm), but reportedly up to 6 inches (15 cm)
Water conditions	Fresh water preferred, but tolerant of slightly brackish (specific gravity <1.005)
Diet	Bloodworms, mosquito larvae, and soft crustaceans such as mysids
Temperament	Usually peaceful, and only infrequently aggressive or a fin nipper
Availability	Common
Ease of maintenance	Easy
Specific problems	Fast-growing teeth

Colomesus asellus

bands, and the underside is white except for a black band that rings the base of the tail. The eyes are golden. As far as behavior goes, these fish are very active indeed, and in the wild they form large, migratory schools that live in rivers and large lakes. In aquaria they exhibit no territoriality at all, and in fact often do best when kept in groups, though it is important not to overcrowd them. A stocking level of around one fish per 20 gallons is about right. South American puffers normally ignore other species, but they are fin nippers, and should only be kept with fast-moving species such as glassfish, halfbeaks, and dwarf cichlids. Livebearers, gobies, and sleepers, on the other hand, are liable to be nipped.

Maintenance of this species is relatively straightforward. It can be kept in anything from a soft and acidic blackwater aquarium to a slightly brackish aquarium, but the one thing it does need is plenty of swimming space. Floating plants are useful, giving this pufferfish something to explore as well as inhibiting its tendency to jump when alarmed. These pufferfish also like to dig, so a substrate of smooth, lime-free sand is useful. While intrinsically nervous, they do become fairly tame, and quickly learn to recognize their keeper.

While Amazon puffers have a distinct preference for bloodworms, it is important to provide them with a varied diet, including foods like snails and unshelled shrimps. Even with the right diet, the South American pufferfish is notorious for having fast-growing teeth, which will need to be trimmed as often as four times a year.

SOUTH AMERICAN ESTUARINE PUFFERFISH—*COLOMESUS PSITTACUS*

Although similar to, and often confused with, *Colomesus asellus*, the South American estuarine puffer, *Colomesus psittacus*, is a much larger fish that needs strongly brackish or marine conditions to do well. Rarely imported deliberately, it has more often been included in shipments of *C. asellus* because it sometimes swims into completely fresh water, particularly when young. Adults, on the other hand, prefer brackish or marine conditions. Unlike *C. asellus*, *C. psittacus* is pale green and has numerous thin, dark bands across its back.

Parrot Puffer

Name	*Colomesus psittacus*
Other names	South American estuarine puffer, parrot puffer
Origin	Atlantic coastline of tropical South America
Size	Up to 16 inches (40 cm)
Water conditions	Strongly brackish or marine conditions (specific gravity above 1.010)
Diet	Chunky invertebrates, particularly snails, clams, and shrimps
Temperament	Usually peaceful
Availability	Rare
Ease of maintenance	Fairly easy
Specific problems	Large size

Brackish-Water Pufferfish

Tetraodon biocellatus

For the most part, treat this fish in the same way as other brackish and marine pufferfish, such as *Arothron hispidus*—given its size, it obviously needs a large, well-filtered aquarium. This fish is neither aggressive nor predatory, though, so it mixes well with other large brackish-water species, including scats and monos.

FIGURE-EIGHT PUFFERFISH—*TETRAODON BIOCELLATUS*

The figure-eight puffer is probably the most widely sold freshwater puffer, and while it seems to occur commonly in freshwater habitats in the wild, it usually does best in slightly brackish water conditions. In some ways, the figure-eight puffer is a very good choice for the aquarist looking to try out a pufferfish at home: it is small, colorful, easy to obtain, generally hardy, and not at all fussy about food. Nevertheless, while many specimens turn out to be good community residents, some become aggressive toward both their own kind and other species. This inconsistency has made figure-eights notorious among fishkeepers— some recommend them as relatively peaceful fish while others characterize them as troublemakers.

Some aquarists advocate taking a conservative approach and keeping figure-eight puffers by themselves. Kept in groups, they establish their own pecking order to be sure, but rarely does the dominant specimen prevent the weaker fish from feeding or swimming around normally. Other aquarists maintain that if you choose a shy, reticent specimen

Figure-Eight puffer

Name	*Tetraodon biocellatus*
Other names	Figure-eight puffer, *Tetraodon steindachneri, Tetraodon palembangensis*
Origin	Southeastern Asia
Size	3 inches (8 cm)
Water conditions	Fresh to moderately brackish water (specific gravity below 1.010, ideally at 1.005)
Diet	Small invertebrates such as snails, mysids, and insect larvae
Temperament	Usually fairly peaceful
Availability	Common
Ease of maintenance	Easy
Specific problems	Unpredictable, with some specimens becoming aggressive fin nippers

from the tank at your dealer's store, the chances are good that you will get a fish that won't turn sociopathic on you. Of course, shy fish can also be sick fish, so taking this approach is not without some risk. Either way, it is crucial to observe your fish once they are home, keeping an eye out for any signs of aggression and acting accordingly.

FUGU PUFFERFISH— *TAKIFUGU OCELLATUS*

The fugu puffer is one of the most attractive pufferfish sold to aquarists, but thus far it has proven to be extremely difficult to keep alive in captivity. Most specimens die within a few weeks or months of purchase. Clearly, aquarists are not providing them with the correct environmental conditions.

Fugu puffers come from the subtropical, southeastern coastline of China, and naturally inhabit waters of varying salinity rather than either completely fresh or marine conditions. This implies that they need lower than average temperatures to do well, with the upper limit being about 64 to 68°F (18 to 20°C). As with other subtropical fish, varying the temperature up and down between summer and winter is probably beneficial as well. And the fact that these are estuarine puffers would suggest that they require a moderate rather than high salinity. Maintaining the aquarium at a specific gravity of 1.010 to 1.015 should be adequate for long-term health, though again, some variation is perhaps useful. Large changes in specific gravity will harm the filter bacteria, but changes of two points on the specific gravity scale, for example from 1.010 to 1.012, will do no harm at all.

Fugu puffers are very active and clearly have a very high metabolism, and it is essential to keep them in the largest possible aquarium. Overfiltering is also a good idea, and these fish should certainly not be kept with gross feeders like scats or any other species likely to result in high levels of nitrogenous waste. Most puffers are intolerant of high concentrations of nitrate, but these puffers are probably even more sensitive than the more commonly traded species, so regular water changes and the use of nitrate-removing filter media is essential. A protein skimmer would be useful, too. And like other subtropical fish, these puffers are sensitive to low oxygen concentrations, particularly during the summer, so it is important to place the aquarium away from direct sunlight, preferably somewhere air conditioned or otherwise kept cool in summer, like a basement.

Fugu

Name	*Takifugu ocellatus*
Other names	Fugu, peacock puffer, orange-spotted puffer
Origin	China, Vietnam, Japan
Size	6 inches (15 cm)
Water conditions	Ideal water conditions unknown, probably mid-strength brackish (specific gravity 1.010)
Diet	Shrimps, snails, clams, small fish, squid
Temperament	Active; predatory but apparently peaceful
Availability	Fairly widely sold and inexpensive
Ease of maintenance	Very difficult
Specific problems	Needs subtropical conditions, so cannot be mixed with standard tropical fish

As far as feeding and behavior go, these fish are much more easily accommodated. They accept all the usual pufferfish foods, such as shrimps and mussels, though they are not beyond eating very small fish. They appear to coexist with their own kind and generally ignore tankmates too large to be viewed as food. The combination of attractive colors and a peaceable character should make this puffer a good aquarium fish, once aquarists have established the correct water chemistry and environmental conditions for long-term health. Besides the fugu puffer, a few other *Takifugu* species are also traded, most notably *T. niphobles* and *T. obscurus*, and while generally larger and hardier, their requirements are otherwise similar.

THE GREEN SPOTTED PUFFERS—*TETRAODON FLUVIATILIS* AND *TETRAODON NIGROVIRIDIS*

Tetraodon fluviatilis and *Tetraodon nigroviridis* are a pair of superficially very similar, medium-size pufferfish that naturally inhabit estuaries, mangroves, and seagrass meadows, and routinely swim between completely fresh water and the sea. They are among the most adaptable and robust of all the puffers, and generally do well in home aquaria.

Tetraodon fluviatilis has frequently been confused with *T. nigroviridis*, and many aquarium books consider them the same species. Since they have identical maintenance requirements, telling them apart is not terribly important, and there is evidence that they can only be differentiated by DNA testing.

Maintaining these fish is very straightforward. Being relative large fish, they need suitably large aquaria, and like all pufferfish, proper filtration and frequent water changes are essential to long-term health. These fish also are sensitive to nitrogenous wastes, and frequent water changes are important. Specimens have been kept in mixed aquaria, but these are not reliable community fish. While youngsters are usually well behaved, they become increasingly territorial and aggressive as they mature. Usually, these puffers are best kept in a single-species aquarium. If you do choose to try combining them with your other brackish-water fish, be prepared to move them if things go wrong!

Green Spotted Puffer

Name	*Tetraodon nigroviridis*
Other names	Green spotted pufferfish, leopard pufferfish, spotted puffer, green puffer, *Tetraodon nigrifilis*
Origin	Southeastern Asia
Size	Up to 5 or 6 Inches (14cm) in the wild; typically around 4 inches (10 cm) in captivity
Water conditions	Prefers mildly brackish to marine conditions (specific gravity 1.010 to 1.018)
Diet	Chunky invertebrates, particularly snails, clams, and shrimps; some plant matter, including algae
Temperament	Aggressive, territorial fish
Availability	Common and inexpensive
Ease of maintenance	Fairly easy
Specific problems	Cannot be mixed safely with other species

Tetraodon nigroviridis

Brackish-Water Pufferfish

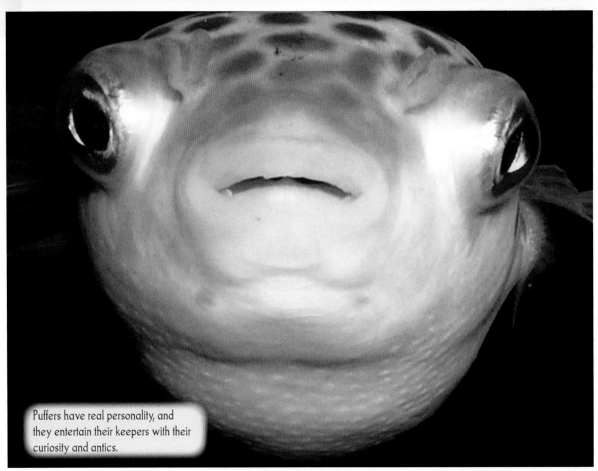

Puffers have real personality, and they entertain their keepers with their curiosity and antics.

Common Spotted Pufferfish

Name	*Tetraodon fluviatilis*
Other names	Spotted pufferfish, green pufferfish, Ceylon pufferfish, topaz pufferfish
Origin	Southeastern Asia
Size	Up to 6 to 7 inches (17 cm) in the wild; smaller in captivity.
Water conditions	Prefers mildly brackish to marine conditions (specific gravity 1.010 to 1.018)
Diet	Chunky invertebrates, particularly snails, clams, and shrimps; some plant matter, including algae
Temperament	Fairly aggressive, but less so than *T. nigroviridis*
Availability	Common and inexpensive
Ease of maintenance	Fairly easy
Specific problems	Unpredictable social behavior: sometimes safe with tankmates, sometimes not.

Although it is difficult to tell *Tetraodon fluviatilis* from *T. nigroviridis*, the former often has reddish eyes, as shown here, and the latter has yellow eyes.

Golden Puffer

Name	*Xenopterus naritus*
Other names	Bronze puffer, golden puffer, *Chonerhinos naritus*
Origin	Burma, Indonesia, Vietnam
Size	8 to 12 inches (20 to 30 cm)
Water conditions	Brackish or marine conditions (specific gravity at or above 1.010)
Diet	Chunky invertebrates, particularly snails, clams, and shrimps
Temperament	The definition of an unsociable fish, they are as nasty to other fish as they are to one another
Availability	Rarely traded
Ease of maintenance	Fairly difficult
Specific problems	Large size; antisocial behavior; often misidentified

BRONZE PUFFERFISH—*XENOPTERUS NARITUS*

The bronze puffer, *Xenopterus naritus*, is a very attractive fish with a very nasty temperament. While it happily eats standard fare like snails and shrimps, it also enjoys biting chunks out of larger fish. Obviously, it is totally unsuitable for the community tank, and is belligerent even to its own kind. While juveniles sometimes get along, adults are extremely hostile toward one another, and invariably end up being kept alone. Overall, this is one pufferfish best avoided by all save the most dedicated hobbyist.

As with other pufferfish, bronze puffers need a roomy, well-filtered aquarium. They are fairly active fish, particularly when young, so swimming space is important. Given their large size, any aquarist planning on keeping a single specimen of this fish (and that really is the only option) will need to set aside a large tank with a good filter. Although it can tolerate fresh water for short periods, this species really needs brackish or marine conditions over the long term.

Bronze puffers can be confused with the strictly freshwater golden puffers of the genus *Auriglobus*. One reliable difference is the color of the belly. *Xenopterus naritus* has a golden belly only a shade lighter than the rest of the body; in contrast, the belly of most species of *Auriglobus* is white and stands in marked contrast to the metallic green of the flanks and back.

While there are many other puffers in the world, brackish aquarists should stick to those discussed in this chapter. Others, like the aggressive Fahaka puffer, might not belong in a brackish tank.

Catfish
By Neale Monks

12

Many aquarists are fanatical about catfish, while others find their interest in these retiring, often ugly, and sometimes highly predatory animals totally inexplicable. But brackish-water aquarists enjoy at least one species that is universally admired: the Colombian shark catfish, *Hexanematichthys seemanni,* a spectacular animal that looks a lot like a real shark but has a peaceful, even gentle disposition and is not at all difficult to keep. Marine aquarists commonly keep a second catfish, the eel catfish, *Plotosus lineatus,* which also does well in brackish water.

These fish represent two important families, the Ariidae and the Plotosidae respectively, which are unique among the catfish because they are primarily marine fish. A third family, the Aspredinidae, consists mostly of inhabitants of the soft, acidic fresh waters of South America, though it includes one subfamily, the Aspredininae. The members of this subfamily routinely occur in the brackish waters of the Orinoco Delta and are able to tolerate marine conditions for extended periods.

Almost all other catfish families are notably intolerant of salt and will not survive in

Catfish

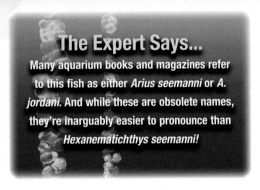
anything beyond slightly brackish water. The hardier members of the Loricariidae, for example *Hypostomus punctatus*, will put up with a little salt in the water, up to a specific gravity of 1.005, but this is far from ideal. Sadly for brackish-water aquarists, there really aren't any algae-eating catfish like plecos, or small housekeepers like *Corydoras*, that do well in brackish water. The few other catfish species that tolerate brackish water are usually large predators of rivers and swamps, and not ideal inhabitants for the home aquarium.

Only two examples from these nonmarine catfish families will be described later in this chapter: the channel catfish of the family Ictaluridae and the estuarine mystus of the family Bagridae.

COLOMBIAN SHARK CATFISH—*HEXANEMATICHTHYS SEEMANNI*

Colombian shark catfish are members of a family of catfish called the Ariidae, named after the largest genus in that family, *Arius*.

This fish is venomous and must be treated with respect. For most people, the venom is mild, no more dangerous than a bee sting, and these fish won't deliberately swim into your hand while cleaning the aquarium or moving rockwork. However, if you handle them carelessly, you might get stung. For anyone sensitive to the venom, the results can be serious enough to require immediate medical attention. Otherwise, placing your hand in water as hot as you can stand will denature the venom and quickly relieve the pain.

The Ariidae are unusual among catfish in being adapted to life in brackish and salt water, and they can be found along the coastlines of every continent except Europe. Consequently they are commonly known as "sea catfish," although a number of other unrelated fish sometimes go by that name as well. All the Ariidae are graceful and powerful swimmers, and most form fast-moving schools that cruise estuaries and coastal

Colombian Catfish

Name	*Hexanematichthys seemanni*
Other names	Colombian shark catfish
Origin	Western coastline of South and Central America
Size	14 inches (35 cm)
Water conditions	Fresh, brackish, and salt water
Diet	Predatory; require a mix of chunky fish, invertebrate foods, and catfish pellets
Temperament	Peaceful schooling fish
Availability	Widely traded and fairly inexpensive
Ease of maintenance	Fairly easy
Specific problems	Large size; must be kept in a group; very predatory; venomous

Hexanematichthys seemanni

Catfish

The Colombian shark catfish can grow much too large for a small aquarium, especially since it should be kept in groups.

waters searching for their prey—primarily small fish and crustaceans. They are somewhat opportunistic feeders, though, and readily eat worms, insect larvae, and any dead animals they come across.

Hexanematichthys seemanni is a fairly large fish, and while normally sold as a juvenile under 4 inches (10 cm) in size, it can grow substantially larger. And since it must be kept in a group, plan on getting a very large aquarium. Although predatory, these are naturally nervous animals— when kept singly, they are very skittish and obviously unhappy, but they do much better in a group of three or more. While they never really become tame in the same way as some other large catfish, they do at least settle down to community life nicely, and when kept with comparably sized species, are tolerant and peaceful.

Ideal tankmates include any of the big, schooling southeastern Asian fish like scats or monos, garpikes, and even the more docile cichlids, such as green chromides. They do not do well with aggressive fish, like territorial cichlids, and of course cannot be trusted with killifish or livebearers, which they will simply view as food.

One of the many nice things about *H. seemanni,* though, is that it is one of the few catfish that is active during the day, and so is always in view.

A peculiar behavior of this fish is the production of sounds. These can be quite loud, normally resembling

The Expert Says...

Another oddity among Colombian shark catfish is their tendency to spend time swimming around in seeming desperation. Sometimes this is manifested as rapid sprints up and down the tank, and at other times the fish simply swim into the stream of water coming out of the filter outlet for hours on end. Many aquarists chalk this up to their migratory instinct, and feel it has to do with keeping mid-size and adult fish in water that is too low in salinity. While the fish will eventually settle down, it is probably a good idea to increase the salinity of the aquarium.

Catfish

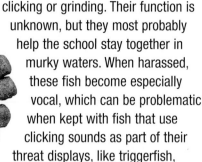

Feeding most catfish is easy—adults and juveniles enjoy good pellet foods.

clicking or grinding. Their function is unknown, but they most probably help the school stay together in murky waters. When harassed, these fish become especially vocal, which can be problematic when kept with fish that use clicking sounds as part of their threat displays, like triggerfish, who can misinterpret the catfish's communication as aggressive behavior. I have watched a blue triggerfish get more and more angry with a school of Colombian shark catfish because of this. At first, the triggerfish merely wanted to shoo the catfish away from his patch, but once the catfish began clicking, the trigger became more agitated and more aggressive. This upset the catfish, which began clicking even more as they started to close up the school for better defense—which of course made the trigger even angrier. While shark catfish are big and robust enough to handle a bit of rough and tumble, they do not enjoy boisterous aquaria and very much like to be left alone.

In addition to a large tank with peaceful tankmates, Colombian shark catfish are not difficult to please. They do not use caves and prefer open water, although some sort of cover, such as artificial roots or bogwood, is appreciated. Gravel, silica sand, or crushed coral are all useable, depending on the needs of the other fish in the aquaria. These fish are not serious burrowers (although they will root around for food) and do not disturb large plants or move piles of sediment around the aquarium. They do like powerful water currents, though, and many specimens spend most of their time swimming in place in front of the filter outlet.

Juveniles are fine in hard, alkaline fresh water for short periods, but they really need slightly brackish water (with a specific gravity of at least 1.002) to do well. As they grow, they need steadily saltier water, and adults eventually need something on the order of half- to full-strength seawater. The exact salinity of the aquarium may vary with each water change; in fact, allowing the variation is probably a good idea, because it mimics their natural estuarine habitats.

Feeding Colombian shark catfish poses few problems. While they will eat live fish such as guppies and goldfish, this isn't the best way to feed them. For one thing, feeder fish can transmit parasites to the catfish. But more importantly, Colombian shark catfish naturally eat a variety of prey, and simply feeding them fish isn't giving them the balanced diet they need. In the wild, crustaceans form a major part of their diet, and Colombian shark catfish relish whole shrimp. Strips of squid and fish also will be taken. Juveniles will readily eat smaller invertebrates, either live or frozen, such as earthworms, bloodworms, brine shrimp, and *Mysis*. Both adults and juveniles enjoy good-quality pellet foods as well.

Other species of shark catfish can be collected from the wild and are particularly popular among Australian aquarists, but they are rarely traded. In general, all the Ariidae are large, predatory fish that must be kept in the same way as *H. seemanni*.

SALTWATER BANJO CATFISHES—*ASPREDO ASPREDO* AND *PLATYSTACUS COTYLEPHORUS*

Banjo catfish of the genus *Bunocephalus* are fairly commonly traded, although they have never become terribly popular. None of these is tolerant of brackish water, and they should only be kept in freshwater aquaria. They are rather small, very retiring, and require copious quantities of small

Banjo catfish like having the bottom of the tank to themselves, so keep them with fishes that swim up higher.

Platystacus cotylephorus

Catfish

Banjo Catfish

Name	Aspredo aspredo, Platystacus cotylephorus
Other names	Banjo catfish, eel-tail banjo catfish
Origin	South America
Size	At least 1 foot (30 cm)
Water conditions	Fresh, brackish, and marine waters
Diet	Live and frozen invertebrates
Temperament	Peaceful
Availability	Rare
Ease of maintenance	Not easy
Specific problems	Require special foods; cannot compete with other bottom-feeders

invertebrates to do well. Also, because they move rather slowly, they tend to lose out during feeding time to more active and aggressive fish in the aquarium. As a result, most don't do very well in community tanks with either more efficient bottom-dwellers, like *Corydoras*, or midwater fish that catch food before it hits the ground, such as angelfish.

However, some brackish-water banjo catfish do exist, and although they are not commonly sold, they are definitely worth looking for. Two that are kept by aquarists are *Aspredo aspredo* and *Platystacus cotylephorus*. Confusingly, the names "whiptail banjo catfish" and "eel-tail banjo catfish" are applied to both species, so when they are sold by these names in tropical fish stores, telling them apart can be difficult. The easiest way to separate them is to look at their coloration: *Aspredo aspredo* is more or less a uniform woody brown, whereas *Platystacus cotylephorus* has a more marbled or mottled appearance.

Maintaining the two species is fortunately rather similar, so even if you cannot distinguish between them, it doesn't really matter. They need a roomy aquarium that fits their relatively large size (though most of their length consists of the very long tail) with plenty of soft sand or peat to burrow into. Neutral to moderately hard, alkaline conditions suit them well. Salinity is not important, and these fish can be kept in fresh water without any problems. Brackish-water aquarists will probably find that a specific gravity of around 1.005 is ideal, as it allows these fish to be combined with suitably sized livebearers and killifish.

It is best to keep these fish with companions that inhabit the top levels of the aquarium, so any food that

The Expert Says...

Over one hundred species are numbered among the Ariidae, but apart from a handful of species kept by Australian aquarists (see Chapter 7), none has established itself as a good aquarium fish. Ambitious aquarists in North America might care to try young specimens of *Arius felis*, the common sea catfish. It requires the same sort of conditions as *Hexanematichthys seemanni* but has less tolerance for fresh water, so juveniles should be kept in at least half-strength seawater. It also needs a larger aquarium, since it is quite a fast-growing fish, reaching its adult size of over 2 feet (60 cm) in two to three years. It also breeds quite readily in captivity.

reaches the substrate is left to the banjo catfish. While these fish prefer live bloodworms and other small invertebrates, they adapt to frozen foods well. Some fish may take catfish pellets, but this shouldn't be taken for granted; watch these fish to make sure they are feeding well, especially when newly introduced to the aquarium.

CHANNEL CATFISH—*ICTALURUS PUNCTATUS*

Channel catfish are much more widely cultivated as food fish than as aquarium fish, but they certainly do well in home aquaria and are not at all shy. The main problem with these fish is their large size—the record length for this species is over 4 feet (130 cm)! Obviously, such big fish demand a huge aquarium with an appropriately sized filter and robust tankmates. In the right aquarium, though, these fish can be very impressive. They can be mixed effectively with large cichlids and gars, for example, and are far less aggressive than *Clarias* catfish, for example. Also, they are active by day and night.

Keeping these fish is easy. They are tolerant of pH and hardness, and can be kept in heated and unheated aquaria alike. They prefer fresh water, but will thrive in brackish water up to a specific gravity of 1.005. Channel catfish are omnivores, and will readily eat catfish pellets, flakes, earthworms, and frozen foods such as bloodworms and *Tubifex*. They also will take strips of fish and squid meat, as well as mussels and other shellfish. It is important not to overfeed these fish; the young are especially active and seem constantly hungry, but they really need no more food than any other predatory fish of their size. Note also that these fish are piscivores, and will happily eat any small fish in the tank, such as livebearers. On the other hand, a mid-size specimen 1 foot (30 cm) long can be trusted with spiny fish, such as cichlids, as small as about half their size.

Other *Ictalurus* species can be found in brackish waters, including *I. furcatus*, the blue channel catfish, which grows even larger than *I. punctatus* and so is less suitable for the home aquarium. A related species, *Ameiurus catus*, known as the white catfish, will also do well in slightly brackish water and does not grow so big—to around 3 feet (95 cm) at most.

Channel Catfish

Name	*Ictalurus punctatus*
Other names	Channel catfish, silver channel catfish
Origin	North America
Size	Up to 52 inches (130 cm)
Water conditions	Prefers fresh water but tolerant of slightly brackish water
Diet	Adaptable omnivore; will eat smaller fish
Temperament	Boisterous
Availability	Common; inexpensive
Ease of maintenance	Easy (despite large size)
Specific problems	Very large; predatory

Catfish

Ictalurus punctatus

Catfish

The white catfish, *Ameiurus catus*, is somewhat smaller than the related channel catfish.

ESTUARINE MYSTUS— *MYSTUS GULIO*

The estuarine mystus is a member of the Bagridae, an Old World family of catfish that resemble the more well-known South American Pimelodidae in form and habit. All the bagrids are predatory, but many are peaceful enough that they adapt well to aquarium life and can be kept in communities of similarly sized fishes. Most are strictly freshwater fish, but many inhabit slightly brackish waters as well. One species, *Mystus gulio*, is almost entirely confined to brackish waters, including mangroves, and in fact does not do well when kept in continuously fresh water. Neutral to moderately hard, alkaline water with a specific gravity of around 1.005 suits *M. gulio* well, but it will not tolerate strongly brackish or marine conditions.

Mystus gulio is not commonly traded and is one of those fishes that turn up unpredictably in aquarium stores specializing in rare and unusual species. However, it is certainly a species to be snapped up when found, because it doesn't grow very large and has the properly robust temperament to do well in a community tank. It is naturally sociable, and so ideally should be kept in small groups.

This is not a demanding fish, and apart from enough room to be able to swim comfortably, it only needs some caves and plants for cover and some soft sand or fine gravel to root around in. It will not uproot sturdy

Catfish

Mystus gulio is a large, predatory catfish that will only be safe with fish of a similar size, such as cichlids and big sleeper gobies.

Estuarine Mystus

Name	*Mystus gulio*
Other names	Estuarine mystus, long-whiskered catfish
Origin	Coastal regions of southern and southeastern Asia
Size	16 inches (40 cm)
Water conditions	Slightly brackish water
Diet	Adaptable omnivore; will eat smaller fish
Temperament	Peaceful schooling fish
Availability	Rare
Ease of maintenance	Easy
Specific problems	Large size; predatory

plants (such as the giant *Vallisneria* species that do well in slightly brackish water), and although it will eat small fish, it ignores suitably sized tankmates. Green chromides, archerfish, and large sleeper gobies all make ideal companions.

STRIPED EEL CATFISH—*PLOTOSUS LINEATUS*

The striped eel catfish is the only catfish routinely kept by marine aquarists, and in addition to the Colombian shark catfish, is the only one that does well in full-strength seawater. The juveniles are adorable: dark, tadpole-like fish with bright, white stripes and a curious disposition that helps them adapt well to aquarium life. They are highly sociable, and in the wild form dense schools consisting of hundreds of individuals.

However, they grow fairly quickly, and as they mature, they become more aggressive toward one another. They also lose some of their attractiveness, turning into a large, brown fish with coffee-colored stripes running along the flanks. Adults tend to hang out in small groups, and as long as the

295

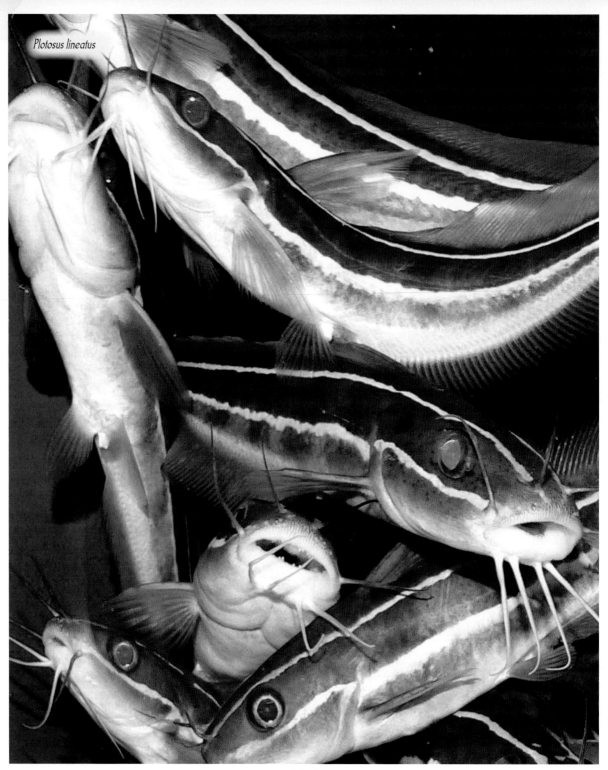

Plotosus lineatus

Striped Eel Catfish

Name	*Plotosus lineatus*
Other names	Striped eel catfish, reef catfish
Origin	Indo-Pacific
Size	1 foot (30 cm)
Water conditions	Primarily marine conditions, though adults will tolerate brackish water
Diet	Adaptable omnivore; will eat smaller fish
Temperament	Peaceful schooling fish when young; territorial as an adult
Availability	Common
Ease of maintenance	Easy
Specific problems	Large size; predatory; venomous

aquarium is roomy and each has a cave or crevice it can call home, a group of three specimens works well in a large community tank.

These fish are almost always sold as marine fish because the juveniles live almost exclusively on coral reefs. However, the adults are somewhat more adaptable, and regularly swim into shallow coastal waters and mangroves, and occasionally into estuaries as well. They will tolerate fresh water for brief periods, but they cannot be adapted to such conditions on a permanent basis. Instead, keep them in strongly brackish aquaria containing fish like scats and monos, and maintain a specific gravity of at least 1.012 (ideally above 1.015).

Plotosus lineatus is not at all picky about food, and while it enjoys live invertebrates such as river shrimp and will eat fish such as small livebearers, it is just as happy with frozen and prepared foods. A good-quality pellet food augmented with strips of fish and squid makes a fine staple diet. To a certain degree, these fish are scavengers, but that doesn't mean they will do well merely on leftovers. Make sure each fish is feeding well, especially as they mature and start developing a pecking order; it is all too easy for the dominant fish to eat most of the food, leaving the other fishes to starve.

The Expert Says...

As with *Hexanematichthys seemanni*, the striped eel catfish bears venomous spines and must be handled with respect. In this case, the venomous spines are in the pectoral and dorsal fins. As with other catfish venoms, if you are stung, immerse the injury in hot water to denature the proteins that make up the venom and reduce the pain. However, the venom is much stronger and more painful than that of other catfish; if stung, you should seek medical attention at once.

Minor Groups and Oddballs

By Neale Monks

13

The vast majority of freshwater fish kept by aquarists are drawn from a very small number of groups, with the carps, characins, catfish, and cichlids at the top of the list, and then the few livebearers, labyrinthfish, and loaches somewhere further down. This reflects quite accurately the actual diversity of freshwater fish: About two-thirds of all known freshwater fish are characins, carps, or catfish. In contrast, the sea is home to many more types of fish, some familiar, like the mackerels and herrings, but others obscure even to marine biologists, such as the deep-sea anglers and oarfish. Consequently, marine fishkeepers get to keep a much greater diversity of fish from many different groups, of which the angelfish, damsels, gobies, surgeonfish, batfish, triggerfish, moray eels, and squirrelfish are just a few of the more popular possibilities.

Since brackish waters occur in habitats where fresh waters meet the sea, it is no surprise that families of fish from both marine and freshwater realms can be found there. Many of these are groups of fish that are diverse and common in the sea, but with only a few species tolerant of brackish or fresh water. Being unfamiliar to aquarists, these are

often called *oddballs*. Some of these oddballs have been covered in depth elsewhere in this book, but a few are either so infrequently seen or so different from anything else that they didn't fit neatly into one of those earlier chapters. This section of the book reviews these oddballs—it really is a list of the weird and the wonderful.

Many of them simply come from families of fish that are otherwise only seen in the sea, like flatfish, pipefish, and damsels. Others are common in fresh, brackish, and marine habitats, but aren't commonly kept by aquarists for one reason or another, like the brackish-water killifish. A rare few come from families that generally have no tolerance for salty water, but in these select cases can be found in slightly brackish as well as fresh water, like the Asian leaffish and the X-ray tetra.

Although some are unquestionably easier to find and maintain than others, they're all interesting fishes with much to recommend them to the discerning aquarist.

Remember, the list of brackish-water fishes available to aquarists is constantly changing, so this chapter cannot possibly cover every oddball out there. Many are imported so rarely that you may go your entire life without ever seeing them for sale, while others make seasonal but regular appearances in dealers' tanks. What follows is a listing of the most frequently seen species, which your local fish shop probably gets in at least once a year. More than likely, you can place a special order for these fish if you so desire.

The experienced aquarist can keep all the fish in this section in an appropriately sized aquarium without any particular difficulties, although a few may need special care for things like feeding and water quality. Do note that the salinity tolerances of many of these species do not overlap: Freshwater lionfish and damselfish, for example, will readily adapt to strongly brackish or marine conditions that would kill X-ray tetras and Asian killifish very quickly.

FRESHWATER SOLE—*ACHIRUS LINEATUS*

The flatfish order, Pleuronectiformes, is an important group for fishermen, but hardly any have become popular with aquarists. Part of the problem is that they don't adapt particularly well to the average community tank, the smaller species at least being rather shy and usually nocturnal. They also prefer live foods, and even if they do get used to frozen foods, they rarely adapt to flakes or pellets. Sadly, the fate of many freshwater flatfish when kept in aquaria is to slowly starve to death. This is a shame, because they are interesting and intelligent fish that make good pets once they settle in.

Achirus lineatus is the most commonly traded "freshwater" sole, even though it is more often found in brackish and marine water. It is a relatively small species, growing to around 4 inches (10 cm) at most in captivity. Thus, despite its predatory nature, it does not pose much of a threat to anything other than very small gobies or livebearers. It is very round, almost circular, and varies in color from olive green to dark brown with a few dark spots and blotches. In the wild, it is not often found in water with a salinity less than half that of normal seawater (a specific gravity of 1.012), although occasionally it will swim into fresh water. Certainly, the aquarist should not keep these fish in aquaria with a specific gravity of only 1.005.

Although basically hardy, these fish do not feed well under the crowded conditions they encounter in tropical fish stores, so many specimens are half-starved by the time the aquarist buys them. As a result, the first priority is often to get them feeding and putting on weight. Live foods make the ideal diet, with small

Like many other flatfishes, *Achirus lineatus* can partially adjust its coloration to camouflage itself.

invertebrates like river shrimp and bloodworms being the most readily available for most aquarists. Tubifex will be taken, but these must be from a clean source to avoid the risk of introducing disease to the aquarium. It is important to feed these fish at dusk and dawn, the times when they are most active. Once they get settled in, frozen foods may be used.

Flatfish need a tank with plenty of open space at the bottom and soft sand to burrow into, and *Achirus lineatus* is no exception. It likes to bury itself under a shallow covering of sand with just its head and eyes poking out. River sand can be used, and its calcareous nature will help buffer the water, but silica sand can be used instead. While ornaments such as bogwood and smooth rocks have their place and will help make the

Freshwater Sole

Name	***Achirus lineatus***
Other names	**Freshwater sole, freshwater flatfish, freshwater flounder, lined sole**
Origin	**Atlantic side of tropical and subtropical Americas**
Size	**4 inches (10 cm)**
Water conditions	**Brackish water with a specific gravity of 1.005 to fully marine conditions**
Diet	**Live foods, frozen bloodworms**
Temperament	**Peaceful, bottom-dwelling predator**
Availability	**Fairly widely traded and inexpensive**
Ease of maintenance	**Quite difficult**
Specific problems	**Needs a quiet tank with a soft substrate and plenty of live food**

If you plan on feeding your flatfish tubifex, make sure they're from a clean source.

other fish in the aquarium feel more secure, they need to be kept toward the edges of the aquarium so the flatfish have plenty of open space in the center. Similarly, plants should not be allowed to encroach onto the sandy area.

Generally speaking, it is best to keep *A. lineatus* only with fish that inhabit the middle and upper levels of the aquarium—they do not compete well with catfish, cichlids, and other more active bottom-dwellers at feeding time. Neither will they be happy in an aquarium with aggressive or nippy fish, such as puffers.

Only a few other freshwater flatfish or freshwater soles are traded. In the United States, the hogchoker sole, *Trinectes fasciatus*, is quite commonly seen, and can be kept in the same way as *Achirus lineatus*. It does get a fair bit bigger though—up to 8 inches (20 cm) long—and it has a more oval rather than circular shape. It can also be distinguished by the lack of pectoral fins and a more salt-and-pepper coloration than *A. lineatus*, although both species can change their coloration to some degree.

Species of *Cynoglossus* from southeastern Asia also might turn up in aquarium stores. These are slow-growing, rather delicate fish that do not readily adapt to frozen foods. They are much more elongated than either *Trinectes fasciatus* or *Achirus lineatus*, and so are commonly called "tongue soles." Not all *Cynoglossus* are brackish-water denizens, though. *Cynoglossus microlepis*, for example, mainly occupies fresh water, whereas *C. bilineatus* inhabits both fresh and brackish water.

Since identifying *Cynoglossus* species (and thus their preferred habitat) is difficult, it is best to use water that is hard and alkaline, but slightly brackish, with a specific gravity of around 1.003. This stands the best chance of being acceptable to all the traded species—it's salty enough for the brackish-water types but not so salty as to be uncomfortable for the freshwater species. Being rather quiet and picky feeders, *Cynoglossus* species are best kept in a species tank, and even then only by experienced aquarists.

Species of *Cynoglossus* are sometimes available, but not all belong in brackish water.

Minor Groups and Oddballs

FOUR-EYED FISH—*ANABLEPS ANABLEPS*

Several species of *Anableps* exist, but only one, *A. anableps*, is at all frequently traded and kept by aquarists. It is primarily a freshwater fish that also inhabits the low-salinity areas of mangroves and estuaries. As such, it is not a fish for high-salinity systems, but rather for use in aquaria with a specific gravity up to 1.005. Generally speaking, the other species of *Anableps* inhabit the same sorts of habitats and must be kept in the same way, but some species occur in marine conditions as well. Regardless of the species, it is important to remember that these are migratory fish that, in the wild, experience continual changes in ambient salinity. Slightly changing salinity with each water change is a good idea to mimic this and make the fish feel more at home.

Anableps are celebrated for their curiously divided eyes, which have a figure-eight shape. The upper lobe is used to see above the water line and the lower lobe below it. This allows the fish to search for food on the

Anableps anableps

The four-eyed fish gets its name from its double-lobed eyes, which can see above and below the fish at the same time.

substrate while quite literally keeping an eye out for predators that might come from above, like herons and sea eagles.

Anableps eat a wide variety of foods, including algae and benthic invertebrates that they collect off the substrate, but they also have a great fondness for insects. In the wild, they almost beach themselves by

Four-Eyed Fish

Name	*Anableps anableps*
Other names	Four-eyed fish, large-scale four-eyed fish
Origin	Atlantic coast of Central and South America
Size	1 foot (30 cm)
Water conditions	Brackish water; specific gravity around 1.005
Diet	Insects and other live invertebrates; frozen foods; flake
Temperament	Peaceful schooling fish
Availability	Not widely traded
Ease of maintenance	Difficult
Specific problems	Large size; must be kept in a group; requires a specially designed aquarium

swimming up sandbanks in pursuit of insects that have fallen onto the surface of the water. Aquatic insects, mosquito larvae and bloodworms in particular, are also readily taken. In captivity, it is not difficult to feed these fish on a mix of frozen invertebrates, vegetarian flake, and live insects as large as crickets. Daphnia, brine shrimp, and clean tubifex worms also may be used to add variety to their diet.

Note that these fish like shallow water, and they will not dive deep to get at food on the bottom of the tank. Use a water depth of no more than 8 inches (20 cm), and build up one part of the tank into a sandbank of some sort—the tank should have a "deep end" and a "shallow end," much like a swimming pool. Given this habitat, the fishes will behave naturally, occasionally diving for food at the deep end, and at other times coming up onto the sandbank to get at any food you leave there. You don't have to use sand, of course; smooth gravel anchored with rocks and bogwood

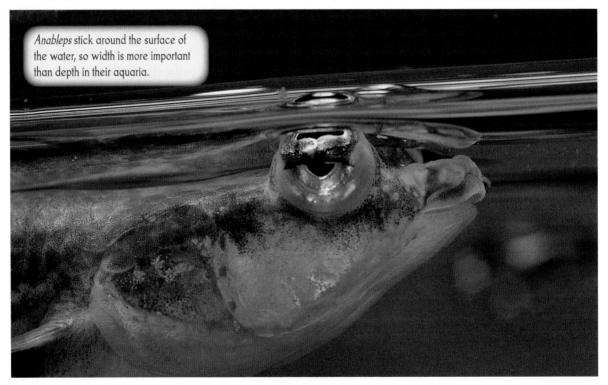

Anableps stick around the surface of the water, so width is more important than depth in their aquaria.

works just as well, as do large, smooth boulders. It is only important that the raised beach area is large enough for the fish to pull themselves onto, and smooth enough that they do not damage themselves in doing so.

Apart from this peculiarly designed aquarium (which, incidentally, would suit mudskippers quite well), *Anableps* also need plenty of heat and humidity. The temperature must be between 75° and 80°F (24° and 27°C), and a tight-fitting hood must be used to keep the humidity high. The hood is useful for another reason, too: These fish are amazingly adept at jumping, and can easily escape from an open aquarium.

These are large, schooling fishes and messy feeders as well, so it is not surprising that a large aquarium with a high-capacity filter is essential. Juveniles will be happy enough in a 4-foot (120-cm) aquarium, but adults will need something larger, around 6 feet (180 cm). Bear in mind though that depth isn't important, so a custom-made aquarium with an emphasis on length and breadth rather than depth is a sensible choice if space is limited. An aquarium 60 inches long and 24 inches broad but only 12 inches deep (150 cm × 60 cm × 30 cm) would be about right, and would allow enough space above the water line for the aquarist to see the fishes' fascinating eyes.

Anableps are livebearers, and breeding is not difficult as long as they are healthy and happy. Gestation takes about two months, after which time the baby fish emerge about as large as a male guppy and ready to feed on tiny live foods such as finely divided flake, daphnia, and brine shrimp. While the parents generally ignore their offspring, it is important to make sure the juveniles can swim freely around the sandbank area and find shelter there if they need to.

ASIAN KILLIFISH—*APLOCHEILUS* SPP.

Killifish are a distinctive component of many brackish-water fish faunas throughout the tropics and subtropics. Two species of *Aplocheilus*, *A. lineatus* and *A. dayi*, are commonly seen in tropical fish stores and warrant inclusion in this list thanks to their widespread occurrences in brackish coastal streams and swamps. *Aplocheilus lineatus* is primarily found in India, whereas *A. dayi* ranges farther east, from Sri Lanka to Malaysia and various Indian and Pacific Ocean islands. Domesticated varieties of *A. lineatus* are quite commonly seen and traded under a number of names such as "golden wonder killifish," and these come in a variety of colors.

These are relatively large killifish, growing to around 4 inches (10 cm) in length, but they are not particularly active. An aquarium around 36 inches (90 cm) long is ideal if you want to keep them in a community setting. Plants and bogwood are essential for providing cover, and unlike some other killifish, these fish tend to swim close to the bottom and like shady corners where they can lurk quietly. These are predatory fish, and they will eat smaller fish given the chance—anything up to the size of a guppy is fair game to these ravenous animals. With fishes of similar size, they are completely peaceful.

Although they like to eat small fish, these killifish also will eat practically any meaty aquarium foods, including bloodworms and small pieces of fish or shrimp. They also will take flake and pellets, as well as live foods such as daphnia and brine shrimp. A slow water flow is preferred, but otherwise they are not picky about water conditions.

Many people keep these fish successfully in freshwater aquaria, and as long as the water is not too soft and acidic, they do not need salt. For the brackish aquarist, the attraction to these fish is that they can be

Aplocheilus lineatus

Sparkling Panchax

Name	Aplocheilus lineatus and A. dayi
Other names	Sparkling panchax, golden wonder panchax, striped panchax (A. lineatus); green panchax, Ceylon panchax (A. dayi)
Origin	Southern and southeastern Asia
Size	4 inches (10 cm)
Water conditions	Slightly brackish water; specific gravity up to 1.005
Diet	Live and frozen invertebrates, flake foods, small fish
Temperament	Peaceful but predatory fish
Availability	Widely traded; inexpensive
Ease of maintenance	Easy
Specific problems	Predatory

kept well with dwarf cichlids such as kribensis and orange chromides, or the larger gobies that need slightly brackish water. They also mix well with large livebearers, such as mollies, though they will eat any livebearer fry they can find.

Both species of *Aplocheilus* breed readily in aquaria. The eggs take around two weeks to hatch and the fry are sufficiently large to be able to eat newly hatched brine shrimp as a first food, later graduating on to daphnia, adult brine shrimp, and finely divided flake. The parents are cannibalistic, though, and should be

Aplocheilus dayi

removed from the breeding tank after they have spawned. These are hardy, long-lived killifish, sometimes living for as long as four years.

COMMON GLASSFISH—*PARAMBASSIS RANGA*

Glassfish are among the most commonly traded brackish-water fish. Sadly, however, the first encounter many aquarists have with them is in a mutilated form known as disco fish or painted glassfish. Fishkeepers

The common glassfish, *Parambassis ranga,* does well in both fresh and slighty brackish water.

Glassfish

Name	Parambassis ranga
Other names	Glassfish, common glassfish, *Chanda ranga*
Origin	Southeastern Asia and Australia
Size	2.5 inches (7 cm)
Water conditions	Suitable in both fresh and slightly brackish aquaria (specific gravity 1.005 or less)
Diet	Live and frozen invertebrates; flake foods; small fish
Temperament	Peaceful fish that likes to be kept in small groups
Availability	Widely traded and inexpensive
Ease of maintenance	Fairly easy
Specific problems	Easily bullied by more aggressive fish; requires live foods

and retailers often think the fish are painted with dye, and assume the process is no more stressful or dangerous than humans coloring their hair, but this is not the case. First, dyeing a fish requires removing its slime coat with an acid bath. Second, these glassfish are not superficially dyed; they are injected with dye. (A study by aquarists in the United Kingdom has shown conclusively that the dye is not on the skin but underneath it, between the skin and the muscles.)

This process of colorizing the fish usually occurs at fish farms in Asia and involves injecting the fluorescent dyes using a hypodermic syringe through the epidermis in several places to build up the desired pattern. Bear in mind that glassfish are small animals, and even a small syringe would be about as traumatic to them as someone sticking a pencil into you. This awful procedure proves immediately fatal for a significant number of the fish, and those that survive are more susceptible to certain diseases, in particular lymphocystis, than are glassfish that have not been dyed.

Thankfully, many fish farms do not dye their fish, and the better aquarium retailers will not stock dyed glassfish, the general consensus among experienced aquarists being that the practice is barbaric and unnecessary.

Healthy glassfish are almost completely transparent except for the eyes and a silvery sac around the internal organs, and the body usually has a slightly yellow or brown tint. Adults, particularly the males, have a blue-white edge to the dorsal and anal fins.

Glassfish must be kept in groups, and single specimens invariably become shy and often pine away. They don't really school, they just like to be among their own kind. They are not picky about water conditions, as long as the aquarium is mature and well filtered, without a trace of nitrite or ammonium. Plants and bogwood are essential, as these fish prefer to make sorties out from some shady nooks rather than stay out in the open all the time. Java ferns are ideal, being tolerant of slightly brackish water, but other plants can be used as well. Plastic plants make perfectly acceptable alternatives.

These fish like sunshine, and their aquarium should be placed so that it receives a bit of direct sunlight each day. Besides encouraging plant growth, sunlight seems to be a key trigger to spawning behavior. The other triggering factor is temperature. While 75°F (25°C) is fine for regular maintenance, increasing the

These fish were cruelly injected with colored dyes. Responsible aquarists do not support this practice by buying such animals.

temperature of the aquarium to 84°F (28°C) is necessary for spawning.

After spawning, the parents scatter the eggs among the plants and exhibit no brood care at all, so it is best to remove the eggs to make sure other fish don't eat them. Once hatched, the baby fish are not difficult to raise, although they are rather small and need infusoria rather than newly hatched brine shrimp for their first few meals.

Glassfish are not difficult to mix with other similarly quiet fish. Ideal companions include gobies, flatfish, pipefish, and halfbeaks. They will not do well with boisterous fish such as livebearers, which will hog the food, or with aggressive fish like cichlids. The main difficulty with keeping glassfish in a community setting is making sure they get enough food, so it is best to choose companions that feed on different foods (such as algae), at night, or at some level of the aquarium other than where the glassfish eat.

Glassfish prefer live foods, although frozen invertebrates such as bloodworms will do fine for a staple diet. While some specimens happily eat flake, it does not seem to be the perfect diet for them; live foods are especially essential for breeding.

As noted earlier, painted glassfish are prone to lymphocystis, an unattractive but not normally life-threatening condition in which cream-colored tumors appear on the fins and body of the fish. There really isn't much that can be done to cure lymphocystis, but fortunately it isn't very contagious either, so it isn't usually much of a problem. Good water management and a balanced diet usually allow the fish to recover by themselves. (Don't expect a sudden improvement—lymphocystis can take months, even years, to clear up.)

Whitespot is also quite common among newly imported glassfish, and because these fish are transparent, it is easy to see and very unsightly, looking as if the infected fish have been dusted with sugar. Fortunately, glassfish respond well to commercial whitespot treatments, but make sure to get one that can be used in brackish or salt water. Alternatively, just up the salinity to kill off the parasites.

A few other species of glassfish are occasionally sold in aquarium stores. *Parambassis baculis* is an Indian species very similar to *P. ranga*—in fact, the two species are probably imported as the common glassfish all the time. For all practical purposes, maintenance of these two species is identical (not surprising, since they might even be the same species).

Parambassis wolffii is a larger version of the common glassfish that grows up to 8 inches (20 cm) long in the wild. In captivity, it tends to stay much smaller, though it's still bigger than the common glassfish. Being a bit bigger, its diet includes larger live foods; in the wild, this includes small fish, but in the aquarium, bloodworms, river shrimp, and small earthworms are adequate. In all other regards, *P. wolffii* requires the same sorts of living conditions as the common glassfish.

Another large but more bizarre-looking variety is the hump-headed glassfish, *P. pulcinella*. It isn't a brackish fish, though, and must be kept in neutral fresh water. Finally, the filamentous glassfish, *Gymnochanda filamentosa*, is one species eagerly sought out by aquarists but sadly rather rarely seen and difficult to keep. It grows to about the same size as the common glassfish and needs the same sort of aquarium and diet, but the dramatic extensions to the dorsal and anal fins of the males set it apart.

Other types of glassfish, like *Parambassis baculis*, are occasionally available.

NORTH AMERICAN KILLIFISH—*JORDANELLA FLORIDAE*

There are many types of North American killifish, but unless you go out and collect them yourself, you are unlikely to find them. One exception to this is *Jordanella floridae*, which, thanks to the alternating rows of red and blue dots along its flanks, has been likened to the American flag and therefore called the flagfish. Many consider it a pupfish rather than a killie, but whatever you call them, these fish are otherwise very easy to keep and breed, and among the best fish for aquarists looking to try out killies.

The flagfish is widely bred on fish farms in America and Asia, and is generally inexpensive. It is also very hardy and adapts far better to life in a community tank than do many other killifish. The flagfish will eat all sorts of aquarium foods, including flake, bloodworms, and daphnia, but a crucial element of its diet is algae. While vegetarian flake foods, such as those used with mollies, can make an excellent staple, it is also a good idea to allow algae to grow in some parts of the aquarium. This is especially true if you want to breed flagfish—live algae is so important, you might as well consider it the required conditioning food for this species.

Other than their requirement for algae, the only other issue with flagfish is territoriality—males of this species can be quite intolerant of one another. In a small aquarium, it is best to keep only a single male, but in a larger tank, it may be possible to keep more than one if ample hiding places are provided. Having said that, keep an eye out for signs of stress in subdominant males, such as reticence at feeding time, ragged fins, and loss of color.

Because they are territorial, it is best not to keep American flagfish with dwarf cichlids unless plenty of room is available. In a sufficiently large tank, flagfish can sometimes be kept with robust fish that stay at the top level of the aquarium, such as mollies, but don't bank on it—be prepared to remove these fishes if the flagfish turn nasty.

These killifish like planted aquaria (use live or plastic plants, it doesn't matter) and plenty of caves and bogwood. In the wild, these fish have numerous predators, so they don't feel secure without a nearby hiding place. As with most other shy fish, the more cover they have, the more secure they feel and the more time they will spend swimming in the open. They are not picky about water conditions, and neutral or slightly hard water

American Flagfish

Name	*Jordanella floridae*
Other names	American flagfish, Florida flagfish
Origin	North America
Size	2 inches (6 cm)
Water conditions	Fresh or slightly brackish water; specific gravity up to 1.005
Diet	Small live foods; frozen invertebrates; flakes; algae
Temperament	Mostly peaceful but sometimes territorial
Availability	Common
Ease of maintenance	Easy
Specific problems	Males can be very aggressive

Male *Jordanella floridae*

is acceptable, as is a specific gravity up to 1.005. And while they will tolerate room temperature, these fish have a subtropical distribution and do much better at a temperature of around 75°F (24°C).

A pair of these fish will be perfectly content in a tank 20 to 24 inches (50 to 60 cm) long, and they can be bred easily. They scatter a very few rather large eggs on floating plants, then ignore them, and the aquarist should have no problems raising the fry; once they hatch, the baby fish are quite large enough to handle small live foods like newly hatched brine shrimp, as well as commercially prepared juvenile-fish foods.

A closely related species is *Garmanella pulchra*, often referred to as *Jordanella pulchra* and known as the Yucatan pupfish in the aquarium hobby. It can be kept in the same way as the flagfish. Numerous other brackish-water killifish from the Americas exist but are rarely seen by hobbyists. Species of *Cyprinodon* and *Fundulus*, for example, are almost never traded commercially, but can be quite easily obtained from the wild in the United States. One species, the sheepshead minnow, *Cyprinodon variegatus*, has some popularity as

You might be able to find *Cyprinodon variegatus* by mail order through scientific suppliers.

317

a lab animal and can be obtained by mail order through scientific suppliers. It prefers brackish and marine conditions, and needs a well-filtered aquarium with hard, alkaline water to do well. A substrate of beach sand and broken seashells is ideal, serving to buffer the water and replicate their natural habitat nicely. Like the flagfish, this fish likes warmth, and a temperature of 75°F (24°C) is essential.

WRESTLING HALFBEAK—*DERMOGENYS PUSILLA*

Halfbeaks are quite commonly traded, despite a reputation for being delicate and difficult to look after. For one thing, they are picky feeders and prefer small live foods such as insect larvae. Once settled in, however, they usually take good-quality flake foods as well. They are also rather nervous, and are unable to handle boisterous or aggressive tankmates. Also, while halfbeaks are livebearers, they are not as easy to breed

Dermogenys pusilla

as, say, guppies, and the parents will eat the young if they are not quickly removed. Finally, halfbeaks are inveterate jumpers; unless the aquarium is covered, it is the fate of many specimens to make suicidal leaps out of the tank and onto the floor below.

The most commonly seen species of halfbeak is *Dermogenys pusilla*, known as the wrestling halfbeak. The name comes from the fighting behavior of the males, which might look fierce but is really quite harmless. Halfbeaks like to swim about in schools of five or more individuals, but to stop the males from pestering the females too much, it is wise to keep two or three females to every male.

Males are easily distinguished by their modified anal fin, which forms an andropodium, a structure similar in form and function to the gonopodium of guppies and mollies. Breeding does not require much effort as long as the adult fish are well fed and water conditions are optimal—the only snag is the cannibalism adult fish often exhibit toward the fry. Since they never produce very many offspring (a few dozen at best), try to remove the fry as soon you see them. A thick tangle of floating plants goes a long way toward giving the baby fish some protection for a day or two before you can get a chance to remove them to safety. They will be big enough to feed happily on finely divided flake, newly hatched brine shrimp, and other small foods.

Dermogenys pusilla appreciate warmth, so the tank should be heated to at least 75°F (24°C). They are not tolerant of poor water quality, and the aquarist should take great care that the water is well filtered and regularly changed. A filter that produces a moderate current is useful, because these fish like to orient themselves into the current. For this reason, a power filter is best. While they do appreciate slightly brackish water, they do not like strongly brackish water and cannot tolerate fully marine conditions. Instead, keep the specific gravity around 1.002 to 1.005.

On the whole, wrestling halfbeaks are not fussy about pH or hardness, but they do not do well with sudden changes in water parameters. Any changes to salinity, pH, hardness, or temperature must be done very gradually. This is especially important when carrying out water changes and when adapting freshwater stock to a brackish-water aquarium.

The best aquarium for *D. pusilla* (and indeed, any of the other halfbeaks) is one that is large enough for

Wrestling Halfbeak

Name	*Dermogenys pusilla*
Other names	Wrestling halfbeak
Origin	Southeastern Asia
Size	2 inches (6 cm)
Water conditions	Slightly brackish water; specific gravity around 1.005
Diet	Primarily small, live foods, such as insects taken at the surface
Temperament	Peaceful to other fish but males aggressive to each other
Availability	Fairly widely traded and inexpensive
Ease of maintenance	Fairly easy
Specific problems	Not as hardy as other livebearers; require live foods

Wrestling halfbeaks will do well in slightly brackish water.

While Celebes halfbeaks will tolerate slightly brackish water, they should only be kept in soft, slightly acidic fresh water.

them to swim freely at the surface without any risk of damaging their jaws against the glass. An aquarium at least 1 foot (30 cm) wide should be the absolute minimum, and the ideal aquarium is 18 to 24 inches (45 to 60 cm) wide. On the other hand, depth is immaterial; generally, these fish stay close to the surface. They will make sojourns down to the middle part of the tank, but rarely will they go as far down as the substrate, so they aren't bothered about what type of substrate you use. Floating plants are useful, because they give the fish a feeling of security and inhibit their leaping to some degree.

Tankmates should be chosen carefully from among those species that occupy the middle and lower levels of the aquarium and lack any sort of aggressive behavior. Guppies and mollies work well, as do the smaller gobies like bumblebees. *Dermogenys pusilla* are also a good choice for combining with slow feeders such as pipefish and small spiny eels: They will greedily snap at live and flake foods at the surface but will ignore anything that drops into the lower levels of the tank. This will give fish in the middle and bottom levels of the tank time to feed at their leisure.

Minor Groups and Oddballs

A second species of halfbeak—*Nomorhamphus liemi*, known as the Celebes halfbeak—is also fairly common. It is a strictly freshwater fish, though, and should not be kept in the brackish-water aquarium.

GAR—*LEPISOSTEUS* SPP.

Gars are handsome, archaic-looking fish that have periodically enjoyed great popularity with aquarists interested in peaceful predators. None of the species is small, as even the smaller ones exceed 2 feet (60 cm)

Lepisosteus oculatus

in captivity. Therefore, these are really only suitable for fishkeepers with a very large aquarium—at least 6 feet (180 cm) long for adults—at their disposal.

Offsetting the demand for a larger aquarium is the fact that these are remarkably peaceful, tolerant fishes that can be combined with big cichlids, sleeper gobies, and catfish without any problems. Unlike many of the other tankbusters, these big fish swim around at the top of the aquarium, are always on display, and do not compete with benthic fish for caves or space. Territorial fish that stick to deeper parts of the aquarium, such as cichlids, usually ignore gars if the tank is sufficiently deep. All in all, these are excellent fish for the robust community tank.

Aquarists generally keep the spotted gar, *Lepisosteus oculatus*, or the long-nosed gar, *L. osseus*. The two fish have a similar pattern and coloration but can be easily distinguished by the length and shape of the jaws: The long-nosed garpike has long, needle-thin jaws almost like forceps, while in contrast, the jaws of the spotted garpike are shorter, robust, and have a rather triangular shape (like the jaws of an alligator when viewed from above).

In the wild, both feed primarily on fish such as minnows and livebearers, but in captivity, young specimens usually adapt quickly to a mixed diet of cichlid pellets, frozen lancefish, strips of squid and shrimp, large crustaceans such as prawns and krill, and live foods such as earthworms. Small pieces of oily fish like mackerel and salmon are also relished, and will tempt stubborn older fish that refuse other dead foods. Foods like these will pollute the water quickly, so anything not eaten at once must be removed immediately. Occasionally, older fish can be reticent about eating anything other than live foods, usually because they do not recognize pellets or frozen shrimps as food, not because they find

Gar

Name	*Lepisosteus* spp.
Other names	Gar, garpike
Origin	North and Central America; Cuba
Size	Typically 2 to 3 feet (60 to 90 cm); some species up to 10 feet (3 m) long!
Water conditions	Fresh or slightly brackish water; specific gravity up to 1.010
Diet	Live foods readily taken, but frozen foods, strips of fish and squid, and even floating pellets will be greedily accepted
Temperament	Peaceful and sociable among themselves, but highly predatory
Availability	Fairly widely traded and inexpensive
Ease of maintenance	Easy
Specific problems	Large size

them unpalatable. Attaching the food loosely to a piece of cotton and dangling it in front of the gar will elicit a strike, and once they have the food in their mouths, they usually eat it happily enough.

Besides a very large aquarium, gar do not place any difficult demands on the aquarist. They can jump very well, so a cover of some sort is essential. Because they are air breathers, however, it is also important to make sure there is a gap between the cover and the surface of the water; otherwise, they will bump their snouts when they come up for air. Filtration must be appropriate for fish of their size.

Gar will tolerate a wide variety of water conditions from soft and acidic to brackish, and some species—not including *L. oculatus* or *L. osseus*—commonly inhabit salt water as well. Generally speaking, *L. oculatus* and *L. osseus* are best kept in brackish-water aquaria with a specific gravity of less than 1.010. Both species are fairly sociable and should be kept at least in pairs. Breeding in captivity is unknown.

FRESHWATER PIPEFISH—*MICROPHIS BRACHYURUS*

Pipefish are closely related to seahorses, and aquarists who would like to try them but don't have experience with marine aquaria can find freshwater pipefish a great alternative. They have the same head as a seahorse, and the same slow, deliberate mode of swimming, but instead of being vertical like seahorses, they are elongated, almost snake-like animals. And like seahorses, it is the male that carries the eggs, although instead of into a pouch, the female places the eggs onto a sticky patch on the male's underside.

Although these fish are not fussy about salinity (a specific gravity of 1.005 or more is ideal for long-term maintenance), they do need hard, alkaline water conditions. This won't be

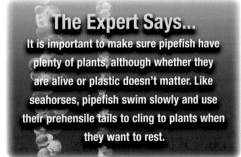

The Expert Says...

It is important to make sure pipefish have plenty of plants, although whether they are alive or plastic doesn't matter. Like seahorses, pipefish swim slowly and use their prehensile tails to cling to plants when they want to rest.

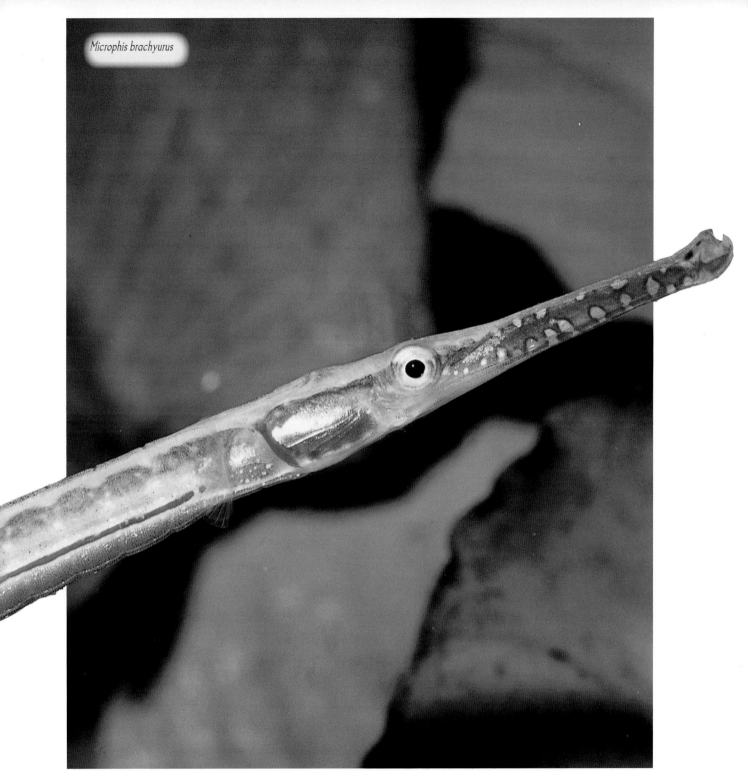

Microphis brachyurus

Freshwater Pipefish

Name	*Microphis brachyurus*
Other names	Freshwater pipefish
Origin	Throughout the tropics
Size	8 inches (20 cm)
Water conditions	Fresh, brackish, and marine waters
Diet	Live foods such as brine shrimp, daphnia, and mosquito larvae
Temperament	Peaceful
Availability	Rarely traded
Ease of maintenance	Difficult
Specific problems	Needs live foods and a very peaceful aquarium

difficult to ensure in a brackish-water aquarium if you use a proper marine-aquarium salt mix.

These fish are not tolerant of lapses in water quality, so good filtration is important. Ideally, they should only be kept in a stable and mature aquarium.

The only real problem with freshwater pipefish is their need for large quantities of small, live foods. Brine shrimp, daphnia, bloodworms, and small aquatic insects are ideal, and the larger specimens will take river shrimps and livebearer fry as well. It is possible to wean them onto frozen foods, such as mysid shrimps, but they will not take pellets or flake. Neither do they cope with greedy or aggressive fish, so they are best kept by themselves or with other slow-moving fish, like small gobies and flounders.

Various subspecies of *M. brachyurus* are known, of which *M. brachyurus aculeatus*, the West African freshwater pipefish, is the most frequently traded. A subspecies, *M. brachyurus lineatus*, is found only in Florida, but it is becoming increasingly rare and should not be collected.

ASIAN LEAFFISH—*NANDUS NANDUS*

Asian leaffish are nocturnal, cichlid-like fish that, as their name suggests, have a mottled brown appearance that strongly resembles a dead leaf. In the wild, they hide in the vegetation, emerging only to snap up any small fish or invertebrate that gets too close to their capacious mouths. Like other ambush predators kept by aquarists, such as pike cichlids and freshwater lionfish, the main problem in keeping these fish is supplying them with sufficient quantities of live foods. In the case of the Asian leaffish, the fact that this fish needs live foods does not mean it will only eat feeder guppies and goldfish—it will also take large insects, bloodworms, earthworms, river shrimps, and other large invertebrates. In a quiet tank, it also can be adapted to certain frozen foods such as prawns, bloodworms, and mysid shrimps, although this will take some time. At least to begin with, newly imported leaffish can be expected to take only live foods.

In the wild, the Asian leaffish is primarily found in fresh, not brackish, water, but many aquarists have found that in captivity, it does best with a little salt added to the water. Therefore, it makes a suitable

There are several types of leaffish, some brackish, some not, and they are so named for their resemblance to a leaf.

inclusion in a low-salinity brackish-water community with other robust fish. It needs a cave or other hideaway, and a well-planted aquarium—dense stands of giant *Vallisneria* and large Java ferns attached to pieces of bogwood are ideal. If plants are used, strong lighting is necessary, but until the plants grow sufficiently to provide adequate shade, the Asian leaffish will stay close to the plants or in its cave. On the other hand, if plastic plants are used, then only dim lighting is necessary, and this will encourage the fish to be a bit more outgoing during the day.

Although highly predatory, this fish is not at all aggressive and will mix well with other peaceful fish of comparable size, such as Siamese tigerfish, spiny eels, and ropefish. While they are commonly kept alone, they also can be kept in small groups, and they have on occasion bred in captivity. Distinguishing

Asian Leaffish

Name	*Nandus nandus*
Other names	Asian leaffish
Origin	Southeastern Asia
Size	Up to 8 inches (20 cm)
Water conditions	Fresh or slightly brackish water; specific gravity up to 1.005
Diet	Live foods including small fish, but also mosquito larvae, bloodworms, river shrimps, and brine shrimp
Temperament	Peaceful but predatory
Availability	Rarely traded
Ease of maintenance	Difficult
Specific problems	Needs live foods and a peaceful, well-planted aquarium

the two sexes is difficult, and practically impossible with young specimens. Aquarists interested in spawning these fish have no choice but to secure a small group of them and then allow them to pair off naturally. Since they are rather large fish, this means using a big aquarium: A tank 6 feet (180 cm) long is about right. Each fish will need its own cave or thicket of plants to feel secure and to avoid territorial squabbles.

FRESHWATER DEMOISELLE—*NEOPOMACENTRUS TAENIURUS*

Damselfish are closely related to cichlids and share many of the same characteristics. They are alert, bold fish that adapt well to captivity and exhibit a similarly high degree of parental care. Like cichlids, they are generally hardy and resistant to disease, and they can be expected to live a long time in a well-maintained aquarium. While the vast majority of damselfish are found in the sea, several species of damselfish enter brackish and fresh waters. These are occasionally traded and make exceptionally interesting subjects for the experienced aquarist.

Neopomacentrus taeniurus is known as the freshwater demoiselle, or damsel, and is probably the most commonly seen species of freshwater damsel. Juveniles have a dusky brown body, similar in shape to the green chromide damselfish, *Chromis viridis*, including the V-shaped tail with extensions to the top and bottom rather like those on lyre-tail mollies. The dorsal and anal fins are the same color as the body except at the back edges, which are yellow. The tail fin is also yellow, except for the top and bottom extensions, which are dark. A little yellow is apparent on the pectoral fins as well, but not on the pelvic fins. Some white spots are scattered on the dorsal and anal fin and on the caudal peduncle, but otherwise the body is uniformly colored. Adults have the same basic coloration, but the yellow fades away completely while the dark bands on the top and bottom of the tail fin become much bolder.

Neopomacentrus taeniurus

Minor Groups and Oddballs

Neopomacentrus taeniurus is widely distributed from East Africa to Australia and New Caledonia. It is always found in shallow, coastal habitats, such as estuaries, mangroves, and harbors, rather than the coral reefs that most other damselfish prefer. While it is found in fresh water, it is never found more than a few miles inland, and in captivity is best kept in brackish water.

In the wild, at least, this fish breeds in brackish water, although it is presumed that the juveniles migrate to the sea, where they feed on algae and plankton.

Keeping *N. taeniurus* presents no real difficulties for the experienced aquarist, as these fish are intrinsically hardy and no more difficult to look after than comparably sized cichlids. They do not tolerate poor water management, though, so good filtration and oxygenation are essential. Beyond that, they will adapt to any brackish-water aquarium with a specific gravity of at least 1.005.

Like other damselfish, these scrappy, territorial fish must be given adequate space. The back of the aquarium should be filled with rocks, artificial caves, and bogwood, with perhaps a few plastic plants here and there as well. This will provide each damselfish with its own territory. Even then, seemingly peaceful fish can suddenly turn aggressive once they become sexually mature, so the best strategy is to introduce two or three juvenile damsels into a 4-foot (120-cm) or bigger aquarium simultaneously and allow them to mature together. Keep an eye out for squabbling; some is bound to occur, but it is only dangerous if subdominant fish are prevented from feeding, or regularly sustain damage to their scales and fins.

Larger, nonpredatory fish, such as tilapia, can have a moderating effect on aggressive damsels, encouraging them to stay close to their hiding places and away from the territories of the other damsels in the tank with them. Really, *N. taeniurus* mixes well with any of the more robust brackish-water species, including scats, archerfish, and monos. It is not a good idea to keep them with very placid fish, such as flatfish or pipefish, as those will lose out at feeding time.

Another Indo-Pacific species, *Pomacentrus taeniometopon*, is known as the brackish damselfish. In shape and coloration, it resembles the popular yellowtail damselfish, *Chrysiptera parasema*, although the body isn't bright blue, but rather a dark blue-black that fades somewhat on the belly. On juveniles, the face bears

Freshwater Demoiselle

Name	*Neopomacentrus taeniurus*
Other names	Freshwater demoiselle, freshwater damselfish
Origin	East Africa to Australia
Size	4 inches (10 cm)
Water conditions	Brackish water; specific gravity around 1.010
Diet	Adaptable; will accept flake, pellets, and frozen foods happily
Temperament	Territorial but not overly aggressive
Availability	Rarely traded
Ease of maintenance	Easy
Specific problems	Requires good water quality; territorial

Damsels and monos make great tankmates.

neon blue markings that pass over the eyes and along the back, with bright blue spots on the dorsal fin as well. They also bear a distinct eyespot on the back edge of the dorsal fin just above the caudal peduncle. The eyespot, and to a lesser extent the face markings, fade as the fish matures and adopts a more or less uniformly blue-black coloration.

This fish can be kept in the same way as *N. taeniurus*, although it is much more rarely found in fresh water. It is best kept at a moderately high specific gravity, around 1.010. It gets a little bigger than *N. taeniurus*, up to about 5 inches (12 cm) in length, but otherwise has the same requirements for caves and a varied diet.

The freshwater Gregory, *Stegastes otophorus*, has the same robust shape as the other *Stegastes* kept by marine aquarists. It is a feisty, territorial fish that, in the wild, lives a solitary life except when spawning. So in a small aquarium, is best kept alone. It inhabits slightly brackish to marine waters but is not found in fresh water; a specific gravity of 1.005 or more will suit this fish well. It grows to about 5 inches (12 or 13 cm) in length.

X-RAY TETRA—*PRISTELLA MAXILLARIS*

As a rule, the characins do not tolerate salty water; indeed, most require soft, acidic water to do well. The X-ray tetra is, however, one species that naturally occurs in a variety of water conditions, including slightly brackish water that is mineral rich and has an alkaline pH. This makes it an ideal fish for use in slightly brackish water, alongside kribensis, orange cichlids, small gobies, and other small, nonpredatory fish. It is completely benign toward its tankmates, never nips at fins or scales, and can be trusted with all companions except perhaps small livebearer fry. Other than well-filtered water and quiet tankmates, it presents no problems to aquarists. It will eat a variety of foods, including flake and bloodworms, and does not need very much space: A school of 10 individuals will be perfectly happy in a 24-inch (60-cm) aquarium.

Although hardy and tolerant of most water conditions, its tolerance of salt is not high. The specific gravity must be kept below 1.003; anything above this and the X-ray tetra will quickly die. Like many other freshwater fish found in slightly brackish water, their salt tolerance is more a reflection of their innate hardiness than any particular adaptations to dealing with excess salt.

X-Ray Tetra

Name	*Pristella maxillaris*
Other names	X-ray tetra, signal tetra, *Pristella riddlei*
Origin	East Africa to Australia
Size	1.5 inches (4.5 cm)
Water conditions	Best kept in neutral fresh water; will tolerate hard, very slightly brackish water up to a specific gravity of 1.003
Diet	Flake and frozen foods
Temperament	Peaceful schooling fish
Availability	Widely traded and inexpensive
Ease of maintenance	Easy
Specific problems	Low salt tolerance

Pristella maxillaris

Rhinomugil corsula

FALSE ANABLEPS—*RHINOMUGIL CORSULA*

The false anableps, *Rhinomugil corsula*, is a rarely traded alternative to the true anableps, *Anableps anableps*. It is not a livebearer but a mullet, and comes from India rather than South America. In both form and habits, it is remarkably similar to the true anableps, right down to having eyes that are modified for seeing above and below the water line simultaneously. When seen in aquaria, the easiest way to tell them apart is the fact that the false anableps has two dorsal fins instead of one, the front one spiny and the second one soft. Naturally, these fish inhabit fresh and brackish water, and although they will tolerate salt water indefinitely, they become notably nervous in it.

Rhinomugil corsula is a peaceful, schooling fish that feeds on a variety of foods at the surface of the aquarium and on the substrate. It is adaptable as far as feeding goes, and will take both fresh and prepared foods greedily. Compared with the true anableps, however, it is much more active and skittish when kept in captivity. A decently sized school is an essential requirement: In the wild, *R. corsula* live in schools containing dozens, even hundreds, of individuals. Single specimens do not do well and die prematurely. The false anableps likes a strong water flow and plenty of swimming space, so a large aquarium with a big filter is essential. The sandbank necessary for keeping *Anableps* is not required for *R. corsula,* as these fish do not deliberately swim into very shallow water.

Because of their activity, large size, and demand for good water quality, these are not fish for the casual fishkeeper. But for the dedicated aquarist looking for something to combine with big but peaceful species, false anableps make good dither fish.

False Anableps

Name	*Rhinomugil corsula*
Other names	False anableps, blue anableps, corsula mullet
Origin	Southern Asia from India to Burma
Size	18 inches (45 cm)
Water conditions	Prefers fresh water but will tolerate brackish and marine conditions; for long-term health, keep the specific gravity below 1.010
Diet	Flake and frozen foods
Temperament	Peaceful schooling fish
Availability	Rarely traded
Ease of maintenance	Not easy
Specific problems	Large size; needs a strong water current and excellent water quality; must be kept in a group

FRESHWATER LIONFISH—*NOTESTHES ROBUSTA*

The freshwater lionfish does not have a great deal to recommend it as an aquarium fish. The negative attributes of this fish are considerable: It is very large; it can be adapted to dead foods only with difficulty; it is

Notesthes robusta

Minor Groups and Oddballs

basically nocturnal; and, like its more well-known marine relatives, it is capable of delivering a painful sting. On the plus side, though, it is quite attractive in its way, hardy, and quite peaceful when kept with similarly sized or larger fishes. Adult scats and monos, for example, are plenty big enough not to be viewed as prey, and large bottom-dwellers like Colombian shark catfish will have little to fear from this otherwise voracious predator.

Freshwater lionfish are usually imported at around 5 inches (12 cm) in length. Even then, they are well able to eat fish as big as swordtails. Adults reach 8 to 12 inches (20 to 30 cm) in captivity, and will be dangerous toward anything less than two-thirds their size. Generally speaking, these are not fish to be combined with livebearers and gobies, but rather with the big, predatory sleepers, sturdy cichlids, adult scats and monos, and the like.

Freshwater lionfish are well camouflaged, have enormous mouths, and like to adopt a sit-and-wait approach to hunting. In the aquarium, they should be provided with soft sand or fine gravel to settle into, and at least some smooth rocks and bogwood. They are not active fish, so if kept alone, they do not need as large an aquarium as, say, Colombian shark catfish. They do, however, demand excellent water quality.

Feeding this fish is a major problem. Although feeder guppies and goldfish can be used, freshwater lionfish must eat a lot of them to do well. This not only becomes expensive, but also runs the risk of introducing parasites and other diseases. Fortunately, freshwater lionfish can be trained to take dead food, but it does take a bit of time. (It is important that, when you select a freshwater lionfish to bring home from the tropical fish store, you make sure that it is not half starved.) As with marine lionfish, the trick is to entice the fish to strike by mimicking the actions of live prey. Frozen lancefish and whitebait can be used effectively for this, being inexpensive and nutritious. (Ideally, use a mix of both white and oily fish to make sure the lionfish is getting a

Freshwater Lionfish

Name	*Notesthes robusta*
Other names	Freshwater lionfish, freshwater stonefish, freshwater scorpionfish, bullrout
Origin	Southeastern Asia and Australia
Size	1 foot (30 cm)
Water conditions	Can be found in fresh, brackish, and marine waters, but does best at a specific gravity of 1.010 or higher
Diet	Live food preferred; can adapt to chunks of meaty foods
Temperament	Predatory loner
Availability	Rarely traded
Ease of maintenance	Not easy
Specific problems	Large size; highly predatory; venomous

338

balanced diet.) The food should be tied very loosely to a piece of cotton, then dangled in front of the lionfish. Don't be too aggressive and bop the fish on the nose, which will merely frighten it. Instead, try to move the food naturally and smoothly around the fish to make it curious. With luck, and if the fish is hungry, it will strike. Once it has the food in its mouth, it generally doesn't care what that food is, and if you tie the prey to the cotton loosely, its strike should pull the food away from the cotton completely.

In addition to small, dead fish, lionfish will also eat large invertebrates like river shrimp and earthworms; juveniles will eat bloodworms and other insect larvae as well. As with predatory fish in general, freshwater lionfish should not be fed every day, and certainly great care must be taken not to overfeed them.

Once they are settled into a large aquarium with appropriate tankmates and are feeding well, these fish do not present any other major problems. They are not picky about salinity and do well in both brackish and marine conditions: Anything in a specific gravity range from 1.005 to 1.018 will be fine. They can even tolerate fresh water for a while, and you are much more likely to see them offered for sale from freshwater rather than marine tanks. Over the long run, however, at least slightly brackish water is essential.

These fish are not overly territorial, but as with all bottom-dwellers, it is a good idea to make sure each fish has its own space, in particular a piece of bogwood or a cave it can call home.

FRESHWATER GAR—*XENENTODON CANCILA*

Despite their similar name and appearance, the gar family Belonidae is only distantly related to the American gars. The Asian freshwater gars are members of the Beloniformes, a large group of torpedo-shaped fish that are all fast-swimming surface dwellers. Other members of this group include the halfbeaks, sauries, and flying fish. *Xenentodon cancila* is one of the few species within the Belonidae that inhabits fresh and brackish water, while most other species live only in the sea. Because of this, and its relatively small size, *X. cancila* is the only Beloniforme that is commonly kept by aquarists.

The freshwater gar is a nervous, delicate, but highly predatory fish that is best kept on its own or with peaceful fish that stay close to the bottom. Surface area is important: In too

Shrimp are a good food for large predators.

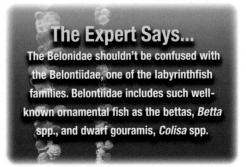

The Expert Says...

The Belonidae shouldn't be confused with the Belontiidae, one of the labyrinthfish families. Belontiidae includes such well-known ornamental fish as the bettas, *Betta* spp., and dwarf gouramis, *Colisa* spp.

Xenentodon cancila

Freshwater Gar

Name	*Xenentodon cancila*
Other names	Freshwater gar, Asian gar, needlefish, garpike
Origin	India and throughout southeastern Asia
Size	1 foot (30 cm)
Water conditions	Fresh or slightly brackish water; specific gravity up to 1.005
Diet	Live foods taken at the surface
Temperament	Nervous but predatory schooling fish
Availability	Rarely traded
Ease of maintenance	Difficult
Specific problems	Large size; delicate; difficult to feed

small an aquarium, these nervous fish will throw themselves against the glass and damage their needle-like jaws. Also, these fish invariably pine away when kept singly, so they should be in a group of three at the very least. An aquarium 4 feet (120 cm) long and 1 foot (30 cm) across will be acceptable for juveniles up to 6 inches (15 cm) in length, but adults need an aquarium at least 2 feet (60 cm) wide. Realistically, the aquarist should plan on getting a $6 \times 2 \times 2$-foot ($180 \times 60 \times 60$-cm) aquarium for a decently sized school of adults. *Xenentodon cancila* also jump readily, so a tank lid is essential.

In addition to space, it is important to ensure that the aquarium has plenty of cover, especially if it is strongly illuminated. Floating plants are especially useful for this, because they provide shade and shelter without using up much of the swimming space, while plants with long leaves, such as *Vallisneria*, are almost as good and often easier to look after.

Feeding is not particularly difficult. Although they prefer live fish, gars also will take mealworms, crickets, and other large insects, as well as river shrimps and earthworms.

The male is distinguished by a black edge to his anal and dorsal fins. After spawning, sticky eggs

The Expert Says...

A variety of fishes are called freshwater gars, and the aquarist should take care to identify a particular fish correctly before purchasing it, as they all have different requirements and habits. American gars are easily distinguished from *X. cancila* by their armor-plated bodies and asymmetrical tailfins.

More difficult are the halfbeaks and pike characins. Halfbeaks are smaller, of course, but look for the modified anal fin (or gonopodium) on male halfbeaks. Also, the jaws of *X. cancila* are of equal length, while halfbeaks, as their name suggests, have jaws of different length—the top jaw is about half as long as the bottom jaw.

Pike characins, *Boulengerella* and *Ctenolucius* spp., can be instantly separated from any of the other gar-like fish by the presence of the adipose fin between the dorsal and tail fins. The adipose fin is a small, soft, fleshy fin that lacks spines or rays, and so cannot be confused with the second dorsal fin of gars and halfbeaks, which is much larger and has a full set of rays.

Gar characins, like this *Boulengerella,* can be immediately distinguished from needlefish by the presence of a small adipose fin between the dorsal and tail fins.

are laid among plants, and the parents take no further interest in them. Once the fry emerge, they eat small, live foods such as newly hatched brine shrimp, daphnia, and, eventually, livebearer fry.

Gars, which in captivity are bred in slightly acidic fresh water, are not really brackish-water fish in the sense of being tolerant of a wide range of salinities. Rather, these are freshwater fish that benefit from a small amount of salt being added to the water. In practical terms, a specific gravity below 1.005 is needed—far less if breeding is desired. The other water parameters are not terribly important, although a neutral pH and only moderate hardness are probably beneficial. Gars do not like the high pH and hardness levels demanded by brackish-water fish from the more marine end of the spectrum, such as scats and monos.

Cold-Water
Brackish and
Marine Fish

PART I: TIDEPOOLS OF WESTERN NORTH AMERICA
By Lori Ziemba

Collecting and keeping fish from North American tidepools and estuaries forms a popular adjunct to the fishkeeping hobby, and can be a fun and rewarding pastime for those who live near the coast. While often overlooked in favor of more exotic species, many cold-water fish, often simply called "natives," are beautiful and hardy, and make excellent aquarium specimens. Add to that the fun and excitement of getting out into the actual habitat and collecting your own fish, and you may find that going to the pet shop and buying fish starts to seem dull by comparison!

One of the things I like best about setting up a native tank using local fish is the

"biotope" concept. This is the idea of duplicating, in a tank, part of an ecosystem. This means that in addition to the fish, you also collect invertebrates and plants from the same area. In this chapter, I will be talking about how to set up an aquarium using tidepool fish. Tidepools are a place of extremes: the temperature, specific gravity, and toxin levels can all change rapidly. This means that its inhabitants are generally pretty hardy and adaptable critters. Let's take a look at some that are suitable for our purposes.

SUITABLE ANIMALS AND PLANTS FOR A TIDEPOOL AQUARIUM

TIDEPOOL SCULPIN—*OLIGOCOTTUS MACULOSUS*

This sculpin is a very cute and amusing bottom-dweller that can be quickly tamed to eat from an eyedropper. They are easily kept on frozen mysid shrimps, brine shrimp, small guppies, worms, and other small, meaty foods. With fish of the same size, they are completely peaceful, but will eat anything they can fit into their mouths—and their mouths are pretty big.

In the wild, sculpins wander among the tidepools at high tide, returning to their home pools before low tide. Their homing instinct is so strong that they can find their way back even when they end up 330 feet (100 m) away from their home patch for as long as six months. Tidepool sculpins grow to about 3.5 inches (9 cm) long.

THREE-SPINE STICKLEBACK—*GASTEROSTEUS ACULEATUS*

The three-spine stickleback is a beautiful, primitive-looking fish that is normally mottled brown or greenish silver in color, though the males develop a spectacularly bright, orange or green patch across the throat and brilliantly green or blue eyes during the breeding season. While commonly referred to as the three-spine stickleback, there is quite a lot of variation in this species, and some individuals have only two spines, while others have four. To me, they look like a tiny barracuda or tuna fish.

Three-spine sticklebacks are found throughout the northern hemisphere, including North America (as far south as California in the west and Chesapeake Bay in the east) and most of Eurasia (south to Algeria and Iran and east to Japan and Korea). Three-spine sticklebacks inhabit weedy, shallow-water habitats including salt marshes and tidepools, where aquarists looking for small fish for a tidepool aquarium are likely to encounter them quite commonly.

There are several varieties of three-spine stickleback, some of which prefer fresh water, and others, brackish or salt water. It is important not to get them mixed up; freshwater varieties will not adapt to a saltwater aquarium and will quickly die. The easiest way for aquarists to tell them apart is to look at their overall coloration and to examine the flanks of the fish in the region between the pectoral fin and the caudal peduncle for a series of tall, bony plates called scutes, rather like those seen on *Corydoras* catfish. Marine forms are greenish silver in color and have 30 or so of these scutes along the flanks. The strictly freshwater varieties are a mottled brown in color and usually lack the scutes completely. The brackish-water forms vary in coloration and may resemble either the fresh- or saltwater varieties, but they normally have at least a partial row of scutes. Freshwater sticklebacks are smaller than marine

Three-spine sticklebacks, *Gasterosteus aculeatus,* resemble small baracudas or tuna.

Clams might not be the most exciting specimens, but they make welcome additions to navtive aquaria.

ones, being full-grown at 3 inches (8 cm); marine sticklebacks can get substantially longer, reaching up to 4.5 inches (11 cm).

Sticklebacks are hardy, adaptable fish, and specimens collected from brackish or marine waters will usually adapt well to a tidepool aquarium. Like the cichlids, the breeding behavior of the three-spine stickleback has been very widely studied by animal-behavior biologists, and part of the attraction of these fish is the ease with which they can be maintained in captivity. Sticklebacks tend to be boisterous, schooling fish most of the time, but during the breeding season, the males become ferociously territorial. Each male builds a nest made from bits of plant material and sand glued together with special kidney secretions. He then makes a tunnel through it, and when a gravid female swims nearby, he entices her to lay her eggs in his nest by swimming in zigzag movements. Several females may lay eggs in his nest. When they are finished, he drives them away from the nest and then guards the eggs and fry.

The male is equally waspish toward potential predators, even ones substantially larger than he is, and will fiercely drive them away if he can. Since male sticklebacks will terrorize any other fish in the aquarium, and it is generally a good idea to keep one alone in the tank.

SADDLEBACK GUNNEL—*PHOLIS ORNATA*

This is a strangely beautiful, eel-like fish with no lateral line and tiny pelvic fins. Unlike true eels, gunnels do have scales, but they are so small as to be almost invisible to the naked eye. Gunnels are also covered in a thick, slippery mucus that in England has led to their being called "butterfish," since they are so difficult to hold onto. The saddleback gunnel lives in eelgrass and seaweed beds, quite often near the mouth of a stream. It can change color from green to brown to match surroundings.

Like all gunnels, the saddleback gunnel is primarily a fish of cold, northern waters and is notably intolerant of warm water and low oxygen levels. In the southern parts of its range it often moves into deeper, colder water during the summer. The aquarist therefore needs to ensure that an aquarium housing this fish does not overheat (by receiving too much direct sunlight, for example), and to provide extra aeration, as with an airstone, during the summer. These fish are also apt to escape from aquaria, so a tight-fitting lid is essential.

Feeding presents few problems, as they will readily take all sorts of live and frozen invertebrate foods, including crustaceans such as shrimps and small pieces of clam and mussel. Saddleback gunnels are fairly large, and can reach a length of up to 1 foot (30 cm).

PURPLE SHORE CRAB—*HEMIGRAPSUS NUDUS*

Hemigrapsus nudus is a beautiful animal that really is purple. They are very amusing creatures that will give you hours of pleasure with their antics. They too like to escape, though, so make sure your tank is well covered, or you may find one in your slipper, like I did. Also, these crabs like to have a spot in the tank where they can leave the water and dry off for a while.

The purple shore crab is a scavenger and eats virtually anything offered to it, but frozen prawns and clam meat make an excellent staple diet. It grows to a shell width of about 2 inches (5 cm).

Snakelocks anemones, *Anemonia viridis*, contain photosynthetic algae and need bright light, but are otherwise attractive and easy-to-keep additions to a cold-water marine aquarium.

KELP OR SPIDER CRAB—*PUGETTIA PRODUCTA*

Be careful when handling this guy, as it is very clingy and can give you quite a pinch. Unlike the purple shore crab, the kelp crab is not really a bottom-dweller. The kelp crab prefers to conceal itself among kelp fronds, and in aquaria will cling to the uptake tube of your filter if it cannot find a better place to hide. Artificial seaweeds make an excellent substitute for kelp and can be obtained inexpensively from most tropical fish stores. Algae grows readily on plastic plants (as long as the lighting is adequate), which is useful for these largely vegetarian crabs. Besides algae, they can be fed on *Spirulina* pellets and seaweed.

Kelp crabs grow to a shell width of about 3 inches (7.5 cm), but they seem bigger thanks to their long, spidery legs. Like most other spider crabs, the kelp crab does not do well in warm water, and is intolerant of low oxygen levels.

BROKEN-BACK SHRIMP—*HIPPOLYTE* SPP.

You can find lots of different colors of broken-back shrimp in tidepools, and all will do well in a quiet aquarium without larger, predatory fish or invertebrates. Shrimps are scavengers, and will eat all types of plant and animal matter, and to some extent will clean up behind the other animals in the aquarium. They will also peck away at algae.

HERMIT CRAB—*PAGURUS SAMUELIS*

An amusing fellow, the hermit crab is the clown of the tidepool and a firm favorite with cold-water marine aquarists. These little guys are black with bright red antennae and brilliant, blue bands around their feet. Having a soft body with no shell of their own, they need to find an appropriate snail shell to move into as they grow. They seem to prefer the shells of the marine snails in the genus *Tegula*, known as top or turban shells, and the aquarist should collect several different sizes of these and place them in the aquarium so the hermit crab can pick from them as it grows. Very funny scenes can ensue when you have one empty shell and more than one hermit; they will squabble and argue over the empty shell, though after trying out the new shell the victor often seems to decide that it preferred the old shell better after all.

Hermit crabs are adaptable scavengers and will eat any meaty foods, including small pieces of fish, crustacean, or mollusk, and grow to about 1 inch (2.5 cm) in body length, not including the snail shell.

TURBAN SNAIL—*TEGULA FUNEBRALIS*

These are the common, black turban snails that you'll find clinging to rocks at low tide. The shell reaches up to 1 inch (2.5 cm) in diameter. These snails are herbivorous and like to eat algae, so their appetite is most easily satisfied by making sure the aquarium is well lit. Without a chiller, though, the lights can elevate the temperature of the tank beyond the tolerances of many cold-water species.

CLAMS

I have to admit to having rescued clams from the seafood department at the supermarket. Plop them in your tank and they will burrow into the substrate and filter feed. Not very exciting as pets go, although it *is* fun thinking up names for them, such as Clambert, Clamentine, Clamity Jane, Samuel Clammens, or Clamuel Clemmens.

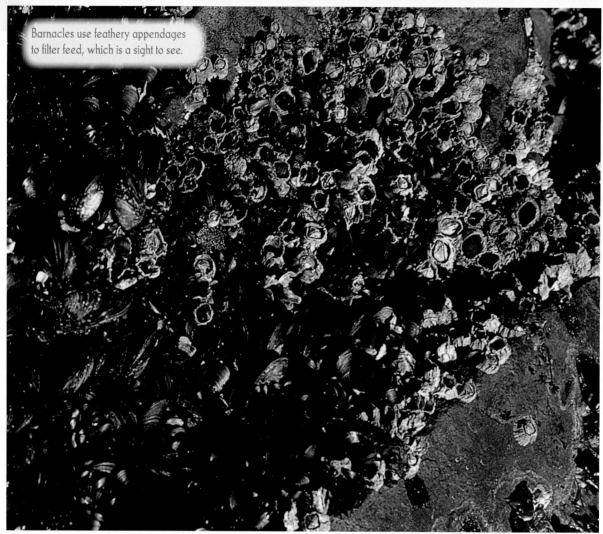

Barnacles use feathery appendages to filter feed, which is a sight to see.

LIMPET—*LOTTIA (COLLISELLA) DIGITALIS*

Like turban snails, limpets are herbivorous snails and need to be kept in the same way. Limpets are not terribly exciting pets, but they are pretty and easy to collect. In the wild, limpets spend a great deal of time out of water, and in captivity may try to crawl out of the aquarium, so keep a tight lid on it.

MUSSEL—*MYTILUS CALIFORNIANUS*

Believe it or not, the mussel is actually a beautiful animal when open. If you plop it into your tank in a corner, it can move by using its foot and will throw out fine threads like spider's silk known as byssus threads. In the wild, the mussel uses these to attach to rocks, but in the aquarium it will just as readily fix itself to glass. Once attached, it will open its shell slightly to filter feed, exposing a beautiful, bright, orange interior.

Live mussels make nice tankmates, while crushed mussel shells can contribute to an authentic-looking substrate.

BARNACLE—*BALANUS GLANDULA*

Barnacles are crustaceans, even though they are hidden away inside shells that make them look like some kind of mollusk. Barnacles cannot be easily dislodged from whatever substrate they are attached to, but small, barnacle-encrusted stones and rocks are easy to gather and add to an aquarium. Make sure you locate them near the front of the tank, where you can watch them filter feed by waving their feathery appendages around.

ANEMONE—*ANTHOPLEURA ELEGANTISSIMA*

This is a beautiful, white anemone with numerous pink-tipped arms that grows to about 2 inches (5 cm) across. You can feed it small bits of shrimp, crab, and fish. Similar to tropical corals, this creature needs good lighting, as it contains symbiotic algae within its tissues. Incidentally, this anemone reproduces by splitting, so you might quickly have a whole colony on your hands.

Many brittle stars grow large, though *Amphipholis puqetana* reaches only half an inch wide.

Brittle Stars—*Amphipholis pugetana*

Brittle Stars are the tiny, starfish-like animals that you likely will find in sand you collect. They eat by sifting through the substrate, keeping it clean and loose, and as such are essentially scavengers that will happily subsist on the leftovers from anything you feed to the other animals in the aquarium. There are numerous larger brittle stars that are more or less similar in habits, but this tiny species only reaches about half an inch (1 cm) from arm tip to arm tip.

Seaweed

There are lots of different kinds of seaweed, and there might be some trial and error in finding which species will thrive in your aquarium. Generally speaking, brown algae (such as kelps and bladderwrack) do not do well in home aquaria and rapidly decompose, but I've had good luck with the fine-leafed, red varieties, and with types like sea lettuce.

SETTING UP THE TIDEPOOL AQUARIUM

One of the nice things about tidepool aquaria is that they can work well with even very small tanks: A 10-gallon aquarium can house a few fish and numerous small invertebrates. As with any saltwater aquarium, it is important to make sure you use one suitable for that purpose, without exposed metal, for example.

Filtration

External filters work best, particularly with small aquaria because they do not waste valuable space inside the tank. The only important thing to remember is to choose a filter that has at least 50 percent more filtration capacity than the size of your aquarium would suggest—cold-water marine fish are notably intolerant of poor water quality. I found protein skimmers to be invaluable with cold-water marine aquaria, and they can really make the difference between success and failure. There are units available that combine filter and skimmer, and these may be a useful choice on small aquaria; otherwise, standard protein skimmers as sold for tropical marine aquarists should be used.

Lighting

Strong lighting is essential for a good growth of algae, something many marine invertebrates, particularly mollusks, require. Compact fluorescent lights are ideal, either as a hanging fixture or with the lamps attached to the hood and the ballast unit located remotely. This helps reduce the heating effect that the ballast units have. Some aquaria come with lights incorporated into the hood, which can be used, but because these have the ballast unit built into the hood, they might heat up the aquarium too much for some species. Actinic lighting is not necessary.

Temperature

Generally speaking, no heater is required, although in a very cold climate or an unheated garage where there is a risk of the aquarium actually freezing over, a heater may be necessary.

On the other hand, unless you have a cool, unheated room in which to keep the aquarium, a chiller unit is probably essential. Until recently, chillers were expensive, costing hundreds of dollars, but several manufacturers now produce small units that cost less than $200. A popular alternative is to cannibalize a small fridge (the mini-bar style is ideal). Drill a pair of small holes through the door, then run a length of pipe from the aquarium's canister filter into the fridge, winding it into a few loops, and back out to the aquarium. The ideal temperature of a cold-water aquarium is in the range 55° to 60°F (12° to 15°C).

LOCATING THE AQUARIUM

Now the fun begins. Clean your tank well, and have the light, filter, chiller, and skimmer ready to go. Set the tank up on a sturdy surface near an electrical outlet. Since the animals and plants you will be collecting come from temperate seas, they absolutely must be kept cool, or they will die. Part of getting this right is making sure that the aquarium is in the coolest part of your house (often the basement or an outbuilding). In a room heated to about 72°F (22°C), a small aquarium chiller will only be able to cool the tank down to about 68° to 64°F (20° to 18°C), quite a bit warmer than most cold-water fish and invertebrates like. So the cooler the room is to begin with, the better the aquarium chiller will be able to do its job.

Besides heating, other factors such as direct sunlight and the type of lighting are important in regulating the temperature of a tank. Therefore it is a good idea to do a "dry run" before putting in any livestock: Set up the aquarium where you think will be best and let the chiller work for one or two days to see what temperature the aquarium settles down to.

It may not be possible to locate your cold-water aquarium and set up your chiller to maintain the ideal temperatures all year, and at the height of summer the water temperature can rise above the safety zone for days or weeks at a time. In emergencies, high water temperatures can be moderated in two ways. The first is to increase the rate of evaporation by using a fan to blow a steady stream of air over the surface of the aquarium, though you will need to watch the water level and replace lost water with chilled deionized or distilled water (not more seawater, which would increase the tank's salinity). The second way is to float a watertight plastic carton of ice in the aquarium. As the ice melts inside the carton it will cool the aquarium, and by keeping several of these in the freezer they can be cycled as required to make sure one of them is always available for use.

COLLECTING

Go to your chosen beach, and collect 15 lbs (7 kg) or so of sand and rocks, taking care to obey any local or state regulations. If you are going to use seawater to fill the aquarium, collect that as well. Both sand and seawater are likely to bring along some stowaway lifeforms, but do not gather any of the larger animals such as fish just yet. Collect the sand and water at low tide, as far down on the beach as you can, and dig a little if necessary to get the wet sand rather than the dry stuff on top. Keep the sand wet and cool, get it home quickly, and put it in the tank as is. It likely contains bacteria, starfish, amphipods,

Many brackish and marine setups use cooling fans to offset the heat generated by the powerful lighting used.

Cold-Water Brackish and Marine Fish

London's Thames Estuary is teeming with brackish life.

and worms—all things you will need to have. Now add enough of the seawater to fill the tank and set up your rockwork, making sure there are plenty of crevices for the animals to hide in.

Red and green seaweed are also worth collecting. Try to get the talus, the "root" of the seaweed, which is usually attached to a rock, and the rock itself. The seaweed grows from the talus, and loose pieces often do not live long. Plant the seaweed wherever it looks good, taking care not to bury the talus under sand.

Attach the filter, skimmer, chiller, and light, and let the tank run. The water will be cloudy at first, but will clear up in a day or so. And keep checking the temperature—I cannot stress enough how important it is to keep the tank cool. It is the single biggest obstacle you will face in keeping a tidepool tank.

Just as with any other type of aquarium, cold-water marine tanks need to cycle, but because of the lower temperatures involved, the process takes noticeably longer than with tropical aquaria. Add a pinch of dry fish food to the tank every day, and using standard aquarium test kits, you should be able to see that the nitrites take a month or more to drop to zero. Only then is it safe to add fish and the larger invertebrates. Start with the hardiest first, such as the hermit crabs and shore crabs, and don't add too many at once; go slowly because your filter still will not be operating at full capacity and needs time to become fully biologically active. Have fun collecting and seeing a bit of nature right in your home!

359

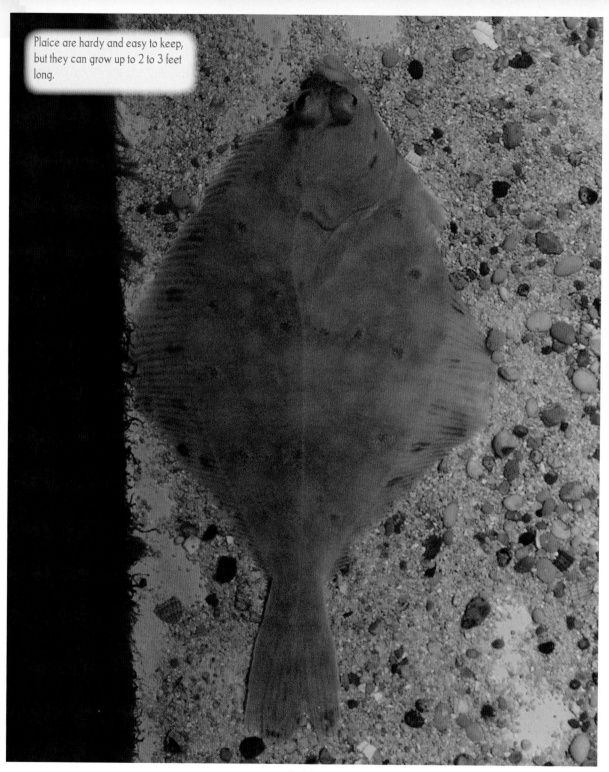

Plaice are hardy and easy to keep, but they can grow up to 2 to 3 feet long.

PART 2: EUROPEAN ESTUARIES
By Neale Monks

Many European cities are built on or close to estuaries. London, for example, spans the Thames Estuary, and it isn't difficult to collect brackish-water fish from streams and salt marshes in these areas. As with cold-water marines, the trick is in picking species that are small, not overly predatory, and tolerant of the relatively warm temperatures they will be exposed to in home aquaria. With a few exceptions, species collected from the English Channel and southward will do well without a chiller if the water is well oxygenated, whereas species from the North Sea and northward, and from the Baltic and Scandinavia, will require a chiller of some kind. In this section, the focus is on species that will not need a chiller and can be kept in an unheated aquarium kept in a cool room or basement.

SUITABLE ANIMALS FOR A EUROPEAN ESTUARY AQUARIUM

SAND GOBIES—*Pomatoschistus minutus* AND *Pomatoschistus microps*

These two attractive goby species are very tricky to tell apart and commonly inhabit the same types of environments, so from the aquarist's point of view they might as well be the same fish. They are easy to collect, inhabiting all sorts of shallow-water habitats, including rock pools, coastal streams, and salt marshes. Of the two species, *Pomatoschistus microps* is the more likely to be found in fresh water, but both are more common in brackish and marine waters, and so a specific gravity of 1.010 or higher should be used.

In the aquarium, these fish present no problems and are the ideal cold-water fish for beginners. They are small: *Pomatoschistus minutus* reaches only 4 inches (11 cm) in length, and *Pomatoschistus microps* grows to no more than 3.5 inches (9 cm). Both species are sociable but territorial, and should be kept in small groups but with sufficient numbers of caves or shells for each fish to have its own home. They will eat all sorts of small, frozen foods, including bloodworms, but they particularly relish live brine shrimp. A soft, sandy substrate should be used, as these fish like to burrow. These gobies are peaceful toward other tankmates, even fairly small shrimps, but should not be kept with more aggressive or predatory fish.

STICKLEBACKS—*Gasterosteus aculeatus*, *Pungitius pungitius*, AND *Spinachia spinachia*

The three-spine stickleback (described in Part 1 of this chapter) is common in Europe, and the brackish-water varieties do well in aquaria. The nine-spine stickleback, *Pungitius pungitius*, is similar, but it is rather less tolerant of high temperatures and usually needs a chilled aquarium to do well. The fifteen-spine stickleback, *Spinachia spinachia,* is a much larger fish—growing to over 8 inches (20 cm)—resembles a pipefish in shape and habits, and is a challenge even for the experienced aquarist. It will only eat live foods, primarily small crustaceans. Like the nine-spine stickleback, this species does best in an aquarium kept cool using a chiller.

Shrimps and prawns can fit into some cold-water tanks nicely.

Cold-Water Brackish and Marine Fish

Peacock blenny—*Salaria pavo*

A charming fish from southern Europe and the Mediterranean, this goby-like fish is alert and intelligent, and adapts well to aquarium life. It grows to about 5 inches (13 cm) in length and bears a spectacular pattern of neon blue spots and stripes on a greenish brown body. There is a distinct eyespot lined in blue on each side of the head, halfway between the eye and the pectoral fin, and on males, the top of the head rises into a small hump. This fish can change its color to some degree, particularly during the breeding season or when frightened.

Most of the time, the peacock blenny stays close to the bottom, propping itself up on its small, white pelvic fins (sort of like a mudskipper). Peacock blennies will take both flake and frozen foods readily, but also should be allowed to graze on algae. Like most blennies, these fish are territorial and need a cave or burrow to call home. They are also exceptional escape artists, and the aquarium must be fitted with a hood to stop these fish from jumping out. In the wild, they can occasionally be found in fresh water, but are much more common in brackish waters. A specific gravity of 1.010 will suit these fish well, but they can also be adapted to fully marine conditions.

Aquarists may come across some other European blennies from time to time. The freshwater blenny, *Salaria fluviatilis*, makes a good aquarium subject but does not inhabit brackish or marine waters. The shanny, *Lipophrys pholis*, on the other hand, is only found in seawater, particularly tidepools, but is extremely hardy and easy to tame, and makes an excellent proposition for a tidepool aquarium including European species.

European Plaice—*Pleuronectes platessa*

Trawling estuaries at low tide with a large net will often yield lots of small plaice and flounders. Juvenile plaice do well in aquaria and are tolerant of room-temperature water. They are uncommonly adaptable, and will take not just live and frozen foods, but also prepared foods such as catfish pellets. Flounders, on the other hand, are more tolerant of low salinity, accepting even fresh water, but they don't do as well in aquaria because they need cold water.

The downside is that while plaice grow slowly, they eventually reach up to 3 feet (100 cm) long. Obviously, such fish are not suitable for home aquaria, and the aquarist will either need to release the grown plaice into the wild, which is never recommended, or donate it to a public aquarium.

Green Shore Crabs—*Carcinus maenas*

The green shore crab is an extraordinarily hardy animal and will tolerate a wide range of salinities, from about one-fifth the salinity of normal seawater and up. In its natural habitat—rocky shores—it may be forced to spend time out of water either in damp crevices or underneath clumps of seaweed, and it is no surprise that these crabs do well in brackish and marine aquaria. They are also quite lively and attractive, and not at all shy.

The problem with green shore crabs is their tendency to be destructive. They are opportunistic feeders, and will catch fish and shrimps, open up clams and mussels, and generally try to overpower and eat anything they can find. So while small specimens can be used with great success, once they get above 1 inch (2.5 cm) wide across the shell, they quickly become a nuisance and need to be removed.

SHRIMPS AND PRAWNS—*CRANGON* AND *PALAEOMON* SPP.

The brown shrimp, *Crangon crangon*, and the common prawns, *Palaeomon elegans* and *P. serratus*, all make good additions to a brackish-water aquarium lacking large or predatory fish. Like the broken-back shrimps described earlier, these animals are primarily scavengers and will eat any plant or animal material not eaten by the other residents of the aquarium. In captivity they are hardy and tolerant of room-temperature water. Just about the only problem with keeping these animals is that they are prone to jumping and often escape the aquarium, only to be found dried up on the floor. Again, a tight-fitting hood is required.

MUSSELS AND OTHER MOLLUSKS

Apart from the crabs and shrimps, most of the other invertebrates you are likely to find in European estuaries tend to be burrowers, such as ragworms and clams. These are not terribly attractive pets: Even if they do adapt to aquarium life, you aren't going to see very much of them. It may be worth collecting a few small clams, but feeding them can be tricky. You will need to use marine-invertebrate food, which is sold in tropical fish stores for things like peacock and feather duster worms.

Mussels are an alternative, and while certainly attractive, they will still need careful feeding to do well. They are tolerant of warm water, as long as the aquarium is well oxygenated. Oysters are a very characteristic element of many European estuaries and need to be kept in the same way as mussels or clams.

SETTING UP AN ESTUARY AQUARIUM

As far as filtration and lighting go, an aquarium based on a European estuary will need to be put together in the same general way as a North American tidepool tank. Locating the aquarium away from direct sunlight and other heat sources, and ensuring that the filter has adequate time to mature, are just as important. Instead of filling the aquarium with mounds of stones and rocks, an aquarium for these estuarine animals should include a large area of open, sandy substrate and a few seashells of various sizes for cover. A pile of rocks in one corner of the aquarium can be used for those species, such as blennies, that prefer to stay close to cover. Seaweeds can be used, but again, brown algae do not adapt well in domestic aquaria and should not be used.

Appendix

Table 1
Commonly traded species best suited to a low-salinity brackish-water aquarium (SG 1.003)

Non-predatory, suitable for most community tanks
Aspredo aspredo
Awaous flavus
Brachygobius spp.
Dermogenys pusilla
Etroplus maculatus
Etroplus suratensis
Gobioides broussonnetii
Jordanella floridae
Macrognathus spp.
Mastacembelus spp.
Moringua raitaborua
Parambassis spp.
Platystacus cotylephorus
Poecilia "black molly"
Poecilia mexicana
Poecilia latipinna
Poecilia reticulata
Poecilia sphenops
Poecilia velifera
Poecilia wingei
Rhinomugil corsula

Aggressive and difficult to keep with other fish
Belonesox belizanus
Sarotherodon melanotheron
Tetraodon biocellatus

Predatory, but otherwise reliable community fish
Aplocheilus spp.
Butis butis
Dormitator lebretonis
Dormitator maculatus
Erpetoichthys calabaricus
Nandus nandus
Lepisosteus spp.
Mystus gulio
Stigmatogobius sadanundio
Toxotes microlepis
Xenentodon cancila

Generally too aggressive for community tanks
"Cichlasoma" urophthalmus
Chonerhinos naritus
Oreochromis spp.
Nandopsis haitiensis
Nandopsis tetracanthus
Synbranchus marmoratus
Tilapia spp.
Vieja maculicauda

366

Table 2

Commonly traded species best suited to a high-salinity brackish-water aquarium (SG 1.010 to normal marine) *

Non-predatory, suitable for most community tanks

Etroplus maculatus †
Etroplus suratensis †
Gobioides broussonnetii
Poecilia "black molly"
Poecilia mexicana
Poecilia latipinna
Poecilia sphenops
Poecilia velifera
Scatophagus spp.
Selenotoca spp.

Aggressive and difficult to keep with other fish

Anguilla spp.
Arothron hispidus
Chelonodon patoca
Datnioides campbelli †
Echidna rhodochilus
Sarotherodon melanotheron
Terapon jarbua
Tetraodon biocellatus †

Predatory, but otherwise reliable community fish

Achirus lineatus
Butis butis
Colomesus psittacus
Datnioides quadrifasciatus †
Dormitator lebretonis †
Dormitator maculatus
Gymnothorax tile
Hexanematichthys seemanni
Monodactylus spp.
Neopomacentrus taeniurus
Notesthes robusta
Plotosus lineatus
Pomacentrus taeniometopon
Stegastes otophorus
Stigmatogobius sadanundio †
Toxotes chatareus †
Toxotes microlepis †
Trinectes fasciatus

Generally too aggressive for community tanks

"Cichlasoma" urophthalmus
Chonerhinos naritus
Nandopsis haitiensis
Nandopsis tetracanthus
Tetraodon fluviatilis
Tetraodon nigroviridis

---

* Mudskippers, pipefish, the four-eye fishes (Anableps spp.), and the subtropical pufferfish, *Takifugu ocellatus*, all have very particular needs. These needs make them difficult to combine with other species, and so they are not included on this chart.

† Do not keep in a specific gravity above 1.010

Afterword
By Neale Monks

Just a few years ago, putting together a book like *Brackish-Water Fishes* would have been very difficult indeed. It wasn't that brackish-water fish weren't being kept in appreciable numbers, it was that the hobbyists who kept them had no idea that others were experimenting with the same fish and figuring out the best way to keep them. The Internet has made it possible for aquarists to communicate with one another far beyond the potential of magazines and fishkeeping clubs, and as a result, aquarists interested in very specific segments of the hobby—in this case, fish from brackish waters—can swap observations and share ideas like never before.

As air transportation of fish becomes ever more reliable and inexpensive, we can expect to see more and more species of brackish-water fish turn up in our local fish stores. In fact, several of the species described here, particularly among the gobies, make good aquarium residents and already are steadily becoming more popular among aquarists. Australian fish fauna is especially rich in species that do well in aquaria, and it is probably only a matter of time before these become as consistently represented in the tropical fish stores of Europe and North America as the characins of South America or cichlids of East Africa are today. One reason this book was compiled was to popularize these unfamiliar and underappreciated fishes, so that when they do turn up in your local fish store, you know what they are and how best to keep them.

But there was another reason for writing this book: to encourage people to keep familiar but challenging species properly. Pufferfish in particular suffer from the ignorance of many dealers and aquarists, beacuse many are kept in the wrong water conditions, fed the wrong foods, and housed with the wrong tankmates. Is it any surprise that they have acquired the reputation for being "difficult fish" despite being intrinsically hardy and adaptable? Sadly, puffers are not the only brackish fish mistreated this way. Mudskippers, pipefish, glassfish, mollies, and bumblebee gobies are all commonly traded and inexpensive, but each in its own way is not exactly suited to the average community tank.

The authors of *Brackish-Water Fishes* are united in their enthusiasm for fishkeeping and the hope that their efforts will encourage others to explore the biology and behavior of brackish-water fish in their home aquaria. Brackish-water fish make an excellent speciality for the aquarist who has already mastered the basic community tank, as well as a proving ground for the ambitious freshwater fishkeeper with an eye on graduating to marines. In the world brackish-water fishes, there really is something for everyone.

Resources

BOOKS

Dawes, J. 1995. *Livebearing Fishes: A Guide to Their Aquarium Care, Biology and Classification.* Blandford, London, England.

Ebert, K. 2001. *The Puffers of Fresh and Brackish Waters.* Aqualog Verlag, Germany.

Glass, S. 1997. *Mollies: Keeping & Breeding Them in Captivity.* TFH Publications, Inc., New Jersey, United States.

Ralph, C. 2003. *Practical Fishkeeping Guide to Pufferfish.* Interpet Publishing.

Schafer, F. 2005. *Brackish Water Fishes.* Aqualog Verlag, Germany.

Scott, P. 1995. *Complete Aquarium.* Dorling Kindersley Publishing Inc., New York, United States.

MAGAZINES

Tropical Fish Hobbyist
1 T.F.H. Plaza
3rd & Union Avenues
Neptune City, NJ 07753
Phone: (732) 988-8400
E-mail: *info@tfh.com*
www.tfhmagazine.com

INTERNET RESOURCES

Brackish-Water Aquarium Mailing List
http://php.indiana.edu/~pdmckinn/Brackish/brackish.html
Brackish FAQ
http://users.macunlimited.net/n.monks/fishkeeping.html
Brackish Systems
http://www.wetwebmedia.com/BrackishSubWebIndex/BrackishSubWebIndex.htm
Neale Monks Fishkeeping Page
http://homepage.mac.com/nmonks/aquaria/aquaria.html
Pufferfish Guide
http://www.pufferfish.co.uk/
Tropical Fish Forums
http://www.fishforums.net/

American Cichlid Association
Claudia Dickinson, Membership Coordinator
P.O. Box 5078
Montauk, NY 11954
Phone: (631) 668-5125
E-mail: IvyRose@optonline.net
www.cichlid.org

American Livebearer Association
Timothy Brady, Membership Chairman
5 Zerbe Street
Cressona, PA 17929-1513
Phone: (570) 385-0573
http://livebearers.org

Association of Aquarists
David Davis, Membership Secretary
2 Telephone Road
Portsmouth, Hants, England
PO4 0AY
Phone: 01705 798686

Canadian Association of Aquarium Clubs
Miecia Burden, Membership Coordinator
142 Stonehenge Pl.
Kitchener, Ontario, Canada
N2N 2M7
Phone: (517) 745-1452
E-mail: mbburden@look.ca
www.caoac.on.ca

Federation of American Aquarium Societies
Jane Benes, Secretary
923 Wadsworth Street
Syracuse, NY 13208-2419
Phone: (513) 894-7289
E-mail: jbenes01@yahoo.com
www.gcca.net/faas

Bibliography

BOOKS

Allen, G.R. 1991. *Field Guide to the Freshwater Fishes of New Guinea.* Christensen Research Institute, Madang, Papua New Guinea.

Allen, G.R. 1989. *Freshwater Fishes of Australia.* TFH Publications, Inc., New Jersey, United States.

Allen, G.R. 1997. *Marine Fishes of Tropical Australia & South-East Asia.* Western Australian Museum, Australia.

Goodson, G. 1996. *Fishes of the Pacific Coast.* Stanford University Press, California, United States.

Graham, J.B. 1997. *Air-Breathing Fishes.* Academic Press, Massachusetts, United States.

Grant, E.M. 1995. *Fishes of Australia.* E.M. Grant Pty. Ltd., Queensland, Australia.

Herbert, B. and J. Peeters. 1995. *Freshwater Fishes of Far North Queensland.* Queensland Department of Primary Industries, Queensland, Australia.

Horn, M.H., et al. 1999. *Intertidal Fishes: Life In Two Worlds.* Academic Press, Massachusetts, United States.

Lake, J.S. 1978. *Australian Freshwater Fishes: An Illustrated Field Guide.* Nelson, Melbourne, Australia.

Larson, H.K. and K.C. Martin. 1989. *Freshwater Fishes of the Northern Territory.* Northern Territory Museum of Arts and Sciences, Darwin, Australia.

Leggett, R. and J.R. Merrick. 1987. *Australian Native Fishes for Aquariums.* J.R. Merrick Publications, Sydney, Australia.

McDowall, R. 1996. *Freshwater Fishes of South-Eastern Australia.* Reed Books, Sydney, Australia.

Merrick, J.R. and G.E. Schmida. 1984. *Australian Freshwater Fishes: Biology and Management.* Griffith Press Ltd.

Munro, I.S.R. 1967. *The Fishes of New Guinea.* Department of Agriculture, Stock, and Fisheries, Papua New Guinea.

Schmida, G.E. 1985. *The Cold-Blooded Australians.* Doubleday, Sydney, Australia.

Sterba, G. 1967. *Freshwater Fishes of the World.* Studio Vista Ltd., London, England.

Whitley, G.P. 1980. *Handbook of Australian Fishes.* Jack Pollard Publ., Sydney, Australia.

Zim, Herbert S. and L. Ingle. 1955. *Seashores, A Golden Nature Guide.* Simon & Schuster, New York, United States.

Zim, Herbert S. and H.H. Shoemaker. 1956. *Fishes, A Golden Nature Guide.* Golden Press, New York, United States.

ARTICLES

Clayton, D. 1993. Mudskippers. Oceanography and Marine Biology: An Annual Review.

Murdy, E.O. 1989. A Taxonomic Revision and Cladistic Analysis of the Oxudercine Gobies. Records of the Australian Museum, Supplement 11.

Murdy, E.O. 1986. The Mudskippers of Malaysia: Lords of the Mudflat. Freshwater and Marine Aquarium, Nov. 1986.

Nursall, J.R. 1981. Behaviour and habitat affecting the distribution of five species of sympatric mudskippers in Queensland. Bulletin of Marine Science, Volume 31.

Swennen, C., et al. 1995. The Five Sympatric Mudskippers of Pattani area, Southern Thailand. Natural History Bulletin of the Siam Society, Volume 42.

Takita, T., et al. 1999. Distribution and habitat requirements of oxudercine gobies along the Straits of Malacca. Ichthyological Research, Volume 46, No. 2.

Index

About the Authors

Neale Monks was trained as a zoologist at the University of Aberdeen in Scotland and, following a brief stint as a marine biologist, moved to London to begin work on a paleontology Ph.D. at the Natural History Museum there. Neale has since been a full-time researcher, a lecturer on astronomy and the history of science at Pepperdine University, and an events and exhibitions developer at the University of Nebraska State Museum. In 2005, he moved back to England.

Neale's interest in brackish-water fish stemmed from his time at Aberdeen, where he had the luxury of big display tanks to fill and a research aquarium at which to study. Fascinated by the ability of certain fish to adapt to changes in salinity, he has for the last ten years maintained the most detailed web site on brackish-water fishkeeping on the Internet.

Michele Kraft is an artist and writer living in Wisconsin. After many years as a freshwater-aquaria hobbyist, she began keeping brackish-water fish in 2001. An admitted amateur by comparison to the other contributors to this book, she is nevertheless enthusiastic about this diverse category of fishes, and about the generous and kind experts she's met while keeping them. Visit Michele online at www.michelekraft.com.

Catherine Burnett, a Canadian pharmacy technician with an IT degree, has been keeping fish of various salinities, as well as many other aquatic and land creatures, for nearly 20 years. When not maintaining her aquariums, she likes scuba diving to visit fish in their natural habitats, ranging from the colorful fish and corals of the Red Sea to the green and brown gobies, zebra mussels, and shipwrecks of the St. Lawrence River.

Naomi Delventhal is currently researching goby systematics at the University of Manitoba, in Winnipeg, Canada. As part of her work, she has had the opportunity to scuba dive and collect gobies in the Indo-Pacific and the Caribbean. Her first aquarium gobies were a pair of *Awaous flavus*, and she has since kept over forty different species.

Bruce Hansen has had a life-long interest in aquarium fish, which for the past 30 years has focused more on the native fishes of the Australian region. His expertise with these brackish fishes grew from extensive collecting experience and his strong affiliation with ANGFA, the Australia New Guinea Fishes Association.

Bob Edwards was introduced to the hobby by his parents when they set up a community tropical aquarium in their living room. For his 10th birthday, Bob received his first aquarium, and went on to breed guppies like most kids do! Twenty-five years later, Bob has three aquariums running: and has bred and raised a variety of different tropical fish and corals.

A graphic designer by trade, Bob has had no formal education in fishkeeping. Instead, he has learned through his own and other peoples' experiences, offering direct insights by people who have been there and done it. He feels the authors' collective experience is why *Brackish-Water Fishes* is so unique and useful.

Richard Mleczko was trained as a physicist and has a master of science degree. About 10 years ago, he developed an interest in mudskippers after seeing them at a public aquarium and realizing that there existed little factual information on the fish. After searching the scientific literature and making contact with mudskipper scientists, Richard set up the world's first web site devoted to educating would-be mudskipper enthusiasts.He has visited mangroves many times and has collected his own mudskippers and mangrove seedlings, and he has kept numerous other species of fish as well.

Richard is married with two boys and lives in Australia, where he studies tsunamis for the Australian federal government.

Lori Ziemba was born and raised in New York City. She has kept and bred many types of fish since her dad taught her how at the age of 8. She moved to San Francisco in 1983, and worked at the Steinhart Aquarium for a time.

Lori's favorite tank was a native marine aquarium, which she set up a few years ago and for which she collected all the inhabitants from her local shoreline.

Rory McDaniel is one of the rising generation of young fishkeepers. He has been surrounded by tropical fish most of his life and has been keeping brackish fish ever since his first encounter with an Atlantic mudskipper. Among his favorite fishes are mudskippers, puffers, and Colombian shark catfish. He currently lives in Roanoke, Virginia.

Acknowledgments

Neale Monks would like to thank Samana Schwank, Bob Ralph, Deb Thomas, P. Doug McKinney, Robert R. Ricketts, Frank Schäfer, the staff at TFH, and everyone on the Brackish Water Aquarium Mailing List and the Tropical Fish Forums

Michele Kraft would like to offer sincere thanks to all the brackish experts she has met over the years for everything they've taught her, and hopes the readers will enjoy and learn as much from this book as she has from its authors.

Bruce Hansen is grateful for assistance and information from his colleagues in ANGFA (national and local groups) and the Brackish List, and his two superb fish-photographer friends, Gunther Schmida and Neil Armstrong.

Richard Mleczko would like to thank the following people for their help and support with this book—Laura Stapleton, Guillaume Perrotin, John Visor, Toru Takita, and Alex Rufle. He also would like to thank Akinori Kamiya, Michael Losch, Masako Tanabe, Joakim Liman, Yuko Nakazato Ikebe, and Hans Horsthemke for kindly donating pictures of mudskippers for this book.

Lori Ziemba would like to thank her dad for teaching her all he knew about fishkeeping. She would also like to thank Neale Monks, who put this whole thing together.

Photo Credits

Dr. Glen Axelrod: 281; John Brill: 231; Dr. Warren E. Burgess: 56, 312; Chris Downing: 160-161, 268-269; Michael Gilroy: 142-143; Andy Goodson: 282; Jaroslaw Grudzinski: 358-359; Stephen David Harper: 22; Joshua Haviv: 11; Hans Horsthemke: 207; Yuko Nakazato Ikebe: 199; Vladimir Ivanov: 194-195; Matthew Jacques: 20; Akinori Kamiya: 210, 218; Sabine Kanzaria: 8-9, 46-47; Danish Khan: 18-19; Karl Knaack: 159, 168, 264; A. Kotchetov: 294; Gennady Kudelya: 33; Tan Yoke Liang: 201; Andy Lim: 81; Cecilia Lim: 24-25; Joakim Liman: 214-215; Michael Losch: 213; Ken Lucas: 69, 72, 73, 305; Theresa Martinez: p. 1; Hans J. Mayland: 154; Neale Monks: 350, 360, 362-363; Aaron Norman: 10, 242, 286; Klaus Paysan: 59, 227, 263; M.P. & C. Piednoir: 252-253; Gianluca Polgar: 197, 200, 206, 209; Sasha Radosavljevich: 254; Hans-Joachim Richter: 157, 290-291, 333; Andre Roth: 52, 99, 105, 222, 306; Ruslan: 15; V. Sato: 122; Gunter Schmida: 147; Ian Scott: 36; Seriousguy: 344-345; Stan Shebs: 296; Stan Shubel: 16-17, 49, 108-109; Mark Smith: 7, 26, 31, 35, 44-45, 53, 55, 60-61, 63, 64, 66, 67, 68, 75, 77, 78-79, 92, 97, 115, 117, 124, 127, 132, 134, 136, 140-141, 144, 146, 151, 161, 180-181, 182-183, 216-217, 220-221, 224, 228, 230, 233, 234, 235, 257, 258, 263, 275, 278-279, 285, 286-287, 303, 304, 308, 309, 310, 316, 317, 322, 325, 331, 334-335, 340, 383; Jurgen Tappe: 353; Edward Taylor: 30, 101, 127, 145, 170, 243, 337; Mario Tomic: 23; Dale Wagler: 348; Wunson: 2; Mike Yamamoto: 125

All other photos courtesy of TFH photo archives.